THE WHOLE HOG

Aidan Higgins was born in 1927. *Langrishe, Go Down*, his first novel, won the James Tait Black Memorial Prize and the Irish Academy of Letters Award, and was later filmed for television with a screenplay by Harold Pinter. His second novel, *Balcony of Europe*, was shortlisted for the 1972 Booker Prize. The novel *Lions of the Grünewald* appeared in 1993 and a collection of shorter fiction, *Flotsam and Jetsam*, in 1996. *Donkey's Years* and *Dog Days* were the first two volumes of the Higgins Bestiary which concludes with this volume.

ALSO BY AIDAN HIGGINS

Aidan Higgins

THE WHOLE HOG

A sequel to *Donkey's Years* and *Dog Days*

VINTAGE

Published by Vintage 2001

2 4 6 8 10 9 7 5 3 1

Copyright © Aidan Higgins 2000

First published in Great Britain by
Secker & Warburg 2000

Vintage
Random House, 20 Vauxhall Bridge Road,
London SW1V 2SA

Random House Australia (Pty) Limited
20 Alfred Street, Milsons Point, Sydney
New South Wales 2061, Australia

Random House New Zealand Limited
18 Poland Road, Glenfield, Auckland 10,
New Zealand

Random House (Pty) Limited
Endulini, 5A Jubilee Road, Parktown 2193,
South Africa

The Random House Group Limited Reg. No. 954009
www.randomhouse.co.uk

A CIP catalogue record for this book
is available from the British Library

ISBN 0 09 928635 1

Printed and bound in Great Britain by
Cox & Wyman Ltd, Reading, Berkshire

For dearest Zin,
again

Contents

PART V: Danish Blue

PART VI: Contretemps at Cranley Gardens

PART VII: Down Mexico Way

PART VIII: How the Century Ends

Circumstances are never fully our own because they contain another person, we forget that. We thought of the other person as part of our perplexity: in reality that perplexity is part of the other person.

Djuna Barnes, *Nightwood* (variorum edition) (1936)

Why yes *he thought* it ain't a place a man wants to go back to; the place don't even need to be there no more. What aches a man to go back to is what he remembers.

William Faulkner, *The Mansion* (1959)

Prologue

Getting On

It began a long time ago, though it seems but yesterday. The lies, the notion of privilege, of being safeguarded by right, was ours in perpetuity; that at least was the notion put about by our loving parents.

But it wasn't so at all. Those were merely mother's lies, the lies you tell a child. The life we were to lead seemed to confirm this, declare it: that we were special.

But we we weren't, that wasn't true at all. What follows is the stark truth about those bare-faced lies. We were not special.

Good News for Pisceans

In order to achieve the best rhetorical effects a diary requires a ready readership of but one. Therefore a perfectly petrified readership – James Joyce's 'ideal reader in search of an ideal insomnia'. The diary is a device calculated to shut the average reader out. To shut him or her up.

This then is suitable for your specialists in doubt, subterfuge and confusion, sad wenchers, lost domainers, *flâneurs* and night-walkers, midnight imbibers of Greek brandy at the Four Lanterns on misty Muswell Hill, the haunted hill of a black transvestite ('Call me Dolores like dey do in de storybooks!'), haunt of ambitious Greeks saving to return home to Naxos; haunt of retired minor criminals from Soho, long oddsmen and those reckless poker players who are prone to draw injudiciously to inside straights.

The Lost Ones

Those who believe in fresh starts never get around to it. A seaman in Brady's sordid Irish pub, frequented by National Front louts and head-butters at the Oval, is a widower, having lost his wife in Korea, to some incurable disease. She was buried there.

He consulted a shaman as to the whereabouts of her immortal soul. The shaman consulted his oracles, then declared: 'At Number 6 Caldwell Street at the Oval, guv.' Cor blimey, it's his own address! His ghost wife occupies the upper storey and can be heard at night, moving the furniture about and sighing deeply.

Pisces (20 February–20 March), my birth-month. Sensational planetary aspects have to be utilised to the full and not for a single second should you imagine that anyone can outmanoeuvre or outpace you. Good news for Pisceans everywhere.

PART I:

Only Family Matters

A Bit of Strange

T hough my parents never made any money they knew how to spend it, spendthrifts both of them in their different ways. They watched the Irish Grand National at Fairyhouse every Easter Monday, motoring there very grandly in the Overland, my mother in a cloche hat with demi-veil and fur coat, my father gripping the wheel in pigskin gloves as though 'she' was getting away from him, though the Overland could not go faster than a moderate 40 m.p.h. because of a tendency to overheat.

Grogan the groom told me of the big stakes laid and won by the rich Aga Khan. He rolled in the hay with a local girl, who wore powder and lipstick, frizzed out her hair, and was our part-time maid of all work.

'Would you fight your match?' Grogan would ask, cocking his head to one side like a bantam boxer, striking a pugilistic pose.

He had bow legs and wore leather gaiters, hobnail boots and smelt of carbolic soap, though he washed his hands with axle grease, in a bucket. He said he would wear out Lizzie. He had a tense white face on him from the wearing.

In August my parents drove to Galway for the Galway Plate and put up at the Great Southern in Eyre Square. They drank whiskey and walked through the Spanish Arch holding hands and Mumu told me that the Arch was named after the Spaniards washed ashore in the Armada. The living ones were hidden from the English and the dead ones were buried by the Irish. Mumu and Dado arrived home next day in a not too sober state and went to bed early.

Mumu's gums were an odd colour, the colour of rubber, kept in a glass by her bedside, attached to false teeth. She drank a morning glass of lukewarm water and Epsom Salts.

My Uncle Jack was a great sportsman and sucked raw eggs; he won the Grand National with a horse called Workman (Tim Hyde up). Uncle Jack bred and trained racehorses and had better luck than my father, who preferred to play golf at Lucan and the Hermitage to attending sick livestock on his estate.

Mumu's younger brother Jimmy Boyd rode three times in the Liverpool National. He came in second; the following year he was third. The Dote and I sucked bull's-eyes and shot birds with a Daisy air-rifle. Plum puddings hung from bags suspended on hooks from the kitchen ceiling, so we shot holes in one and it leaked and old Mrs Henry told us we were bold boys and she would tell Mumu on us, so she would, but she never did, so we stopped shooting holes in plum puddings hanging from the kitchen ceiling.

Dado dressed like a swank. A dark three-piece suit with display handkerchief in the breast pocket and handkerchief up one sleeve. Gorgeous tie and patent leather pumps, relics from his dancing days. When the patent leather pumps wore out he wore my cricket boots, with wads of newspapers as undersoles. The paper came out in shreds, he shed the stale old news that was just beginning to be forgotten: the stamp scandal, the fellow who had absconded with all the funds. When these functional undersoles protruded, Dado became Pegasus, the winged horse that caused the fountain Hippocrene to gush upon Mount Helicon.

Springfield (Ideal Hunting Box or small Racing Establishment, suitable for Stud Farm) was sold. Another breeder, more methodical in his ways, took over the running of the farm that had never been properly farmed in Dado's day, the acres of lush grass let out for grazing. Other horses now exercised in the seventy or so acres where Ringwood Son and Cabin Fire flew over the jumps and Grogan (on One Down) had come down.

I left home.

2

Largo: Three or Four Miseries, 1956–85

Coppera (Rijeka Harbour, summer 1956)

An awkward squad of Yugoslav soldiers in baggy pants and ill-fitting tunics line up on the quayside near steps that descend into the still blue water of the harbour toward which a launch with some visiting dignitary aboard is chugging, its flag fluttering in the breeze.

A volley is fired and a small pompous figure on the launch offers a brisk salute. The launch draws in alongside the steps and a stout little man in a linen suit darts nimbly up to where a stiff squad of awkward soldiers come to attention as the white smoke of the gun salute drifts over the water. It is 6.30 in the morning of August 1956 and the Adriatic sun already hot in the port of Rijeka, in the long ago and far away when I went with my first wife weeping with exhaustion and vexation, on the way to Cavtat, Mlini, Dubrovnik, working as puppet operators and stage managers for John Wright's Marionettes, touring Yugoslavia, Austria, Germany and Holland, before embarking on *Die Waterman* for Cape Town.

When Coppera Hill (née Anders of King William's Town in the Eastern Cape) weeps she means it, and oh how she weeps; she is converted into a child again, becomes herself again in King. Everything has been taken from her, so the child understands, and is cast down.

It rends her to bits, so it does; she liquefies, weeps her heart out, for that's her way. Coppera's in tears again, hand her a hanky! Woe is me.

So it went.

Hanne (Grand Hotel de la Loire, Paris)

At 20 rue de Sommerard off the rue St Jacques downhill from the Sorbonne you'll find it, a hotel of narrow rooms used by students who sometimes use the toilet as a place for copulation. The owner wants to know when the money will come to pay the rent; we stay until it arrives, first not eating much, then eating nothing. We eat each other. We have begun to smell; an overwhelming longing for sweet white wine forces me to steal a noggin of Scotch from a shop fitted out with mirrors. I await an influx of funds from a Dublin bank, for reviewing work, but no deposits are being made. I walk in the Luxembourg Gardens, see Beckett striding past the line of statues of famous French dead, his hair stiff and erect like a cockatoo.

Dream: a high-ceilinged double room perhaps in Paris, with interleading doors open wide. On the parquet floor crouch shadowy listening forms. Squatting on the floor but a little apart from them Beckett is playing a strange musical instrument, half lyre, half washboard, with lead pieces inset but without any strings. How can he play a stringless instrument? Only Beckett could do it. He plucks this strange unknown instrument, head cocked, chanting to himself. Music and words are very odd, delivered at unheard-of tempo. In the darkening apartment Beckett plays and I, unseen, listen to this disturbing music. It's the music of snakes.

There are long silences to achieve effects. Now he rises, approaches. Someone whispers to me: 'Now he sings of Judas.' Beckett's high apartment is not far away, on Boulevard St Jacques overlooking Santé prison.

I have returned from Parc St-Maur with a bad conscience. Behold Judas, the betrayer.

At the Closerie des Lilas he had hardly looked at me, a few

sharp mistrustful glances vouchsafed, then he left abruptly, up
and away after three whiskies, hardly acknowledging my beloved
Hanne. The blood-soaked sheets from her difficult menses are
changed without comment or complaint by the Spanish maid,
who cleans out fifty rooms every morning. Hanne, who has good
Spanish, befriends her, is told her troubles.

After a night of twisting and turning in those sheets I am
standing at the window looking down towards the rue St Jacques
just before first light. As daylight begins to ebb into the street
a fellow comes walking down the hill and stands outside the
unlit Hotel Diana. All that side of the street lies in darkness.
He stands on the kerb with hands in pockets and looks up. He
appears to gesture. Out of the darkness of the hotel entrance she
emerges just then, dressed in a red coat. They embrace and
walk off together down towards the rue de Sommerard. I watch
them crossing. Soon the butcher shop opposite will open; the
pavement had been hosed down the previous night. The owner
takes his first Gauloise outside the shop, under the awning. We
have begun hallucinating now on the third day without any food;
inhaling Gauloise makes the head swirl. No deposits are being
made. The manager is very patient, but what else can he do? It's
3 January 1973.

Hunger had weakened us and misery had ground us very small.
When we began to stink, we turned against each other. Three
days without food and we were very strange to each other. Do
you take us for utter fools? We were in flitters.

3

Forgive My Silence

A card of mourning, handwritten, came to me when I was least expecting it. She wrote:

Forgive my silence.

My sister is dead. I'm living in Rørvig mostly in this weeks. Kos journey suspended. My mother is near going mad. I don't know myself how to be normal again. I'm freezing in this lovely summer.

She committed suicide, flinged herself out from a tower. I'm sick, we are all sick, please write something to me. She was so lovely, so weak and lovely. Pisces.

Anna

No address, May 1978.

It was in North Zeeland, in Little Russia that I turned into a mare in a lovely meadow there. Nearly all kinds of nature is there in Little Russia – meadows, hills and certain kinds of wild flowers growing in dry places where snakes like to be. It was ten days after my sister's funeral and I was there with the painter chap that I told you about. I was mad there, mad of unhappiness. I was dead of misery, wanting to be with her, look after her, but she wasn't there.

I must say the painter chap was very kind; he just stayed
with me and said nothing. There was nothing you could
say really. She was buried, had gone away; I couldn't
understand why she had done it. All her clothes were
there and the flat was the same, as if she had gone out
for a minute.

I was not myself; I had turned into a black mare prancing
about in the meadow. It was gleaming and I could see the
sexual parts opening and closing like a flower.

The painter chap was Torbin Thimm, a former lover who grew
roses commercially with his sister in Jutland. He had rented a
studio across from Anna's apartment in Østersøgade.

On the *Litfasssäule* by the Gedächtniskirche with its head blown
off by a Red Army tank, the piercing eyes of Beckett stare
accusing from a poster and follow Rory. *Nicht ich* comes to the
Schiller Theatre annexe, a chilly place.

The convenience stood up as Teutonic as anything else in
Berlin; whereas the last Parisian *pissoir* behind Santé prison was
as Gallic as garlic or Gauloise.

Hannelore (Prinzregentenstrasse, Berlin)

Wasn't I very hungry, pfennigless, when Beckett's eagle eye,
hooded, found me walking by the café patronised by Georg
Grosz? It was a freezing day with cold air from the Baltic Sea
coming up Kurfürstendamm and I was thinking of a currywurst
bread roll garnished with pepper and washed down with one
of those heavy warming dark beers that the Germans drink in
winter; but I hadn't a tosser, not one pfennig. And there were
the ravaged ascetic features glaring at me from the *Litfasssäule* near
the bombed-out Memorial Church.

February (German) 1974. *Nicht ich* running at Schillertheater
Werkstatt.

From Berlin on 18 September 1971 she had written to me:

No telephone call, no little handwritten letter – awful

silence. What about welcoming the New Year together? Christmas will be already quite dull for me without you – and then dearest, that horrible waiting.

I have put gin and vodka in the fridge instead of food. The first things for you, the missing things for me as I stated that my figure seems to concentrate in my bottom and my bosom although I have lost some weight. I become more and more restless. At night I hear my heart beating and my mind seems to work with a heavy uneasiness.

It's very cold outside. Yesterday I heard some birds singing in the Tiergarten and I thought that Christmas might be an error ... I'm doing a carpet to calm my nerves after I had made a blue and black cap.

I finish this little letter now because the sleeping pill I took seems to pull me from the chair.

[Written along margin:] 'All the time I'm painfully longing for you. Hannelore.'

But by 1974 when she was pregnant by me the gilt had worn off the gingerbread enough for her to be understandably sour and snappish. Who was it said that when the Germans shut themselves up in their silent resentment they prepare a blow – Harold Nicolson or Count Ciano?

When she hitch-hiked with a plain girlfriend she never accepted lifts in cars that hadn't four doors; she sat in the back, with a *shiv* in her sock. Once a hairy truck-driver stopped at a small beach and suggested they swim in the altogether. *Nein, danke.*

Her first boyfriend was French – Pierre, let us call him, who played the guitar quite well. She had met him driving through a mist on the road to Nîmes or was it Montpellier coming down off the Cévennes in her Karmann Ghia. They hit it off at once.

Her first German boyfriend was, oddly enough, a replica of Pierre; let us call him Hans. He didn't play the guitar but in all other respects he was a German Pierre: same port, disposition, voice, manners, as if a continuation of the same, except he had no French.

Then there was a long silence. She wrote to him but received no answer. Time passed. One day, months later, her mother handed her a letter, an official notice from a hospital, to say Herr Hans so-and-so had died during an operation on such-and-such a date. He had gone in to have an operation to change the shape of his nose. The letter was handed over months later.

Who was in the right – the vain boyfriend trying to change the shape of his nose, the mother trying to protect her daughter?

> Finding is the first Act
> The second – loss,
> Third, Expedition for
> The 'Golden Fleece'
> Fourth, no Discovery –
> Fifth, no Crew –
> Finally, no Golden Fleece –
> Jason – sham – too.
> > Emily Dickinson

One morning in our perambulating around Krumme Lanke we saw a heavy-set, hairy he-man swinging from a liana bullock naked with a big loaded cock semi-erect; and she had pretended not to see him, as she had averted her eyes from certain explicit nudes in the Neu National Gallery.

Flora (Connemara, winter 1985)

There's no use pretending that there are no constraints; naturally there are, must be. There was Flora Rossiter who had married a man called Jessup, so now she was Flora Jessup but wrote under her maiden name of Rossiter.

I said: OK, by all means let us live together but no hanky-panky, and she had agreed to that, and found a modernised cottage for us to share in deepest Connemara, across the first of three causeways joining up Annaghvaughan, Gorumna and Lettermore. It was a thatched cottage in a group of four or five, later torched by one of the local disgruntled lads who had been refused employment by our kindly landlord Johnny O'Toole, owner of the cottages and landlord of An Hooker pub opposite, where he slept with his wife Lucy and a shotgun for protection. Against arson and grudges of course he had no protection, in a remote place where grudges were assiduously cultivated.

We drove to Galway town in her green Ford for provisions, washing, Gauloises and spirits, and it rained for six weeks without stopping. The old postman came cycling over the causeway to deliver damp parcels of books, with a permanent drip depending from the tip of his old discoloured nose and I offered him morning shots of Jameson, fearing he would otherwise never make it back to the PO.

We were to share the cottage for the duration of an honorarium paid out on condition that I live in my own country for ten months and engage in a work of fiction or biography; but when the honorarium ran out in the ninth month I returned to London, found it impossible to live there and left for Spain. Flora wrote to me, on a postcard.

Emor Street
17 October 85

Dear Rory
  Would you ever write?
  I find I'm so upset and confused all the time. I can't understand what happened after a time of so much closeness and nearness and now nothing. I felt so strongly that we would be together, I don't know, some very deep gut feeling that what we had was so good and you telling me to rely on that and not be impatient and ever since you went to Spain this numbing awful silence. What changed so drastically for you? We're so good together in every kind of way – I feel as if the whole thing was a farce now. I know it will be hard for you to try and explain but I feel as if I'm going bananas. Please write, hey? Much love – Flora xxx

4

The Genesis of *Langrishe, Go Down*

For the son the first hard loss is the loss of the mother and there never will be another loss like it, for later losses are partly of one's own devising. Wasn't it Gertrude Stein, that heavy Red Indian totem, who said fathers are depressing. Mothers may not be cheering but they are not as depressing as fathers.

Well, one can bear the loss of a father, but what unmitigated anguish is the loss of a home! You have only the one home, the one you were born in; but the break-up of the family means that you have lost it for ever. As one day (for the son) comes the first involuntary erection and emission, so one day there goes the last, so too for the daughter when menopause follows hard upon the last menses.

My younger brother swore that the very stones which he had dug out of last year's potato patch had come up again this year. 'The constant renewal of nature is impressive in contrast to the necessity to renew the man-made, with an evidently opposite tendency to decay,' he informed me in a letter. The balanced antithesis was worthy of Ruskin himself, a suggestion of fussy overshoes, whaddyacallem . . . galoshes.

The ultimate privacy is to be found only in the sleepy stagnancy of the grave. Even if that privacy is an illusion, upon our becoming a part of the multitudinously teeming subatomic microbe life that exists underground, now with all vanity obliterated.

My first novel, *Langrishe, Go Down*, was about the death of a house and the break-up of a family. It took me two years to write, two more for a dilatory publisher to bring it to the public eye; the final editing took twenty-four hours non-stop (but for dinner in Jammet's) and I stayed up all night, wearing out two copy-editors. *Langrishe* sold just over 2,000 cloth copies in the first fortnight after publication in September 1966, after which sales sank to a dribble. And it has consistently sold in a dribble ever since, in five or six European languages. Beckett called it 'literary shit'.

Later, move on thirty-three years please, another publisher commissioned a sort of sequel; and this was finished in two months. Were I a painter of the stamp of Magritte, I might have suggested the decline of the Higgins family in one significant image: Virginia creeper leaves from above my father's room now blown into the gutter of the small balcony above the long windows, one opened about a foot at the bottom for fresh air. The leaves would change colour from spring into autumn, first green, then scarlet, then orange, then purple, then dark plum-coloured, blown about the little balcony by various winds, then clenched together in a ball by frost, reduced to the size of a clenched fist, now the teak colour of Tollund Man dug out of the Danish earth.

The narrow room must have once been a changing room for the big bedrooms on either side, and here my father, the narrow fellow in the grass, the great sunbather gone the colour of rhubarb, then the livid red of a turkey-cock's comb, had withdrawn when my mother withheld or withdrew her favours or had tired of sharing a double bed in a large echoing windy room with rattling venetian blinds (for Mumu was claustrophobic) or the embarrassment of using two chamber-pots drawn out at different times from under both beds; this narrow room commanded a view of the Dublin hills with Buck Whaley's Hell Fire Club on the summit, where at one time the smoke of the steam-driven Blessington tram must have made pretty patterns over towards Hazelthatch station and Baldonnel aerodrome.

*   *   *

I have always been troubled by the strangeness of strange places. The otherness of places I didn't know, assailed by their smells and strangeness, announced along the Dublin quays by a sulphurous stench rising off the river at low tide, suggestive of loss of control and God knows what else, as we waited with Dado for the single-decker bus (bound for Birr) to take us home. The sulphur stinks and the sickening Virginia cigarette fumes from Gold Flake and Player's and Sweet Afton were the prelude to a bout of vomiting. As effective as the mixture of a haircut at Maison Prost's with stiffener that made the scalp go rigid, and a large-size sixpenny ice-cream wafer at Woolworth's that produced splitting headaches, as the preliminary states of discomfort and stomach upset, before the wild stinks of the monkey house and lion house in the Zoo put the kibosh on it, with more vomiting. On the bus home I always vomited, and sometimes even on the gravel before the house. The visit to Maison Prost in Suffolk Street was followed by a visit to Woolworth's in Grafton Street and then the Zoo regular as clockwork, for Dado was at a loss how to amuse 'the lads', who were then taken to Eason's in O'Connell Street or Combridge's in Grafton Street, to buy books: Baroness Orczy and Rafael Sabatini, then Sapper and Leslie Charteris.

The unfamiliar was always threatening – fresh-ground coffee aromas outside Bewley's suggested Africa, heat, wildness; for which the methane fumes mixed with slag and coal around the Kingsbridge goods yards gave fair warning. The warning whistle of the Great Southern and Western steam train puffing into Kingsbridge Station made me want to throw up, as did the seaweed and sewage stinks around Dun Laoghaire, when we went walking along the pier with Dado.

Dado had parked the Overland some way down the front avenue at Killashee and in the back seat with curtains drawn we consumed the cakes and buns baked by Mumu with all her love. Sundays were visiting days but the Overland seemed strange to us with its rabbity smells which reminded us of home and what we were missing, and the knowledge that it would soon be back in the garage there made us sad. Under the care of the French nuns, La Santé Union, or later under the Jesuits it was the same sadness of departure for us both; the nuns were all Irish but the sadness was the same, the same sadness when Dado had departed; the visit was soon over, the cakes eaten, the newspaper cuttings collected, and Dado drove away.

Premonitions of this oncoming loss were conveyed in a subtle way by Mumu when she read Grimm and Hans Andersen to us, those terrifying tales of the overgrown castle with the sleeping beauty within, the dank and dripping cellar through which hurried the cruel queen, the woodland house made of sugar where the witch lived, the giant's castle above the clouds, the old woman who lived in the shoe; all were premonitory hints of that first ejection from the home and intimations of the places and the ordeals to be encountered later.

The strange house the Dote has found so hard to finish was perhaps another such dwelling found only in dreams and fairy tales. The house that he couldn't complete was the house that didn't exist, the home that wasn't there; no more the abode of parents long dead and gone; say rather one of Piranesi's fanciful ruins.

He whom we call the Dote was no doubt a singular fellow of undeviating probity, positively Quakerish in his austere ways and grey functional clothing. Faithful to his religion through the Latin Mass and after; faith was proven in work, a spur to morality; right-doing was just part of one's duty. As altar boy he had served at Mass, rang the little joined bells to make them chime prettily at the Consecration, rotated the thurible to send out puffs of incense.

A nature indentured to work gave him a settled distrust of flamboyance; solely on the evidence of *The Guermantes Way* volume two, which was in the study at Springfield, the Dote preferred Ruskin to Proust, who was too neurotic and rather too purple for the Dote's taste. He was as set in his ways as an Amish quilter. Sometimes when exasperated by him, Mumu said he was thick; obdurate meaning obstinate.

My brother Colman was first called the Dote in his infancy, because he was the last, and then (as a lad) the Dowd. The Dote, the Dowd, the Scholar, the Architect, the Town Planner and now (alarmingly) the Litigant.

The *litigant*! A bit of something strange all right.

5

Ordeal at Mealtimes

When summoned to table by gong or handbell with dindins getting cold, little Rory's face fell and his little heart sank into his little boots (size 12) too, and with what laggard step he made his weary way table-ward! Indeed he brought a sinking heart to the table, where he preferred to take his meals in reverse, not from soup to dessert but the other way around, *pari passu*, starting with what he liked best (jelly or trifle) and working his way back to what he liked least, the soup, which was frequently refused. And Mumu indulged him in all this, sneered at by brother Bun for being too lenient and accommodating, he himself, ever a hearty and not particularly fastidious eater who, it was said, would eat *anything*.

Monday meant mash again that smelt of mouse droppings; then came Tuesday's corned beef, Wednesday's soggy dumplings; Thursday was greasy mincemeat day and with it the week declined; when Friday came around again, it brought with it some really smelly fish whose purposeful pong would turn your stomach, and for sure young Rory had one fastidious stomach. He was forever throwing up whatever didn't agree with those queasy insides of his; so much disgusted him; *too* much, I'd be inclined to say.

'He's a true Hill anyway,' murmured Mumu as if speaking to

herself, proudly and possessively, munching on those loose dentures of hers in that way she had. 'At least he's no greedy-gut.'

Young Rory was no greedy-gut, but a real Hunger Artist. At best, mealtimes at Springfield were onerous occasions; at worst, penitential.

'Don't you want to grow up to be a big strong man like your father?'

'No I don't.'

Brother Bun, poker-faced, kicked Rory under the table.

'Bun just kicked me, Mumu.'

'Nonsense! Pure imagination. Just eat up what's put in front of you. Cook has taken great pains with this.'

'This' was streaky silverside of beef with valves sticking out of it and gnarled tentacles that seemed to writhe in agony on the plate.

'This thing's still alive . . . ah feck it!'

Dado's fork was already snaking out for the tasty portion, 'I'll eat it.' Mumu showed me a face frozen with disapproval and brother Bun kicked my shins harder under the table, looking innocent as pie.

Truth to tell, Dado was a small fidgety bantam cock of a man, vain as any peacock, who was sometimes mistaken for this or that famous jockey, as happened once outside the Monument Creamery in O'Connell Street. 'Aren't you Morny Wing?' A big stout woman had stopped him in his tracks. Vanity pure and simple.

His cramped sleeping quarters was a narrow chamber of trapped ambient air stilled by Dado's scorching farts, for he had a heavy hand with the emetics and was forever dosing himself with Milk of Magnesia and Eno's Fruit Salts to clean out his stomach and bring his guts – much referred to – back into proper working order again.

'Ah Rory, the old guts are killing me.'

If it wasn't that, it was stabs and darts of appendix, which excused him from the pumping chore ('The old appendix is at me again'). He was tricky, evasive, sly, my father.

Dado was probably now letting off sly farts under the bedclothes, his nostrils arched free of the quilt, his eyes closed like a dead man's.

'What kind of a day is it out? It's a bit stuffy in here. Throw open the window, there's a good lad.'

I did as I was bid, waded through the miasmal scorching air towards the window that opened out on to the little balcony, the view of the Hell Fire Club on the summit of distant Dublin blue hills in the distance beyond Baldonnel aerodrome.

In Mumu's big bedroom alongside Dado's, the windows were always thrown open and the venetian blinds flapping inwards, and there were many flowers in vases, to make the room fresh, like Mumu's flowers in her tiered arrangements amid the burning candles on the high altars at Celbridge and Straffan churches. You'd almost expect birds to be flying around Mumu's head in the gusty swirl of the bedroom.

'The days are getting a great stretch into them, thank God, aren't they?' murmured Mumu, propped up on great mounds and escarpments and embankments of pillows. She was reading *Flotsam*, a dirty book translated from the German, lent to her by Helen O'Connor, who was as voracious a reader as herself. It lay now face down on the upended orange crate that did service as a bedside table, her place marked by a hair-clip. Mumu surfacing from deep sleep, casting aside sheets and quilts and emerging to take deep breaths at the beginning of another day, was like a whale blowing.

If she was badly overweight then Rory was grievously under-weight and Dr Sheehan gave his professional opinion that what I needed was iron to build up my bones, Metatone or Virol to bring the roses to my cheeks when feeling not up to it and 'peaky'; and that was the way I generally felt. Worse still, I was 'looking pasty-faced', which meant constipation and dosages of herbal remedies to bring about a 'motion' or stool; and all little Rory's stools were hard, hard, hard.

'Get him to eat bananas,' Dr Sheehan advised Mumu; 'lots of bananas. Feed him up with Fyffes, ha ha ha!'

'Oh doctor, he's terribly faddy about his food. He won't *touch* bananas.'

'Oranges then, lots of oranges. Fill him up.'

So I was given lots of oranges which Dado peeled with his penknife all in one knacky revolving peel, before handing the slices to me and drying his hand on a large pocket handkerchief.

When he cut an orange for himself, he bisected it and sucked away part; the rest he threw away; as he always left a few Player's No. 3 in the discarded packet. For he was wasteful and extravagant by nature, never having had to earn a living by the sweat of his brow, nor done an honest day's work in his entire life.

By not eating, by refusing this or that dish lovingly prepared by a mother's hand, by flatly refusing to eat what is put before one, the mother's love is tested. For sons have that power from a very early age; from the time the difficult child has been weaned, ceased to be a suckling, the mother can be controlled.

The child can refuse titbits offered as bribes. Judge of the poor mother's mortification and discomfiture when her little pet, previously so tractable, so manageable, now declines to accept whatever goodies are placed before him and begins to bawl! Or a flat refusal to accept any such bribes, with an aplomb as upsetting and deadly as the power of veto. Now the mother must beg and grovel before her small tyrant.

By refusing tasty morsels and little treats, the brat, embryonic tyrant that he is, finds himself in a strong negotiating position, with a bargaining strength to obtain what he wants, that which he can hardly name, not yet able to talk; and the mother, weighed in the balance, has been found wanting.

Little Rory, the famously faddy feeder (fff), the picker at food, the *more* than fastidious eater, refused eggs and butter (the latter associated with womanly flesh and early superior strength) and had to be coaxed to drink milk. Sago that resembled frogspawn or semolina pud with a skin or scum on it enlivened with a dab of raspberry jam were 'sweets' not enjoyed by the skinnymalink fusspot who sat next to the silent Dodo, silent but for the methodical chomping at his food. Rice puddings and bread puddings and nice spaghetti puds were tolerated, brown sugar was spread liberally on soda bread and a red-hot poker laid across it to produce the consistency of glazed marzipan, crystallised fruit, angelica and ginger.

Woe betide the cook who offered butter or eggs in no matter

what form. Meat had to be cooked until carbonised before I would consent to touch it. ('Don't pick at your food, Rory, there's a good boy!')

As a consequence, I weighed no more than four stone, give or take a pound, by the age of six or seven. Four stone avoirdupois, if that, a thin shivering shank of a child permanently anxious: witness the living skeleton of Booterstown Strand captured in the Box Brownie *circa* 1933 with matchstick legs and rickety arms when stung on the forearm by a wasp that must have mistaken little-meat Rory for some half-starved mongrel stray.

The Hill family table, the great groaning board, was indeed a battleground and the meals served up were occasions for skirmishes and strategies for survival ('*Don't* pick at your food, child!').

Dado, who had the palate of a dog, once accepted dishwater lying on the pan for gravy. Pulling back from the table and crossing his legs as a signal that the 'sweet' (trifle or stewed apples from the orchard, served up with Bird's Eye custard) should be brought in, he gave his opinion, picking his teeth with a spent match in lieu of toothpick, that you would hardly get better gravy at the Shelbourne or the Gresham than the dishwater on the pan. 'What's wrong with it then? The lad is too fussy altogether.' The lad had refused to accept it; when it was poured forcefully over my tiny portion of carbonised silverside of beef by the irate Dado, I had pushed my plate away and burst into tears.

'*Now* what's got into him?'

Old Mrs Henry, our cook, said that my stomach must be one mass of worms, full of sugar and jam and sweet things.

Sometimes, to emphasise the point he was making and bring it home sharply to Mumu, Dado struck the edge of the table with his clenched knuckles, as a court beadle might strike the floor of the chambers for silence; or as the judge, clearing his throat, might rap the dais before him with the gavel, before pronouncing sentence.

Dado referred in most disparaging terms to 'that mincing two-faced bitch' whom we know to be none other than Miss

Pasty-Face Dermody who had once called uninvited, come over the fields; but only once and had never presumed to come again in her tight home-made tweed skirt that demonstrated how tightly laced she was into a corset.

You might suppose that the Dodo had a second stomach, as cattle have, for he masticated his food in a slow methodical way just like a cow, moving his lower jaw from side to side. He had some theory about digestion, ways and means of extracting the best possible nutritive results from the food consumed, subjecting every blessed morsel speared on the prongs of his fork to the most exact scrutiny at close range, before bringing it to his lips, hesitating, then popping it into his mouth to begin grinding from side to side, eyes closed, a bovine 'Fletcherising' guaranteed to extract the maximum of good from his meat, brought to the kitchen door in a butcher's basket by the bowsie Murray himself, smelling as usual to high heaven.

It was as though he (the Dodo) suspected that his meat might be spiked with nux vomica or cyanide. He ate in silence. But sometimes, when some remark tickled his fancy, he emitted a high-pitched witchy cackle; otherwise he ate in stoic silence. Never a word of praise had he for the food put before him; never a good word for the cook, old Mrs Henry or Mumu.

'What's this thing, then?'

He was holding it up on his fork, peering at it.

'That's cauliflower, dear. Don't you like it?'

'Not much.'

'Then we won't have it again,' said Mumu, always ready to defer to his wishes.

The Dote and I were very much in awe of him. The eight and ten years that separated us made him appear a very senior brother, already fully vested in authority, a stern prefect to reeky fags; it was an awesomeness which he did nothing to modify. On the contrary his silence at table seemed to make it clear that he thought very little of us, a wormy pair.

Seldom did he speak and when he did it tended to be either dismissive or outright alarming, and always the imperative ('Hey, you!' risen up suddenly to tower above us, down in the ditch, remorseless and heavy as lead – the *Golem!* – 'Hey, what's the big idea?').

The strained silence that followed was indeed strained. The Dodo was rolling the whites of his eyes ceiling-ward and then fixing his napkin into its silver ring, preparing to leave the table.

We sat frozen in embarrassment. It was all for some innocent question the Dote had put to Dado, which the Dodo had taken as cheek. We were the pups from the convent with thick provincial accents (mudder, me brudder, dis, dat) who fraternised with the snotty-nosed Keegan boys from the front lodge who used the plantation as an open-air latrine, for the Dodo to tread in and bring into the house.

It was as though he and brother Bun were the true sons of their father and mother and Springfield was their true home and Clongowes Wood College was their rightful Alma Mater and their airs and graces were the only possible attitude to adopt towards the brats (the Dote and I), who were just worms to be trodden into the ground.

Giving cheek at table, making cheeky remarks, from the likes of *that* (the Dote reduced to the size of nothing) was no better than *lèse-majesté*, 'Infernal cheek!'

We saw ourselves as a humble, ignorant pair at garden parties given by Helen O'Connor, at Dr O'Connor's residence near the National School (which we would attend for one day), or at Springfield with the wild relative who joined the Royal Navy and played very rough games involving barricades and repeating air-rifles, stumps as swords and pads as bucklers, bamboo canes as pikes, and pellet slugs. We were sons adopted by fosterage, taken from a poor family to be brought up as little gents, but gents never accepted by our elder foster-brothers, who described us as whelps. We would have to watch our Ps and Qs.

If he (the Dodo) was the stern prefect with power to punish, set lines and use the cane, we were the shivering wretches with bums bared awaiting punishment, a cruel punishment meted out with an impartial severity which made it all the more cruel. He was never a big brother to us.

Maybe it was some idea he got from his reading – *Teddy*

Lester's Schooldays was a sort of Bible at Springfield, and Mumu had read it to all of us in turn as we grew up. Slapton School, where Teddy Lester was the hero, was run on Sandhurst lines of military strictness, a reign of terror with heavy caning in the dorm.

We had no option but to grin and bear it; take our gruel like a man, bent over a chair, for the Dodo to lay on with a will, grunting at every whack.

The Dodo, padded up, school XI cap down over eyes, collar up to the nose in the Sutcliffe manner, stands at the crease and defies the umpire (Harrison of Notts, the school cricket coach) to give him 'out'. Up goes the finger and the Dodo snaps to attention, rams the bat under his arm (subaltern with swagger stick) and retreats to the pav with a slowness intended as silent comment on a poor decision. But no matter how cruel and unjust the punishment, the heavy caning in the dorm, no matter how great the sadistic pleasure in those inflicting it, it simply wasn't done to peach on a fellow. Certainly not in Slapton School, where we learnt many ways of the world, of which we had previously known nothing. Through Arthur Digby (fullback on the Slapton XV) we learnt of true English grit and bulldoggishness, tenacious loyalty, endearing thickness.

A very curious England emerged from these pages; perhaps useful to us later when we discovered the real England for ourselves. Slapton School seemed to be run on sadistic lines, the Beak in a wax again, cane in hand; rites of passage occurred in playing fields and dorms. It prefigured the drill grounds of later military academies. The pallor of Teddy's complexion worried the Dote and me, for we knew him as our friend; in the background perhaps was a weak mum deferring to her authoritarian husband determined to make a man out of unpromising material and who gave short shrift to lily-livered sons.

This brave but pallid youth and the stern father were to us (the Dote and Rory) as quintessentially English as the Eton wall game, being sent to Coventry, the Windmill (naughty theatre) and chorus girls scantily attired, the Changing of the Guard, rough and ready executions in the Tower, the bloody end of Mary Queen of Scots, pig-sticking in the Punjab, running the

gauntlet, the Royal Navy and its strict regulations, foaming
tankards of ale quaffed by the Lubber and his cronies in a local
hostelry before visiting the bookies, with a nod in the direction
of the bursting beer belly of the ogre-monarch Henry Tudor,
who got rid of his several wives as soon as they tired him, callous
as Bluebeard; all this seemed as familiar as the roast beef of old
England and we cried out in a rhapsody of fond memories, 'The
day of the big match dawned fine and clear!' For we seemed to
have been there, cheering on Slapton School.

There were complications, naturally.

The dorm prefect, a betting man, was in the hands of the
village bookies; this fact is discovered by the school bully,
the Lubber, who puts it to his own nefarious uses by forcing
the betting prefect to cane Lester and 'the little yellow chap' Ito
Nagao, the white hope of the school XV as scrum half; Lester and
Nagao are given the father and mother of a caning in the dorm
on the night before the big match, which memorably 'dawns
fine and clear'.

Lester and Nagao, crippled by the heavy cane used, cannot
give of their best, and take the field half crocked. The illustrations
in colour show the Slapton XV in loose-fitting drawers and
collarless rugger singlets of shocking pink. The Slapton team
appear to be running in on tiptoe like stage fairies waving
wands in an end-of-term masque. Were they apprehensive of
the outcome? And, sure enough, they lost. This was somehow
endearing, like the inaccuracies of old oil paintings in the time of
Stubbs that showed a long-bodied racehorse with a small head,
never with all four feet off the ground in a gallop; this had to
wait until the invention of photography and the neat hand of
the dandy Degas to get it right.

We were worried by the paleness of Teddy Lester's face.
But we learnt of drill, of class, swotting, flogging, paper-chases,
ritual punishment taken for granted, meted out and executed
and accepted in stoic silence, the heavy cane rising and falling,
the beater grunting, the others watching from their beds. The
unutterable strangeness, the unspeakable, unforgettable *foreignness*
of all foreigners, particularly those of another pigmentation living
in paper houses in their millions thousands of miles away on

islands scattered about the Sea of Japan (where Ito Nagao hailed from), which was the home of Ito the nippy Nip, scrum half of the Slapton XV, the famously plucky half-backs Lester and Nagao. We were for them; we were madly cheering them on the sidelines.

'Will you call your brother and tell him his meal's on the table?' cried Mumu from the depths of the kitchen. She was banging pots and pans about and sounded flustered.

We went out with a torch, the Dote and I, passed under the yew tree's spread of branches and stood by the sagging tennis net, waiting for the Dodo to make an appearance on his never-changing exercise path alongside the beech hedge. The Dodo, who could wear away the patience of a saint, had worn a smooth path there, worn away the gravel surface and superimposed his own path upon the existing one, by incessant marching up and down, methodical as his mastication of food at table.

There was no sign of him. We doused the torch but stayed put, for Mumu had told us to tell him that his supper was ready, that it was getting cold, he should come in at once, so we stayed at our post and waited patiently.

Then the astounding figure burst forth again from beyond the flowerbeds and the small orchard of young apple trees and the heavy bush of Scottish thistles. He hove into sight, moving like an automaton or a soldier on sentry duty, arms pistoning, marching robot-like, his head thrust forward, taking short choppy strides.

When he had reached the end of his outward march by the rose bushes, he would turn on his heel and resume his inward march, and there we would lose him until he appeared again.

The Dodo took short fussy steps as if constricted in a tight skirt and corset, heading for the far end of the garden by the potato drills that were diminishing as the winter proceeded, there by the plum trees.

'Ma says your supper's ready!' we screeched in unison and ran for our lives, laughing and flashing the torch beam into the old yew tree that spread its great branches all about, not waiting for a reply or any acknowledgement that he had heard and understood, only the wart-hog grunt of assent to tell us that he would be on his way.

He was, if that were possible, even more terrifying at close quarters at table, where we were too timid to open our mouths except to put in food; watching him go through the exact and precisely unchanging ritual that began with him sitting down, the thoughtful removal of the napkin from its silver ring, engraved upon it his initials, D.B.J.H. Esq. and the circumspect spreading of double damask linen napkin on the stout thigh, his lap.

Then began the secondary ritual with knife and fork and the sighs of resignation when the fare wasn't up to scratch and always the peremptory duck-like nods and mouthings of the sign language deployed to get what he wanted, the salt, the pepper, the gravy boat, bread (the staff of life).

Fastidiousness of manners and deportment had been instilled into him by the nuns at Killashee prep and made him ultra-finicky and obsessional; witness his constant manicuring of fingernails, running his fingers along the emery board with an anguished expression on his face like the great American cellist Steven Doane playing Bach.

I thought later of another figure perhaps closer to the Dodo in his seclusion: Rudolf Hess trapped in the Spandau exercise yard, draped in his old military cloak, pacing up and down stiff as a board, not speaking to the guards now, wrapped in silence, grimly serving out his life sentence.

Some days he seemed to us dank and evil-smelling, as if the Bogey Man had hauled himself up the cellar steps, smelling of dampness and mould and decay, come to take his rightful place at the family table and gratefully accept whatever food was placed before him.

On other days he was heavier, slow-moving and monumental as if hewn from stone, from granite, even more silent than before, withdrawn deeply into himself or into whatever it was that troubled him, for assuredly something *did* trouble him, something was eating him. Sitting there as impassively as the Golem, and so heavy he might break the chair he sat on, seated between Mumu at the foot of the table and myself, the Faddy Feeder, the picker at bones, to his right hand.

Dado and Mumu in turn addressed each other in coded terms which we only partially understood and had to make some shift to decode; references to a mysterious Mr K and a Mrs B and the unforgettable Miss D who had called once but never again, and Charlie Twybell and the Ruttles and the Dempseys and youknowwhat and youknowwho and youknowwhere, and a certain Mr Curiosity Box, which I took to refer to myself, all ears at table, or hiding under the long table, hidden by the drapes of the tablecloth.

My parents were constantly glancing out the long windows as if these coded parties were massing on the front drive and coming on with much chattering and shouting to trample all over Dado's recently scuffled gravel, leap up the front steps and burst into the dining room where we sat at table, all risen up appalled.

Hey, what's the big idea?

Don't play with your food, dearie.

Latterly, in the darkness of the confessional, the priest would murmur behind the wire grille, 'Don't play with yourself, child.'

I was the ever-so-thin little monkey in the cage of the Dublin Zoo absently squeezing pawpaw rinds in tiny simian hands, goggling out past the bars with flaming orange eyes, apparently without any shame living amid his own dirty excretions.

For as the lost monkey will masturbate himself all night long in the darkness and seclusion of his stinking cage, in the extremity of his loss (his lost forest home, the wilderness, the swaying tree-tops) at night in the Zoo when all the gaping humans have departed; so Rory played with himself in the darkness of the dormitory, pulled his wire into oblivion, from the beginnings in the Third Line, through the Lower Line and on into Higher Line, for so was the school divided into three, like the three persons of the Blessed Trinity; from Grammar through Syntax into Rhetoric, Rory played himself out. As likewise did some three hundred other pubescent schoolboys approaching manhood and a job in Esso Oil or the Bank; and

Revd Father Perrot SJ (nicknamed the Michaelmas Daisy) and
Father Meany SJ and the oozy Father Ffrench (who had a bad
stutter), hearing of this sin whispered into their inclined ears in
the semi-darkness of the confessional, in turn urged me not to
play with myself.

'Don't play with yourself, child.'

'No, Father.'

So I received absolution and said my penance.

The Dodo, who never got to bowl for the school XI, for no
skipper had ever asked him to 'turn his arm over' and try a
few overs from this end, nevertheless put in hour after hour at
patient practice, bowling into a long net erected on the tennis
court in early summer by Tommy Flynn. One stump stuck in
the ground to mark where he released each grunting delivery,
another twenty-two yards away which he attempted to knock
out of the ground and into the net; pounding in heavy and
truculent as Voce of Notts; throwing both arms up like Bill
Bowes when the ball missed the stump by a millimetre. The
Clongowes purple and white tie was knotted about his portly
waistline as a makeshift belt, in the fashion of a previous age,
adopted maybe by Dr W.G. Grace himself, who had set the
fashion, like Edward when he was Prince of Wales knotting his
tie in a certain way, a style to copy.

The Dodo sent down thousands upon thousands of deliveries,
the white shirt clamped to his back with the sweat of his exertions,
undone several buttons down. He set off from the gravel path
on to the tennis court, six strides to where the arm went over;
then the march down the crease to collect the ball, the rubbing
against his flannelled thigh to bring up a shine and leave a mark
as though he were bleeding; then the thoughtful march back to
the rockery wall, against which he sometimes urinated, splashing
like a cart-horse below us, for the Dote and I had climbed on
to the greenhouse roof and hid behind the tall chimney where
the jackdaws had made a nest and brought up their young, diving
down to feed them worms; it was from there were heard the Dodo
pissing and sending down his thunderbolts, the tail of his shirt now
out, the studded cricket boots much in need of Blanco.

These practice sessions went on for hours, for he had limitless patience. When at last he gave up, the stump stuck in the net, pullover about his shoulders, he sat himself on the garden seat outside the summerhouse and gazed down past the sundial and the palm trees and the pergola, thinking no doubt of the great bowling feats of his heroes.

Once the Dote and I, at a tender age, had escaped from Nurse O'Reilly, who was running a bath for us, and come down from the bathroom, scuttled downstairs and out on to the gravel, naked as the day we were born, and about to run around the house and into the garden when who came from cricket practice with all their cricket gear but our two elder brothers, with caps on their heads, carrying bats and pads and pullovers about their shoulders in the style of Test players quitting the field at the end of a gruelling day.

'Hey, what's going on here?' cried the Dodo in his high soprano voice.

He opened the innings for the school; he was a stonewaller difficult to remove. Having dug himself in, he occupied the crease as though he intended staying there for ever, perfectly satisfied to make few runs, refusing to take quick singles. D.B.J. Hill had to be *pried* out.

Nurse O'Reilly, who was taking a quick puff in the porch, called out that we would certainly catch our deaths of cold, and we should come into the house at once.

'Would you ever run out like good boys and tell your brother that his meal's ready and will be getting cold? Muffle up well.'

So, well muffled up and armed with the torch (its batteries failing, shining weakly on the garden door), obediently we sallied out into the pitch-black night of winter when the earth had already begun to harden with December frost and underfoot the grass of the tennis court was now stiff as astro turf and the net (never taken in) snagged and torn and tangled up with its supports and the sundial just a greyish blob by the palm trees shuffling their stiff sodden fronds and the summerhouse with its clapboard walls and climbing roses (finished now) just a dark thing on its elevation and the cold wind off Mangan's big field soughing through the bare branches of our great beech tree, oh!

Would you ever call your brother? Never never would we call him by his Christian name, Benedict. D.B.J.H. Never never never ever would he call us by ours, Rory and Colman George. Why he hardly seemed to see us, never adverted to us; we might as well not have been there at all. We were like the bell that summoned him to the table, functionally useful at times; at other times, playing games, getting giddy, a curse he had to put up with. D.B.J.H. Esq. The q had a curlicue tail to it that soared up and away, the swirling pretentious signature of a fop. He was named after his father, who had the makings of a fop.

Could the rapidly perambulating one, whose footsteps we heard hurrying towards us, see like a cat in the dark, then? Hardly; but years of incessant path-pounding summer and winter had worn away the gravel surface, as a decayed tooth is worn away to its exposed nerve, and the hard earth underneath shone with its quartz like a stream, upon which he resolutely marched.

The stiff familiar figure hove into sight now, pounding the path by the tall beech hedge, swinging its shoulders, head thrust forward from the trunk like the figurehead on a ship sailing before the wind, sails filling with the wind, turning upon itself and then as it (or he) swung around on his heel we recognised the oncoming Dodo, ready for the return march, and called out together in our shrill trebles, 'Ma says you're to come to supper!' as if that would stop him in his tracks; and ran off screeching with laughter. The pair of us good little brats ran off laughing fit to burst.

Benedict!

6

Mainly Semantics

On their holidays from Clongowes, which after all stood less than ten miles away beyond Clane village and the Jolly Farmers (the lights shining like an ocean liner sailing through Kildare, over fields and low ditches sparkling in the frosty nights), the Dodo and brother Bun seemed to have changed; certainly they spoke a different language to ours, dis and dat and mudder an me brudder and me fawder.

They favoured a strange tacky talk of obscure and puzzling references to unheard-of rituals that took place at the pool and in the three dormitories that segregated the three Lines. They spoke knowingly of the Yak, 'Baa' Keegan, 'Shanks' Lowry, Eskimo Nell (an American girl who came once at visiting time), 'Daisy' Maloney, 'Dog's Hole' Maguire, 'Horny' Ward (the science master), 'The Dog' McGlade, SJ (Classical Greek), 'Spud' Murphy and Father 'Spike' O'Donnell (who parted his black hair with a central parting like Mandrake the Magician and was said to have an ungovernable temper), Father 'Razz' O'Beirne, who discarded his dog collar and bloodied the nose of a Communist who spat on him in Salamanca.

Not to mention pandies, cockers (on the bare bum), twice nine, sleeps, sods, spooning, sowing, sneaks, tacks, snogging, sucks, Square Johnnies and Refectory Johnnies.

'Bags first go!' they cried in fluting voices.

'Crikey, I'm creased!'

Little Micky Kelly SJ was Father Minister, a sort of liaison officer between the parents and boys, much sought after by the loving mothers, much deferred to by the awestruck daddies, walking with him around the Higher Line track or about the castle (formerly country seat of the Wogan-Brownes) or down in the pleasure grounds.

He had a soft small appeasing voice and handshake and he was the authority you appealed to for 'Sleeps' which got you off night study, swotting up prep for next day's classes.

He presided over meals in the refectory thrice a day aloft in a wooden rostrum like the pulpit in St Audoen's in Dublin, with some narrow steps leading up. A nimble little hop on to the first step and then up hand over hand; he threw back the wings of his soutane and seated himself aloft on his throne and twinkled at his subjects below, watching to see that no billet-doux passed from table to table, for the three Lines were divided again here, the Third Liners as far as possible from the Higher Liners, all hoping for a touch, to 'get their hole' before leaving.

The other Father Kelly was Father Brendan Kelly, SJ, back after years in a Jesuit house in Australia to be Higher Line prefect and coach of the school XV; a tall, buck-toothed, quick-striding man whom you attended for easy pandies, unlike the Prefect of Studies, who sat in his office with the door threateningly open. If he heard you creeping by with a punishment tag in Latin, he called you in, whipped out his pandy bat, and would take the hand off you, panting as he struck.

Father Brendan Kelly was an equable sort of a man who coached in sports, track events, field events, relays, cricket and rugby. On Saturday evenings he sometimes took Declamation, a kind of pep talk to the Higher Liners assembled in the games room that got you off study. He asked the Higher Liners to open their dormitory windows at night because it wasn't so fresh in the morning when he came in at 6.50 to see that his charges were dressing in their cubicles and going down to Mass. He asked the Higher Line to desist from defacing the square (the toilets with cubicles called boxes presided over by a square Johnny to see that no hanky-panky went on, no passing of notes under box doors or soliciting messages on the backs of box doors, or bunking over the barbed wire to swim in the Liffey) with graffiti; though he understood the inclination and had heard that the walls of Pompeii were similarly defaced, so someone who had been there told him.

Finally, the local country lads of Clane and environs served at table and were called Johnnies since ages immemorial. Father Kelly said it would be kinder to call them by their given names, Johnny and Micky and Kevin and Paddy. We knew their names and it was rather demeaning to be called Johnnies, all of them. We were given privileges and should not abuse them. That was about all he had to say.

7

An Unwelcome Visitor Calls

O ne fine summer evening about six we were all sitting about the study table taking our supper or high tea (ham and salad with chopped tomatoes, hard-boiled eggs for those who would have them, all but the ham our own produce, with a Swiss roll for 'afters') when a spry figure, undoubtedly female, flitted past the window and presently we heard a timid knocking on the side door which stood invitingly wide open.

The family sat rigid and mortified as stone: Mumu stared at Dado as though it were all his fault, the Dodo stared at brother Bun as if by staring hard enough he could compel the unwelcome visitor to go away, the Dote stared at me in mild surmise: I was the one who wouldn't touch hard-boiled eggs or be persuaded or coaxed to drink a glass of milk.

'It's that one from Maynooth,' piped up the Dote, who sat facing the window, facing Dado who had his back to it. 'Miss Carmel Noseyparker Dermody!' sneered Dado, who had been 'getting a colour up' in the long grass of the orchard, stark naked on an oil-soaked rug, and was lightly dressed in slashed running shorts and sandals, his combinations or 'combs' cut short at the middle, and was hardly dressed for 'receiving'.

'Carmel Dermody, what a lovely surprise!' we heard Mumu's most dulcet tones in the hallway.

The Noseyparker, or Two-Faced Bitch in Dado's scornful appellation, had already entered, getting no response from her timid knocking, and was standing in the hallway outside the lamp-room where the Aladdin lamps were kept and filled, staring at a great pile of coke that mounted to the ceiling, uncertain how to proceed further.

'It's that bitch from Maynooth,' Dada said in a strangled aside, staring at the Dote's innocent little face as if it were a burnished mirror wherein was reflected Mumu being gracious to Miss Smarty Pants in the hall, and now saying, 'Come in, come in! You must take a cup of tea with us. I'm sure you must be famished after your walk.'

And in they came; the family rising as one.

Mealtimes were always a little charged, what with the demands of the faddy eater, the Dodo's silence and pointing and 'Ahems' for the procurement of condiments out of reach, Dado's table-rapping with knuckles and coded references addressed to Mumu; the meals, sometimes soon over, at other times indefinitely prolonged, arbitrary as inter-parliamentary debates (but here carried on in silence with innuendo and sign language, eye messages), this person vindicated, that one damned. It would put you in mind of the complexities of our unfair and lopsided Statutes of Kilkenny, the Codicils of the Elders of Zion or the archaic and long obsolete Manx laws, procedures and protocols to control an island less than a third the size of our own, the stocks and the gallows barely dismantled, flogging still popular in sentencing.

'Yes indeed, Mrs Hill. I'm *famished*.'

She lived with her old cranky mother somewhere on the way to Maynooth and had 'run up' three tweed skirts, after two sittings, lined and zipped, that Mumu was so delighted with, she said she would order more. But calling for sittings and calling unannounced was not the same thing; as long as she knew her place (and stayed in it) socially she was acceptable at Springfield; otherwise not. She had come across the fields to pay us a surprise visit, it was such a lovely day for it and she loved walking; she wore booties and ankle socks and the booties were yellow with pollen, and she never stopped talking, the cup balanced on her lap and her little finger raised when she sipped in a delicate ladylike fashion. She wore one of her own tweed skirts and under it a corset that attempted to flatten her pronounced rump. The deep imitation leather armchair bought at cost price from Jack Ellis, whom Dado called a Jew-boy, was as awkward to get out of as the deepest bunker in Portmarnock links and groaned deeply and embarrassingly every time she moved as if involuntarily emitting wind, dry farts.

She sat sideways on, sipping tea and flattering Mumu, offering to my abstracted gaze a disconcerting view of fleshy female inside leg and fat thigh and she was asking Mumu where would she (Mumu) be without them (the Dote and myself, the second-last born faddy feeder and the last-born who 'was no trouble at all').

'Run along now, boys. Go and play in the garden,' Mumu bade us in a grand affected accent, as the chatelaine giving orders to a groom. 'Say goodbye to Miss Dermody.'

So we ran out into the summerhouse and did murderous imitations of the unwelcome guest. Speaking in prissy tones and balancing an invisible cup of tea on the lap, we were in turn Miss Carmel Dermody, the guest who had called unannounced but would not come again; for behind all her gush she had watched us, and saw us judge her and find her wanting. She was no fool.

'I'm not overstaying my welcome, am I?' the Dote asked, giving me a sly look. 'You have a lovely place here. How do you manage to keep it so clean?'

'I don't bother,' I said in the voice of Carmel Dermody.

'Your two manly little lads must be a real blessing,' the Dodo ventured boldly, and we fell about pissing ourselves laughing.

'Oh not a *tall*,' I gushed, 'we love to have you.'

'Do you know Dunmanway?' shrieked the Dote.

'I'm sure you must be famished!' I got in.

It was as good gas as the Gaiety.

'To tell you the truth, I *am* famished,' squeaked the Dote.

'You're really famished?'

'What a bummer,' said the Dote.

It was the new word he had recently discovered: bummer. Miss Carmel Dermody was a *real* bummer.

8

The Handbell and the Gong

To stay immobilised was the Dodo's dream, since all action was suspect, tarnished back to its source. As an opener who refused to open up he was most himself, forever standing guard, an emblem or graven image: Len Hutton of Yorkshire and England, obdurate and unflinching as Yorkshire granite.

Always at his fingernails, buffing, snipping, trimming, blowing on them; like one of Faulkner's devious rustics a-whittling slivers of wood on the back porch of Mrs Littlejohn's kitchen, whittling in order to disguise what he was thinking or waiting for the summons to food, 'Vittles is up!'

What was that imperious term he used?

I SAY!

The handbell rung vigorously by Lizzy told him what he wanted to hear, namely, that the food was in the oven awaiting his arrival. When the meal was over he rose, pushed his chair in and left as silently as he had arrived, at the summons of a gong. A gong for lunch, a handbell after dark. He never flew combat missions in the dark when he was serving in the RAF, and when the war ended he came back and was working in an office on Stephen's Green in Dublin, studying to qualify as a quantity surveyor, had laid out cartridge paper and tacked it down with drawing pins on the study table, brought in his T-squares and rubbers, mapping pens and marking ink, HB pencils sharpened keenly as his fingernails, and set to work there every evening, before Ovaltine and bed, cackling at Tommy Handley ('It's That Man Again!') on faulty transmission from the BBC, as if the Irish Sea had got into the works and Handley and his jokers were drowning. The family was obliged to eat elsewhere and took meals in the drawing room, in the dining room empty of furniture except the table and chairs, and even in Mumu's bedroom with a view of distant blue Dublin hills, with Lysanders and Avro Ansons rising up from Baldonnel aerodrome.

'Stay!'

The Dodo's poses at the non-striker's end were dramatic in the extreme; he remained rooted to the spot, gloved hand rigid as the tall Civic Guard who directed the traffic over Capel Street Bridge and along Ormond Quay in both directions. None of your cheeky Compton creeping down the pitch before the bowler's arm was well over.

It was an illustration of one of Mumu's favourite quotations (was it from some novel by Brinsley MacNamara, whom she had known in her youth?): 'Wanted: a detective to arrest the course of time.'

The left forearm vertical and stiff from the elbow up, the palm (white-gloved) extended to stop oncoming traffic; the right hand making an accommodating gesture of 'free flow', under the rigid left elbow as though paddling the air, 'Proceed!'

All Civic Guards had to be six foot or over in those days, clomping down in outsize boots from the training depot in Phoenix Park past where Gina Green had taken the Dote and me to the Dublin Zoo, past where I went later when playing cricket for Phoenix with Jimmy Boucher, who bowled bodyline, with Dick Greer and Brendan Fox and David Pigott, and crouched in the leg trap with the Quinns, Frank, Brendan, Paddy and Kevin.

Boucher had once bowled out the New Zealanders. He kept his jock-strap in a canvas bag used for small change, silver coinage in the bank, having once worked in the Munster and Leinster.

You could hear the click of his fingers as he released each

fiercely flighted delivery that broke either way, after the high-stepping, chest-out bustling run-up had the shiny red ball whipping off the pitch; the click was as menacing as the Xhosa tongue-click; and the leg-trap that had been crouched behind the batsman and to one side rose upright again. The six deliveries came buzzing down the pitch like a hive of wild bees.

'Nice one, Jimmy,' someone murmured.

When Phoenix played the Free Foresters, both teams lunched in the Dublin Zoo and a cheerful fellow who had been a British Army officer in Soviet Russia during the war said he had slept with a Russian woman and that it was like sleeping with a she-bear. But what was a British officer doing in Stalinist Russia? Were the Allies fools enough to share their Bletchley Park code-breaking knowledge with Uncle Joe?

The Dodo, as I say, was always at his hands, attending to his fingernails, buffing, trimming, clipping, pushing in the cuticles, blowing on his fingernails and holding them up for closer inspection with the quiet complacency that a cat, when engaged in toilet, gives its paws.

The Dodo was as one of those dandies you find in paintings by Carpaccio forever fondling one of those terrible little dogs called Tenerife, or as the butterflies that flitter about a Whistler canvas. Such vanity!

9

An Unwelcome Visit Recalled

D ado said that she was 'country cute' and he had a good mind to give her a flea in her ear if she had the neck to come calling again. The cool cheek of her!

'Underbred,' said Mumu with a dismissive sniff that put the upstart back in her place. 'But what more can you expect with parents like hers? A big thick cattle dealer and his big lump of a wife with no more social graces than a heifer. That sort of woman should *never* wear beige. The daughter is making sure not to take after her.'

So that's how it was.

As long as Carmel Dermody knew her place, and stayed in it, well and good; she was acceptable. Acceptable, that is to say, as a talented seamstress who could 'run up' skirts and blouses to order. She was most definitely not welcome as a casual visitor who dropped in uninvited for tea and a chat, wearing sensible brogues for walking across the fields and a powerful girdle that attempted to control that big behind of hers.

She was after all just the country-bred daughter of a big thick lug of a cattle jobber who had an unprepossessing wife and an ugly big house somewhere up there near Maynooth.

Neither Mumu nor Dado would seek or accept any reciprocal hospitality from the Dermodys; nor would Miss Two-Face attempt to offer any; that was clearly understood by all parties concerned.

The truth of the matter is that my dear departed parents were in some ways strangers to this world. Both had their own particular brand of ingrained self-centredness, a lethargy, akin to the apathy of the stars, the indifference of the galaxies floating away into space. They preferred to let things slide.

They were cast down twice, twice blew all their wealth away, all security, ending up in a damp underground basement fit only for rats. There they lived on the dole, and for four years on the money Rory sent them from Johannesburg.

When, through no choice of theirs, they began to go down, they went far down; finally they found themselves in a place where I couldn't reach them.

Inherited money, money for which you hadn't sweated, was funny money, hardly money at all. Dado had no compunction in asking for and getting large overdrafts to 'see him through', very condescending to bank managers and then cringing before the same official when the American dividends finally ran dry. Dado stopped picking his ears with a match and began poking up both nostrils with his little finger, letting off a barrage of farts, poised at some strategic point.

Mumu was no help at all, except at helping him to spend it, the cab at the door, Phoenix Park races, dinner at the Royal Hibernian and the Red Bank, Jammet's; the dividends rushed away. 'Keep it and you'll always have it,' Mumu said bitterly, her lipstick awry, her awful hat at an angle, like a ship sinking.

When they ran into debt (and 'ran' is the operative word), she protested that she was at her wits' end; now the bank manager was losing patience; stiffly phrased letters began to arrive. Dado, hands in pockets, was off, whistling to himself. Inherited money wasn't money at all.

Though Catholics were discouraged from holding a lease in the Burnaby, the most Anglican of enclaves within a mainly Protestant community, Dado found a small holiday bungalow up for sale on Kinlen Road on the extreme border of the Burnaby. Even though he was still nominally a Catholic, though no longer a practising one, he became a member of the Greystones Golf

Club. In time, with the passing of years and schooldays ended, Rory joined him, proposed by 'Brandy' Ball and seconded by Simon Pettigrew.

Having lost or spent one fortune, Dado and Mumu began resolutely to throw away another. With the proceeds of the Springfield sale, for which Dado had got a good price, he bought 'Caragh' (Gaelic for 'friend'), and complacently saw it go to rack and ruin over the years.

The cycles of extravagance were repeated, the squandering went on apace, dinners at the Grand Hotel and the Horse and Hounds in Delgany, hacking on a hired horse, on a four-day whiskey binge with Captain Ball, and him with only one leg (the other he had left behind on Anzio beach). Until at last, for the second time, it was all gone again; but this time for good. There was no house to sell, just a load of debts; not even the furniture was theirs. They quit Greystones in ostentatious poverty. After sixteen years of ever-dwindling resources the American annuities dried up, their poor effects were piled up on an open wagon and they left for a new life in Dalkey 'like the Joads setting out for California', the Dote reported to Rory who was living in London.

Notions about social inferiors and betters remained with them: that was all they had left, their illusions. The American money dried up when the real estate (the Hill Building in LA) was sold.

When the herd of cattle that had grazed in the seventy-two acres at Springfield were sold and the land steward Tommy Flynn got his walking papers and returned home to Longford, the downward spiral had begun.

The farm was not worked, the fields lay fallow, were rented out for grazing, the idlest form of farming for gentlemen disposed to a life of ease. Dado did some light scuffling, did a few chores around the house and farm, counted the eggs laid in the mangers, occupied his days in unrelenting idleness.

After Springfield was sold, they moved to Greystones; after the Burnaby they moved to Dalkey; after Dalkey to Dun Laoghaire. Going down into the Haigh Terrace basement flat would 'do' for them both; and indeed it did, given time and enough dampness.

A brain haemorrhage in the night did for Mumu; cancer finally caught up with Dado two years later. Their last years were not happy ones. They gave me my life and I should be thankful to them.

In Haigh Terrace (ominous mnemonic!) they were already halfway into the grave; Dean's Grange cemetery wasn't too many furlongs off. Their mouldy underground quarters were situated midway between the Garda station and the spired church built by Italian POWs.

10

A Fragment of the True Cross

My earliest and fondest memories were of the Dote dressing himself on the thin strip of carpet worn threadbare by constant usage on the floor that separated our twin beds in the unheated nursery.

Solemnly vesting himself in a mealy-coloured woollen gansey knitted by his mother; applying himself to the task in hand with all the intense seriousness that was habitual to him; for that was the way he was made, that was the way he was and nothing could change that. Never exactly 'the glass of fashion and the mould of form' but the cheap striped tie knotted about the neck so fragile, the shirt worn for three or more days slipped over the head; then on with the boots with turned-up toes and brassy eye-studs, dull clothes that proclaimed duty, duty, duty, before the slick of water to settle the quiff, the comb run through the parting. His everyday clothes were as keepsakes flung into a drawer and forgotten by this careful brother of mine who never threw anything away, whose earliest ambition, so he averred, was to be a crow.

A crow; cor!

Were not clothes 'weeds' for poet Edmund Spenser, as 'wonted weeds' were mourning apparel in Shakespeare's day? My younger brother would have looked neat and chipper if kitted out in silken knee-britches or half-hose, ruffs and powdered wig, the face powdered too, cheeks rouged and a touch of lipstick and eyeliner, in the time of Haydn and Schumann; to bring a touch of natural colour to anaemic cheeks, a sparkle to the anxious eye.

He had a nose on him thin and keen as the nib of a pen; not a fountain pen, mark you, not a Bird or a Waterman with little sac and clip, but a penny pen with disposable nib and a cheap wooden grip ink-stained and chewed with mental effort, frustration and long usage, dipped into the inkwell of Quink, giving off a whiff strong as chloroform or smelling salts; in order to attempt joined-up writing, copying out the adage set forth on the top line of the exercise book. A penny pen in First or Second Infants of the Holy Faith Convent hidden behind the walls of Celbridge in the care of the nuns in the time not long after the Eucharistic Congress of 1932.

Now divesting himself of his drawers and pullover (stitching had already run along one arm), rumpled shirt and combinations (his 'combs'), the daywear; to climb into his nightwear, crumpled pyjamas as bedraggled as the items he had just discarded and folded neatly at the end of his bed.

Pulling the shirt over his head with arms crisscrossed in a fussy way that never failed to irritate me, his face – when it appeared again – screwed tight and anxious in a purposeful scowl as though caught in the act of somersaulting headlong over a vaulting horse or 'pulling off' some daring trick of the loop which contrived to whisk the gymnast back the way he had come, arms now outflung for applause, before running off, vanishing like Harry Houdini over the fearful fall of Niagara in a barrel.

Well, it takes a worried man to sing a worried song. The finite is ever trapped within the infinite. All good things must come to an end. It never rains but it pours.

Abhorring laxness, the sluggishness that leads to backsliding, the Dote was ever his own man. When he applied himself to the task in hand it became a mighty serious matter, an act of single-mindedness. Firm and even-handed in his dealings with others, he was as honest as the day is long; his character had been formed early and nothing would change it. Humanity is its work in itself; our daily bread can only be earned – and we have this on the very best authority – by the sweat of our brow. When he pulled the ganzy over his head the face that reappeared was an Aztec or Mayan mask of suffering.

He drove me from the Holyhead ferry in his beaten-up Mini Minor through Wales and across England via Stratford-upon-Avon where a company of merry Spanish bakers was working in a bakery at six o'clock in the morning, from whom we bought a loaf of warm bread. And off via Edgehill, site of a famous battle. Coming at last with swollen feet to the two-storey semi-detached house sublet to slutty hippies at 18 Ludlow Road on the way to those sad-sounding places, Ongar and Hounslow, home of howling dogs.

My poor brother was distraught and all but in tears when he saw what havoc the hippies had perpetrated against his house somewhere off the Great North Road, amid the onward-spreading sameness of the great urban sprawl.

'LYNN WAS HERE!!!!' haggishly screeched one wall, daubed and besmeared with what looked like menstrual blood. 'HIS 'N HERS!!' was splashed slapdash in runny purple humpy lettering athwart the defaced headboard, roughly as evacuations voided on counterpane and sheets. The cramped rooms were livid with shrieking psychedelic colours, porno magazines crammed into the overflowing privy, its cistern blocked with nameless filth. All the signs of hanky-panky were there, as though the rascally sub-tenants had just departed, leaving their foulness and smells behind. All the never-ending mess of other lives had been toppled pell-mell over my now thoroughly confused and upset brother, so careful in his own way; his privacy and security had been breached, torn apart.

Didn't Wordsworth have some scatterbrained theory that houses should be the same colour as the land they stood on? In some primitive cultures human dwellings are glued together with excrement.

In Stieglitz, West Berlin in the years of the Berlin Wall, the former 'brown district' with many of the grim Nazi villas still standing aloof behind their high protective walls, there lived Walter Waldmann in deep seclusion, a 'scraper' by profession; that is to say an illegal abortionist.

In Andalucía on the coast, the walls of the fishermen's cottages are precariously put together with rubble masonry, rocks, driftwood off the beach and sea-sand in the cement likely to 'give' in heavy rain; as happened the morning Trevor Callus drove back from the Málaga nursing home with his Norwegian wife and newborn daughter Camilla in his DKW. My wife and I were passengers. We had hardly turned the key in the door of our house when we heard the rumble of one of the poorer cottages opposite collapsing into the street down which the rain was pouring. Calle Carabeo in Nerja always had a high pong of sewage, human waste, which delighted Callus, who liked to quote statistics of what *caca* was flushed daily into the Hudson in New York.

An old-fashioned taste in clothes was part of the Dote's habitual reserve, of not drawing attention to himself: socks pulled up over trouser ends for cycling; shabby woollen gloves in need of darning. One thought of Freya Stark travelling through the Arab lands with riding-shirt buttoned up to the throat, woollen stockings covering her head, shirt worn over riding britches, making her way through Bouzai Gumbad into Bistritza and on over the Parmirs.

Colman was transparently honest, honest as the day is long, incapable of cheating, notorious for never accepting bribes, straight as a die. As they say nowadays, he 'hung in' there tenaciously, a person of set habits fixed as his formal attire, reticent by nature, even secretive – to every nook its cranny. Conscious of his obligations and set in his ways, he had long ago put himself in order. In his view we had not been put on this earth to enjoy ourselves; think rather on frugality, on decorum.

The unchanging ritual of dressing was as mannered and composed as Colman's way of saying his night prayers, when whispering into joined hands as he prepared for bed just across from me; enacted with the same ritual care that he used when vesting and divesting himself as an altar boy serving Mass, careful with cruets and thurible, immensely slow in measured genuflections, solemn as a crow digging in a potato drill.

Behind all this there was something obdurate, fine and

unflinching, as true to form as a splinter from the True Cross. Colman, donning surplice and soutane in the sacristy at Clongowes, holding the paten under the chins of communicants with their eyes shut tight, was as solemn and subdued as a convict donning prison garb in preparation for serving out a stiff sentence; the clothes themselves were the token of bondage, a penitential vesting correctly meek, a humbling investiture.

With eyes lowered, he invoked the Scourging at the Pillar in the ritual he was partaking in, marking the progress of the Holy Passion. He himself, the humble altar boy, the suppliant, a veritable pillar of rectitude and correctness, robed in red soutane to his ankles, verily washed in the Blood of the Lamb. In the fringed white surplice stiff with bleach and ironing, he became the Lamb Bled White.

The little white puffs of incense sent out of the perforated thurible boat sedately swung by my brother, told in Latin, *Castitas! Castitas!* Be chaste, sin no more, Heaven is nigh. A whiff of that stuff assailing my nostrils caused my giddy head to reel.

Hands joined at breast level, eyes downcast and pale as a sheet, Colman moved slowly and gravely as in a trance, for himself and for the other altar boy from Second Syntax, preceding the celebrant priest – and this morning it was to be Father Eamonn Diffilly himself, republican and Gaelic revivalist – through the arch of the sacristy door, moving together in a phalanx towards the high altar as the school of over three hundred boys knelt as one, a field of growing wheat ruffled by a sudden breeze.

He was by nature a *kneeler*. He liked to get things right, liked to obey; it became him. In retirement in his later years, free time became a burden; he fed the half-wild moggies, worried about the weeds, began to be a little autocratic in shops, bossing shopkeepers about, keeping them on their toes, glad to serve Mr Hill (no informality please) who had been a big noise in the Planning Department of the Wicklow County Council. He ordered wood and milk, took in the *Irish Times*, was (I suspect) somewhat of a tyrant in the home.

The half-finished home had all the chilly ambience of a

Bavarian *Kursaal* out of season, water dripping on to deserted landings, the phone ringing and no one there to answer.

His wife Stella Veronica didn't answer back, didn't give any lip, seemed contented enough to live in the past, with her memories of Greystones, which after all wasn't so far away.

The ugly cats glided about, were fed regularly. They had been found lean and starving on some building site and taken back and fed and had lavished upon them all the love that couldn't be lavished on the children that hadn't come. In that sense their life together had a certain shape to it, though admittedly an uncomfortable shape, as the lives of others always seem to have; the chill of nothing much.

For so frail a being he seemed to carry on his back an enormous freight of irresistible sorrows, as *der buckelige Männlein*, his hump.

Sincerity was the *sine qua non* of his existence, that which propped up the whole shaky edifice and kept it standing. When duties were respected and honoured, as they should be honoured and respected, then the emoluments would flow; how could they not?

This I sensed in the stink of the swirling incense that drifted back from the altar; but Catholicism for me was like the luke-warm milk Colman fetched in old-fashioned bottles at a certain shop in Wicklow that sold newspapers and processed 'turf', known as briquettes. That was the Catholic Church on its wobbly foundations, a leaning tower of Pisa seen in the incense fumes and the two altar boys robed in red, kneeling and genuflecting when the priest came to the altar rail holding the ciborium with the hosts in it and the altar boys suddenly sticking out their tongues at the priest and then swallowing the blessed oval dissolving on their tongues.

That to me was all humbug, like the hand-shaking and the Pope prostrating himself on the tarmac of strange airports, purporting to kiss the ground, a lowly and unhygienic act. The Blessed in Heaven in their serried ranks, supposing they were observing this malarky, must have been in stitches.

Now wasn't it typical of my brother that his lowly dwelling should be nameless? That veritable Crusoe stockade of his was

'The House With No Name', Ye Olde Moncken Holt, haunt
of coot and hern, abode of otter; which went with the subdued
genuflection, meek mien, the serving. 'Lurkyne in hernes and in
lanes blynde,' (Chaucer).

Not for Colman such grandiose notions as Frank Lloyd
Wright's Falling Water by a river cascade in the woods of
Pennsylvania or the Robie House in Chicago; not the dwelling
place that Luis Barragan had designed for a rich client in Mexico
City; nor the stupendous eighteenth-century wooden chalet
where Balthus hid himself away in the Swiss Alps; nor Gaudi's
gaudy edifice in Barcelona – a witch's house built of sugar; nor
Branson's grandiose Caribbean hideaway, an island retreat fit only
for high-flyers such as himself.

It would certainly be more subdued and darker, along the lines
of the Roman villa built for Alberto Moravia (born Pincherle) by
an architect father in a small thickly wooded garden somewhere
behind the Hotel Excelsior; a darkened abode purpose-built,
suitable for a melancholic at his own depressing dinner party.

Pliny the Younger owned summer and winter villas, Malaparte
and Dali had their exotic Mediterranean belvederes and eyries
built to puff up their own vanity; but a whiff of Bauhaus
simplicity and austerity would better suit my brother's spartan
taste.

Nabobs like Maugham and Berenson owned palaces with
Lamborghinis and Astra-Romanas stashed in spacious garages,
with gardeners and droves of servants at hand to gratify every
whim; but my brother was having none of that. Maugham, the
milk-drinking nonagenarian multimillionaire, was irascible as a
stoat, staring down the table at his uneasy guests dining off his
silver plate; the host convinced that they were hatching schemes
against him; while his French servants, having already devoured
his dogs, had proceeded to rob him blind. Riches didn't amount
to much under such circumstances; or at least hadn't produced
happiness.

The luxurious homes of the very rich, private pleasure domes
of the Côte d'Azur battlemented and buttressed and with flag
flying that announced the owner was in residence, once the
property of some duc or vicomte but now more likely owned

by a film star the likes of Rex Harrison; these were fortresses of wealth perched on a hill.

The benign old codger Berenson paced gravely about the manicured grounds of I Tatti and all's well with the world; at least so believed the not-so-decrepit Rex Harrison in San Genseio at Portofino.

11

A Rude Country Habitation

The House With No Name in Dunganstown West was hidden behind its protective escarpment of earthworks and cramped weed-choked ramparts and had already a dilapidated look, even before completion. The Dote had taken to heart Mumu's bitter axiom that you can't have too much of a good thing. She had a repertoire of such old sayings: what was sauce for the goose was sauce for the gander, a little learning is a dangerous thing, a little goes a long way, it never rains but it pours, you've got to be cruel to be kind.

Eat every scrap, she bade us at table, confronted with reheated beef and dried-out swedes, stewed apple and custard after school; and we would again be reminded of the starving millions in China.

The House With No Name, the unfinished home, was duplicated on another scale in the drab clothes he wore and seemed to prefer above all others, the trusty Balbriggan surtout as snug a fit as feathers on a Rhode Island Red, the pens and pencils of his profession protruding from his breast pocket, the jacket so well worn (worn seven days a week) that it already had a reach-me-down second-hand appearance soon after he had bought it off the peg in some old-fashioned Talbot Street, Dublin haberdashery away from the fashionable quarters; duplicating the jacket just discarded, a herringbone tweed in mustard twill. No question of taste; taste didn't come into it. Appearances didn't count, after all, didn't amount to much; for behind all fiction loomed the undisputed fact. As behind Citizen Kane's Xanadu stood Hearst's real foursquare San Simeon, the stately pleasure dome erected with no regard for cost on the deserts of the Gulf of California, just as Branson's men had dynamited the crest off a deserted Caribbean island to build his House on the Hill (Necker), his bailiwick seventy-four acres of sun-blasted scrub and cactus and screeching seabirds. As behind Sutpen's Hundreds (Faulkner's fancy) stood the remnants of some honest-to-God antebellum Mississippian mansion with shadowy colonnades fit home for the loon bird and the coon; empty slave quarters somewhere decently out of sight, in that time and that place fragrant with wisteria and magnolia sweet and fresh, where Southern belles in hoop skirts did not walk but floated.

My sober, level-headed brother, set in his spartan ways and normally so sparing of praise, declared that a good two inches separated every word in Scott Fitzgerald's 1925 novel, *The Great Gatsby*, one of those American moralities on the theme that wealth does not buy happiness, which came out the year before I was born.

But hold your hearses, Golubchik, wasn't 'Jay Gatsby' already an assumed name, a disguise for 'Jimmy Gatz', and the mansion built there on West Egg in the great wet barnyard of Long Island Sound with its marble swimming pool and forty acres of rolling lawns just as much an invention as the vast palace faked by Welles's small ingenious models as conceived by his special-effects man Vernon L. Walker and executed by his Art Director Van Nest Polglase?

The grandiose mansion was itself a surrogate, an imitation of some grand hotel de ville that the rich but alcoholic author had once seen like a drunken vision and had tabulated and stored up in his acquisitive and retentive writer's memory for later use; to be there, immutable, transfixed as a figment of the imagination, a dream.

A stranger called Lou Harrison built himself a house on a high spit of land overlooking the Pacific, because he couldn't stand the constant din of the metropolis. 'The thing roars all day long and there's no getting away from it. There are no woods to go to. Too much turbulence, too many goddamn people, too much noise.' He found a safe retreat in the Mojave Desert, where he built his house entirely of densely packed bales of straw fixed to cement foundations, with soundproofed rooms.

Charles Olson thought that he had recognised the origins of the mosque dome in the curvilinear tents of the nomads pitched by oases, and the form of the minarets in cypress trees. These, to frequently drugged eyes and brain, were indeed deceptive likenesses, beguiling in their winsomeness as certain imaginary ruins found in Venetian Masters depicting parts and relictae, broken monuments of dead generations, roofless ruins and the dust of ancestors, perfect parts of an impossible whole.

I remember the holy old man who had built himself a corrugated iron hut away from the sea, held down with wire hawsers and sods of earth on the roof, near the sand dunes at Baltray golf links when I played in the East of Ireland Golf Championship and bought a set of irons off the pro, Mick McGurk. Dado had been incautious enough to give me a blank cheque signed by his own fair hand. I made it out for £20 and traded in my old set of woods and irons.

The hermit had returned home after spending a lifetime herding cattle in Canada. His step was long and slow and when he said 'Praise be to God' (the weather was fine) it was like seeing a feather dropping off an angel's wings. He put in time chipping old gutta-percha balls on to the greens with hickory-shafted clubs. A little girl came across the fairways with a pail of fresh milk every evening and a plume of blue smoke that rose straight up from his makeshift chimney informed her that old Barney the holy man was at home.

I called on him once but, on hearing the drone of the rosary within, left him to his devotions. He was a reflective self-contained man with skin the colour of old parchment, from his years on the prairies; he kept himself to himself. I never got talking to him.

In my mind's eye, the eye in the back of the head, I imagined or thought that I saw a stone house standing by itself on a desolate headland facing an immense ocean that lay to the west; and where on earth could it be but a plot of land at Carmel Point on the Monterey Peninsula to the north of Big Sur – the house that Robinson Jeffers built with his own hands, hauling granite rocks from the shore with strong horses and pulleys.

In the pavement outside the front door of Tor House was inset a piece of Yeats's Thoor Ballylee and fragments of George Moore's ancestral home in Mayo that had been destroyed during the Civil War.

Gift-stones were cemented into Hawk Tower and in the wall of the courtyard (as a small blue unmarked casket containing the ashes of Orson Welles were cemented into a wall on the bull farm of his *amigo* Antonio Ordoñez outside Ronda); these were fragments from the Great Wall of China and the Great Pyramid of Cheops, toted hither by the hawk-faced man who, as a lad of seven years, had Latin slapped into him by a severe father, a minister of the United Reformed Church, a gifted preacher and pastor, a student of German and French, a scholar of Greek, Latin, Hebrew, Aramaic, Syriac, Arabic, Babylonian and Assyrian, a professor of Greek and holder of various chairs in biblical and ecclesiastical studies.

Colman, two years my junior, believed in work as a God-given duty and obligation; not for him any platitudes about work being a curse, soporific or negative reality: to my brother's way of thinking, that just didn't wash. He was as sound as Galusha Grow himself, the homesteaders' champion, member of Congress and defender of the prairie farmers who had built their sod huts *sans* foundations and sanitation on the windy western plains, where every man was his own fertiliser, and every woman too. Every man had a right to as much of the earth's surface as was necessary for his support and well-being, even a plainsman of Nebraska.

Well do I recall the little tits and wrens in their ovoid nests of moss and twigs and sheep's wool and leaves with their false entrances and tiny unseen fledglings twittering within; and weaverbirds that built their basket nests daringly suspended over the Orange River outside dusty Vryberg, an Afrikaanse township in what is now Nomaqualand, and their colony of nests that weighed down the telegraph poles on the borders of the Kalahari Desert, seen when touring with the marionettes out of London on a two-year tour of South Africa and the Rhodesias in the time of trouble for the downtrodden tribes of Africans, the time of apartheid, with Colonel Spengler and the *swak van du bloed* ranged implacably against them.

Those ingenious avian architects had contrived their habit-ations with a makeshift perishable look to them, swinging out over the water, casual as tinkers' encampments; sagging loose as spider webs over the river, intimating that time and fate and the turning seasons would deal harshly with them. And in my brother's unfinished house, I had had that feeling too.

The parsimonious deployment of building materials, the exposed brick and timber, the mounds of rubble in tarps on the ground, the gaping holes for absent front door and outlines of missing windows, the whole unsightly and unshapely pile seen against the darkening sky across which passed a scattered assembly of raucous crows returning from their feeding grounds; all this put me in mind of nothing so much as the Temple of the Crossed Hands at Kotosh at the headwaters of the Huallaga river in Peru; of the adobe – and thus perishable – city of Chan Chan built by the rulers of the ancient Kingdom of Chimor and later levelled by stout Cortes in his meteoric passage of destruction across Mayan territory; of legendary Cuzco of the Inca Empire in the fastness of Peru.

I thought too of the children given to be sacrificed in Mayan times, whose tender lives were not to be spared, the little innocents led in procession to a place where they would be put to death by the priests; to reappear the following spring as flowers, placatory emblems to the sun. And I recalled the hideous beasts that destroyed Nineveh in the prophecies of Zephaniah.

It (the darkly speculative outline of the house-to-be) seemed all interstices, all its insides falling out, like the quarterings of some carcass with interior exposed by the butcher's knife; a skinned beast hung up for butchering purposes, suspended on the hook and already beginning to subside, pulled downward by its own dead weight, crawling with bluebottles. There in the falling darkness it appeared as an unwieldy structure, something dark and undefined, wavering as if underwater.

In the raising up of it – and my brother was ever-sceptical of any rash venture undertaken without sufficient forethought, raising expectations that were bound to be dashed, running ahead of all reasonable hopes; for such failure was inherent in all human enterprises – that failure was already evident, as intimated in the sad sag of the rafter beams off true and the dejected appearance of protective sacking thrown over mounds of stuff drenched by downpours of incessant rain, for the place was sited in a double rainshadow. Here too I detected only stages of dereliction. He was going to have trouble fitting windows.

Not much daylight was admitted. It was a shabby place of stale spent air and awkward angles. This sanctuary was a chosen haunt, a final retreat. The sadly sagging bed, a sorry spectacle, appeared to subside, supported by piles of yellowing outdated newspapers and magazines packed tightly together, supporting the bed-sag, holding the whole miserable contraption up. The bed, mother of all hiding places, was an unsurpassable hideyhole. For, as said before, all was perishable here on earth, so my brother understood; certainly we were not put here to enjoy ourselves. Earthly Paradise was not for the likes of us. He was quite capable of not saying anything, when he wanted to (and if that house was mine, what part of me was buried in that grave?).

Dervorgilla Doran's cottage *ornée* was as true to herself as anything that remains true to itself, as neatly aligned as her Japanese-inspired fencing to its ground. Don't change a thing, darling Derv; it's *you*.

Of course the perfect fit, *vis-à-vis* landlord and rented property (whatever about awkward sub-tenant) was and is a myth: it may look grand (Dervorgilla graciously serving Earl Grey tea, sipping the brew, little finger elevated as in the painting, *Five O'clock Tea*, by Mary Cassatt) but is as false as the fit of frontal dentures in bridgework that tends to induce a frightful grimace when a winning smile was the effect intended. (All that had happened ten years ago. Now the Grand Hotel is up for sale, now Dervorgilla is a mother, by a German.)

★   ★   ★

Dressed as if in cast-off clothes, apparel of beggars, my brother and his wife had appeared by the door with the suddenness of an apparition and the exhausted look of nomads on the march. The *noli me tangere* look, veiled with suspicion, the look askance of those perpetually on the move, begging, the shifty look that will not engage your eye, was here made manifest. Then they made their way shyly and circumspectly across the breadth of the Grand Hotel lounge bar as if crossing tundra or shifting ice-floe, approaching where I was seated by a fire of great logs, gin and tonic to hand, and Werner Herzog's *Of Walking On Ice* (*Von Gehen im Eis*), which I had picked up in an Austin bookstore in the degrading heat of August in Texas.

Pastoral nomads came to mind, tent-dwellers, Bedu of Donakil footing it down the *routes horribles* known to Rimbaud burnt black by the sun, or Sanburu cattle-herders of northern Kenya, the denizens of the Empty Quarter where I had never been. That, those there, or the spring migration of the elusive and backward Bakhiari; or the Kaffirs of the Hindu Kush.

A decayed and moth-eaten wolfskin coat (similar to that worn by Brossette, the chauffeur of Octave Mirbeau) would not have looked too amiss on Colman's back. Casting anxious looks about them they came on, making their way down the crowded bar through the press of people that ignored them, uncertain smiles frozen to their bloodless lips, frozen to the bone. How thin and ethereal were those evasive vegetarian smiles hovering on anaemic lips as if too timid to declare themselves as true smiles, any gladness of heart at seeing me; no, merely appealing ghosts of smiles, vapoury, sepulchral smiles. The motto *Horreur de Domicile* was their true blazon; it suited them down to the ground, for no house would hold them.

'Long live the living!' I cried effusively, rising. 'Success to sailors' wives and greasy luck to whalers. Take a pew. You both look frozen, as if you've come a long way. From Alaska or Archangel, I fancy.'

'Timbuktu, actually,' breathed my brother with a lost faraway look in his eye as he lowered himself cautiously into his seat.

'My, my! A body does get around.'

'Quite.'

They had seated themselves opposite me, the guarded semi-smiles still hovering about their lips but already melting away in the great heat thrown out by the fire; doubtless too by the warm anticipation of potent spirits about to be ordered up.

'Never throw a stone at dogs in Timbuktu,' said I, seated now. 'What'll it be? Your pleasure, Mistress Stella?'

She had the timid and reserved manner that went with demi-veil and fluttering fan to hide blushes and cover any embarrassment, now squinting up at the ceiling as if at *trompe-l'oeil* angels with bare bums blowing cornets or little trumpets along the pediment frieze that ran about the entablature.

'What are you having yourself?'

'Gin and tonic.'

She said that she would try that.

Hadn't I once seen them walking together in wellingtons along the muddy road that led to St Kevin's church and the pub there, appearing to float inches above the ground, wobbling as they advanced, their centre of gravity imperilled, the next puff of wind certain to blow them both away?

Off with the pair of them now wibbleywobbley in their clodhopper boots wading awkwardly forward along the road, stiff as penguins tottering along the ramp of the Dublin Zoo, in their bluchers, top-boots, gumboots, waders, galoshes or whatever you care to call the damned things, wobbling wraith-like on down to Laragh, not linking or laughing. Not looking around nor yet stumbling, not talking, together and apart; and the thin shanks on them weak as gruel.

Theirs was indeed a strangely tripping and vacillating tread; not so much wobbling as toppling.

12

Brother Bun and the London Labour Mart

Brother Bun never had a girl.

Never rolled in the hay nor put a bun in any oven. Never took off for foreign parts nor travelled much in any direction except in a dead straight line that led direct from London to Dun Laoghaire via Holyhead once a year for his 'holliers' with his 'buddies', the lifelong chum Doran, or was it Dolan? As if to atone for privilege, his slang was scrupulously downgraded and low. 'What class of caper is that?' He spoke of 'buck' privates, once had tried to enlist as a private in the Irish Army. Dado sent Civic Guards out after him to drag him home; but his flat feet had already disqualified him for any military career.

His travels had been as circumscribed as Poldy Bloom's. A long streak of religious and racial bigotry (which we must touch upon presently) was a very Irish bias and came from our common progenitor's mistrust of strange people resident in remote climes and speaking in unknown tongues and all too familiar with strange customs and unnatural practices, doing strange things to one another at odd hours of the day and night, gabbing away in funny voices at the latter end of the world.

A strain of melancholy befitted the affrighted misogynist. The lonely bachelor who lusts privily after hot female flesh, the Other whom he is too timid to approach, is surely doomed to disappointment and disaffection. His racial prejudices were merely the unacknowledged half-hidden fears of those other strange parts into which he had never dared venture, whose wholly unfamiliar currencies were drachmas, rupiahs and ringgits, bahts, the Brazilian *real*.

(Fearing to have a goitre lanced by a surgeon in a white smock, carefully brandishing a scalpel, the young Dado had hatched his plans for escaping and did so in the classical manner, knotting bedsheets together, and so made good his escape to freedom through a third-floor hospital window, as do cowardy custards and those who cannot face very much reality – to which category my dear father-to-be assuredly belonged – to the great annoyance and chagrin of the nurses and the Ward Sister when all at once they came running to discover the bed empty, the window open and the bird flown.)

So when brother Bun awoke one day to find himself in a strange hospital bed surrounded by several 'darkies', coal-black medics from Barbados with shiny faces on them as black as tar and jabbering away in their own dark lingo, one with what appeared to be a snake – an adder? – draped about his neck and all gathered close as carnivores about a kill, grouped about his bed with the curtains drawn, he knew that his hour had come, the death knell was surely nigh.

What was it he lacked, apart from life? He lacked bottle.

He was surely now in Hell, out of which there is no escape, and about to receive fit punishment for a dilatory lifetime of self-abuse, beer-swigging and futile longing. When strong black fingers undid his collar and dug into him to commence the auscultation they were as red-hot pincers and he let out an almighty howl and began to fight for his life in the arms of the black men trying to pacify him.

But he saw no National Health internees from Lahore, Madras or Bombay with clipboards in hand, nor an Indian doctor with stethoscope about his neck, nor the black nurse, all white teeth and glittery eyes fixed steadfastly upon him, nailing him to the hospital bed.

What he saw were gutta-percha black pricks fully extended in the monkey house, as gruesomely active black capuchins sprang from branch to branch and began bouncing off the bars of their cage, glaring impudently down upon him with his little bag of nuts.

And he saw black men squatting on high sand dunes laughing at the antics of the brazen brown-skinned girls darting about like snipe, quick as quails, and nude but for the leis swinging about their necks, flashing horny grins and making lewd niggery gestures, wobbling their bums at him, giving him the come-on with thin double-jointed wrists and prehensile hands, inviting him to join them for a bout of jig-jig in the sea or make out with their screaming sisters splashing about buck naked in the surf, apparently all running amok.

All this he perceived in a flash of revelation, or imagined that he saw, before his reeling senses began to slip away from him again, dropping him into a bottomless pit of darkness unfathomably deep.

The dark singsong voices uttering incantatory words intended to be comforting and make him easy in his mind had no such effect but on the contrary terrified him out of his wits. All the more so for brother Bun, not understanding one single syllable of what was being said or rather chanted; hearing only voodoo incantations and wicked spells and niggery maledictions and sorcery thrown his way.

While being thus roughly manhandled and abused by the jabbering nig-nogs, brother Bun attempted to let loose one last almighty howl but all that issued from his mouth was a blood-curdling, unmanned soprano scream, a castrato's unhinged shriek, the expiring babble and dribble of exhausted civic dementia; the true cream of the White Nightmare.

As with the migratory habits of birds of the air or the unseen passage of fish through the deep channels of the sea, compelled upon some course whether they wist or nay, so too some centrifugal force or compulsion (necessity?) propelled brother Bun across the Irish Sea by mailboat, the *Princess Maude*, sailing from No. 2 pier in Dun Laoghaire bound for Holyhead and thence whisked by train to London Town, to be rushed by tube to Ealing Broadway at the end of the District (green) Line where a manifest destiny awaited, as it had awaited many another such Irishman, like him or as unlike as it was possible to be (men of the pick from Blacksod Bay to the Glen of Imaal); of those who had found themselves at the end of the same line, to be marooned in the great English Labour Pool, ever churned up afresh by new arrivals and dispatched hither and thither, whether it be into drainage ditches, manhandling heavy JCBs or hung aloft in the swinging cabins of crane lifts above mucky building sites from Kensal Rise to Kensington where a numerous and ever-renewed Irish workforce found itself to be positively indispensable with shovel and pick, every man jack of them as good as (if not better than) the man before him, or the man next to him or the man coming after him; until along came a true giant from Carraroe in Connemara, six foot six in his stockinged feet, to beat the bejasus out of every man jack of them, every fucker before him.

In this mighty subdivision of a largely ignorant semi-skilled migrant Irish workforce, in a movement akin to the compulsive migratory force that impels birds and fishes about their business toward specific destinations, the seasonal urge that carried them from one habitat and feeding ground to another, so innumerable Irish passed across the Irish Sea singing their doleful songs, orange visages now gone green, then white, all the colours of the tricolour, and puking black draught Guinness into the quaking passageways and thence through British Customs, distraught and already feeling homesick, in great distress, in flocks and shoals.

Some ended up in the Liverpool area, some were headed for Kilburn; for others (among whom brother Bun and after him Rory) it was to be Ealing in Middlesex on the outer perimeter of Greater London, flushed hence out of the King's Cross labour exchange.

Brother Bun found himself 'quids in' there and settled into a 'cushy number' (his the dated slang of a previous era) in an office job connected with the film library of the BFI at their Greenford branch. Once in the course of his years there, until its premature closure, he had spoken 'on the blower' to none other than the famed film director Tony Richardson of *Saturday Night and Sunday Morning* fame, who had been most obliging and indeed courteous to him, Bunny Hill of 16 Windsor Road in the borough of Ealing, London W5, who had a Polish landlady, Krystine Szynanska, to look after him.

After the closure of the film library, brother Bun had found employment in the vicinity near the Hoover factory at Perivale where eventually he was 'put in charge of a roomful of gabby women', whom he could boss about to his heart's content, or not, as he saw fit.

He found digs for me near the tube station beyond Ealing Common on Fordhook Avenue. The two-storey semi-detached was kept as neat as a new pin, all chintz and floral motif and polished banisters and cut flowers in the hall, run like a ship by a retired French couple, a long-suffering worried pair who feared that the end of the world was nigh – this was 1952 – with a rain of atomic bombs falling on Ealing.

They spent most of their time in the kitchen, listening to the news, venturing out now and again for necessary provisions. They were a sweet pair.

Much of my free time I spent soaking in a bath in the spotless bathroom, immersed in a copy of *Lilliput* (a Douglas Glass photo of a nude girl sprawled in the surf) which I had found in Kevin O'Sullivan's room. I had played many rounds of golf with him over Greystones and Delgany; he was red-haired with gingery hair on the backs of his hands; now he was working shifts in the motor factory at Acton Town, blowing up outsize tyres for the African market. Presently he was to vanish into Canada.

It was a beginning, the froth on the dream. At least it was *my* beginning. Although now it seems like someone else's life and about as remote in time as the Crusades; it would have been the same for many another migrant Irish labourer in light and heavy industry before and after me, until I made my escape into South Africa and found work in Johannesburg.

The centrifugal force, I have heard it said, is really inertia. When brother Bun, eager to defend his country against all invaders, had joined the Local Defence Force during our Irish 'Emergency', he went marching off on his flat feet down the avenue past the lodge (then unoccupied) and Killadoon (seat of the infamous Lord Leitrim) back gate, in his field-green LDF uniform proudly worn with forage cap set at a rakish angle and brown boots and smart puttees highly polished; he was proud as punch, marching off to defend his country, even if unarmed (arms, in the form of Lee Enfields, last used at Arras and Mons, were promised), off to drill at Straffan Town Hall facing the Catholic church with the legless and armless Christ in the polychrome stations.

He wore the determined *Weltschmerz* expression befitting one in uniform, a compound of sadness and resignation. The face that he would surely have worn had *Wehrmacht* paras come floating down on to neutral Irish soil, to sweep all before them. Then his goose would have been cooked for sure.

Meanwhile the Dodo was undergoing training at Cranford for RAF night-fighters, going into the West End on leave to see Pat Kirkwood at the Coliseum, very leggy and toothsome in fishnet stockings, belting out 'Oh Johnny, oh Johnny, how you can love!' He saw Terence Rattigan's *Flare Path* and probably some naughty stuff at the Windmill ('We Never Closed').

Neither brother Bun nor Mumu was exactly the type for route marches. Both of them moved badly. Overweight and top heavy, Mumu advanced awkwardly as if walking on broken glass or fire, or crippled with corns. Her long period in bed had left her in a semi-comatose state.

All his life brother Bun had the indecisive broken gait of an old man, catching his breath, puffing if he exerted himself, snoring when he slept, Guinness his preferred tipple. He died one Sunday in October 1998 of liver failure in Ealing where he had lived for most of his life under the care of Mrs Szynanska, thirty-two years after his mother died, twenty-nine after his father's death. Now they have all gone away.

None of the three surviving brothers had attended his funeral. The Dote stayed where he was in deep retirement in County Wicklow. I stayed put at World's End. The Dodo was thought to have settled thousands of miles away in Tasmania, home of the pademelon, the quoll cat, the possum and the Tasmanian Devil.

Mumu had died first, of a brain haemorrhage in the night, and went hence to Heaven. Two years later Dado followed when galloping cancer carried him away.

Then there was a pause, to allow the graves to settle in Dean's Grange cemetery, then brother Bun followed unobtrusively into Ealing earth, slipping out of life without much to-do.

Sixty or more mourners attended his funeral in Ealing Abbey and someone read Yeats's 'Four Ages of Man' over the mortal remains of my brother who had never 'walked upright' in his life, being sorely afflicted with wicket keeper's stoop. He walked with a sort of waddle or shuffle, with toes turned out as though wearing snow-shoes, humpbacked as Humpty Dumpty.

The mourners were mainly the members of St Benedict's Club, buddies of my brother. St Benedict of Nursia, shortly before his death *circa* 547, looked up from his prayers and saw in the darkness outside his window that 'the whole world appeared to be gathered into one sunbeam and thus brought before his eyes'.

The last time I saw brother Bun was when we invited him down to Kinsale. Most of the other passengers disembarking from the Dublin train had dispersed when he slowly emerged on his flat feet from the Gents at Cork railway station, with no particular expression of welcome on his face, no offer of handshake or fraternal embrace, no back-slap, God forbid; for we were never a demonstrative lot, and nothing had changed between us in a long interval.

That night at the Blue Haven bar when he was in his cups, he addressed a total stranger standing next to him, threatening (as once before in an Ealing bar) to 'sort me out'. He was still the elder brother.

'I'll soon put manners on that fellow.'

Me, Rory.

All three had died in winter and all three are in Heaven now, above the clouds. No, they have all gone into the world of light, become one with their grandparents and great-grandparents before them, the leavenings of the Hills (not to mention the Higginses) and the Boyd clans from Carrick-on-Shannon and Longford and Granard. Isn't that saying enough?

13

Ancestral Voices

T he perennial myth of the Great Irishman is as old as the hills. Old and hoary as the beard of the Patriarch himself, dim holy man and humble sheep-farmer of Anglia who was reputed to have slept all over Ireland, generally in the open on exposed hillsides, as frequently as Queen Victoria had slept in ornate four-poster beds all over England.

The heroes who belonged by right to the renowned generations, the powerful strong men of the past, Finn McCool, Brian Boru and Cuchulain, have deteriorated into Dan O'Mahony the wrestler from Ballydehob who invented the Irish Whip, a throw in wrestling; and the heavyweight boxer Jack Doyle, who had famously bedded and wedded the movie star Movita, renowned for her knockout beauty; he himself perhaps more famous still for a proclivity to being knocked out cold in the ring. At least so he was mocked by the cartoonist Tom Webster.

The Horizontal Heavyweight became an all-in wrestler, the Gorgeous Gael, who then deteriorated into a song-and-dance man at the Theatre Royal in Hawkins Street off the Quays, appearing with Movita in *Something in the Air* with the Royalettes chorus line high-kicking; then deteriorated further still to become a bouncer at Mooney's pub in Notting Hill Gate, lounging at the counter, wearing an eyepatch like Peg Leg Pete.

Some years after that he died in a London hospital, and sure enough Irish obituary notices referred to him as a Great Irishman; sometimes with the rider that he 'had lived life to the full'. The English obituary notices tactfully refrained from mentioning the many times he had been knocked out in the ring, but all agreed that he had lived with *zest*.

The Great Irishmen who had died with their boots on tended to be minor celebrities known throughout the land. Such a one was the actor Noel Purcell, who in a long and undistinguished career on the Dublin stage had appeared in everything from Christmas panto with fake snow, tinsel and reindeer in the Olympia, that gilded emporium of rococo, to one-act O'Casey knockabout farces at the Gaiety and, then, in one final plunge downwards, was given bit-parts in English movies with small budgets.

He sported a long white beard like Santa Claus, or God; possibly in an attempt to conceal his ineptitude as an actor, by typecasting himself as the tall gauche nincompoop with the thick Dublin accent for whom nothing worked out. It was the same strategy adopted by Hollywood in order to broaden the available talents of Joan Crawford, enlarging her beautiful eyes by surgery to extend her range of expressions; give her at least the opportunity to convey more than *one* expression.

Noel Purcell pulled terrible faces, exposed his great horse teeth, caused his eyebrows to fly up, huffed and puffed, shambled about the stage. I saw him dismantle a stage room in O'Casey's *The End of the Beginning*. Finally, being pulled up the prop chimney, still blathering and protesting, the manic head first to disappear, then the awkward body and long legs, the boots last of all, blustery protestations still audible in the flue when the corporeal presence had disappeared. He was the Great Irishman personified. In the end he was only fit for bit-parts, the rear end of the panto horse; that's all he was good for finally. He was definitely a bits-part man, a fit-up artiste.

'When beggars die, no comets fall,' as brother Bun was fond of quoting.

Purcell's cockney counterpart was Alfie Bass, who held down small character parts in British movies and carried a hod in the

Francesco Rosi movie *Christ Stopped at Eboli*. When Bass died he got more flattering and longer obituaries and news coverage than the distinguished movie-maker, Carol Reed, though none thought to describe him as a Great Englishman.

Alfie Bass was the prototypical footsoldier of the old wars, fought in the mud and finished in a day by Nym, Bardolph and Pistol, rough-spoken sods of soldiers. A blocky root of a man with a permanently worried expression, a bulldoggish frown on features as wrinkled as a prune; a racing tipster, small-time gangster or London barrow-boy in our times.

'The more one sees of him, the more the wonder grows.'

I saw Jimmy Bruen once in the dusk of the evening hammering off practice shots with a long iron from a raised tee on Portmarnock links, digging great divots that came slowly back to earth again. A playful giant was sending off cannon-like projectiles up-soaring into the gloaming towards a distant caddy, who was busily recovering the much-bashed-about Dunlops in a bucket.

It was the Hibernian Wonder Golfer himself getting in some practice, Jimmy (The Loop) Bruen of Muskerry in the County Cork. He would have been up in Dublin on insurance business. When a son was born unto James J. Bruen, former Connaught Ranger and bank official who stood well over six feet tall, little did he know that the child of Margaret Bruen would grow up to be a golfing prodigy who won the British Amateur Championship at Birkdale, defeating the great American Sweeny in a titanic final.

The old codger Bernard Darwin, doyen of English golf commentators, had declined to describe the fabled Bruen Loop, the famous whip-like flailing action that sent the ball in a high trajectory to a distant green three hundred and fifty or more yards away. It was something outside our ken, like the Angel Gabriel looping the loop; but was in fact probably an adaptation of the hurling puck, the same whiplash swing of the body that dispatched the *sliotar* far upfield, or over the bar.

It was a shy sportsman who inspired those rhapsodies of praise; and like all true legends he was to die young, in his early fifties early one May day at his home in Cork, of a heart attack, leaving six children fatherless.

But leaving behind the great legend of his doings, the prodigious shots, the records, for us to marvel at all the more; the fierce crack of the contact and the Dunlop 65s soaring away! Great shot, Jimmy!

Bursting free from the chrysalis and imago of his living fame to become yet another of the Imperishable Ones in the legions of our illustrious dead.

Eily Arnopp, of Kinsale, born and raised in Barrack Street, was the mother of nine children by a taxi driver who predeceased her; she is famous in Kinsale as being the only person to have lived in the same house in the same street all her life, and died there. Obituaries in the *Southern Star* said she had lived life to the full. You said: 'Most of the Arnopps are either grossly fat or painfully thin.'

Irishwomen by and large, no matter how gorgeous they had been in their prime, like Lady Eleanor Palmer or Hermione, Duchess of Leinster or Daisy, Countess of Fingall, would never be great Irishwomen unless they became champion horsewomen like Iris Kellett. The moulded forms were of Mother and Martyr – sometimes the terms were synonymous – the beauties had become haggard eccentrics, frowsy widows with their wits astray, lost women, old hakes. The lovely girl (notoriously fast) who loved to slide downstairs on a tray via polished banisters, wearing pink tights, had become the immensely old and frail dowager Duchess of Desmond who fell to her death from an apple tree at the age of one hundred and four, some said one hundred and forty, but much too old to be climbing apple trees. The Connaught Queen Grainne Mhaol, the Pirate Queen, Grace of the cropped hair, who had it all her own way once, sailing her vessel up the Thames to speak to Elizabeth I as an equal and what is more, in Latin, died in penury in rocky Connaught. The ladies who had lost their looks and their wits now turned into Shan Van Vochts and Sheila na Gigs; Cathleen ni Houlihan with a pained expression (as though she had a pain in her hole) became the womanly model on the punt note. Yeats's earlier moth, the lovely Maude Gonne, became a harpie, following in the footsteps of the Countess Markiewicz who had entered Irish polities, that muddy carp pond. The best option was to die young as did Hermione, Duchess of Leinster, chatelaine of Carton in its heyday, with hunt balls and outings to Punchestown races, doing it in style.

14

Harry Allen, J. Pierpoint Morgan and Luis Buñuel

The hooded figure, known to be a woman and a murderess, a husband-slayer condemned to death by a named Judge on a date already specified months before, wearing a smart outfit and with her face carefully made up, fell heavy as a sack of earth into the pitch darkness below; accelerating as she fell, faster than Rousseau's bastards went down the chute of the foundling hospital, her last terrified scream smothered by the hemp rope that gripped and snapped her spinal column.

She was spared further ignominy and shame, what ensued after the loosening of uterus and sphincter muscles, the gruesome descent of the prison doctor into the bowels of the execution shed to disarrange her clothes, her decency no longer protected, the nice ethics of how men should behave with women at their mercy, taking out his stethoscope to auscultate her and pronounce the woman dead.

Ruth Ellis was the last woman to be hanged in England. Justice was seen to be done down there in the gloomy shed. No one would ever be killed that way again, though the hangman slept like a babe. Gravity had almost pulled her head off; falling as from an immense height she voided herself.

★　　★　　★

Our dear mother, one of the Boyds of Carrick-on-Shannon whose father had been Peace Commissioner of Longford, was ever a snob. The French finishing school at Parthenay had done it, had finished her.

She never referred to the people in any charitable way, but always disparagingly, looking dismissively down her nose at the common people, at individuals, 'dreadfully common', the sweaty nightcaps, the *canaille*, not much better than common tinkers, who came begging with their numerous noisome progeny, stinking up the front porch into which they crowded; to be told to wait, she would see what she had for them (the Master was in, upstairs in his study, forsooth); and then out came the cast-off clothes, the bags of apples, the stale soda bread, the fistful of coppers, a sixpenny bit, received with both hands, and the chorus of 'God bless your ladyship, but you wouldn't happen to have—'

The front door closing on the renewed chorus of entreaties and a scrofulous babe, wrapped in a dirty papoose-like shawl, held up like the Host elevated in the clasp of the golden monstrance at Benediction in rising clouds of incense; the door finally closing once and for all on the stinks and the pained look on the face of the Mistress.

I've heard that they left a sign near the gate – a stone turned a certain way – to indicate a house where they were given alms. Such entreaties recurring at irregular intervals (Mumu rather suspected that they used a system of secret signs) must indeed have been music to her ears, for it confirmed her innermost belief that she was not of the common stock, but a superior being, a lady of means.

We were brought up to see ourselves as a cut above the rest, an elitist band of rural nobs, the Higginses of Springfield, all four sons educated at Clongowes Wood College, of parents who dined royally and regularly at the Royal Hibernian Hotel. Mumu was the chief instigator of this fantasy, the elevated status claimed as our birthright and one that characterised us as above all others; so what choice had we, her four abashed and shy sons, but to believe her: that we were indeed out of the top drawer? She could be very sharp when such presumptions were discovered in others, the social upstarts who were 'stuck up', putting on airs and graces that did not become them: they needed to be taken down a peg and shown their place. The note of condescension and quiet superiority I heard a lifetime later in Berlin, in the mouth of a youngish Prussian *Frau* who spoke so proudly of *'mein Mann'*, overtly pleased with her husband and *'alles in Ordnung'* simmered like something rich and good cooking on the Aga.

Having myself turned seventy-one, par for the course plus one extra stroke, with hand on heart I cannot truly say that I have quite shaken off this grandiose notion, implanted so long ago by our mother, who wanted only the best for us.

Seventy-one was Buffon's (Georges-Louis Le Clerc's) age when he finished his great treatise *Histoire naturelle* (1749–67), concluding that the earth would eventually freeze over and all life thereon become extinct. He was then a shade under five feet five inches and afflicted with gallstones, fifty-seven of which were removed from his bladder at the autopsy when he died at the ripe old age of eighty.

At the age of seventy-one Harry Allen, the public hangman, was interviewed by the *Daily Telegraph*. 'It may be eighteen years since I last hanged a man, but even at seventy-one, I'm perfectly ready, willing and able to resume my duties,' said the ex-hangman, flexing his biceps. 'Since the rope was scrapped, discipline has gone right out of the window.'

In his time of tenure he had attended or conducted over a hundred hangings. He appeared at the gate wearing one of his multicoloured bow-ties, so that anti-hanging demonstrators outside the jail would take him for a doctor or lawyer.

'After breakfast I always used to return home, have a bath and go to bed. I slept like a baby for the next eight hours. I've never been bothered by dreams and nightmares.'

Somewhere in the north of England, off the beaten track, don't you know, he had run a quiet pub called Pity the Poor Traveller (or was it Poor Straggler?) Our 'arry was the publican and genial host. Before you could blow the top off your pint of Thwaites real ale, he'd have 'topped' his man. Pulling pints or hanging felons was done with the same aplomb. He sounded like a married man. And children too? Had he topped Ruth Ellis?

Harry Allen had succeeded Albert Pierpoint as chief execu-
tioner in 1956, and conducted his last public office in Britain in
August 1964, just a year before parliament abolished the death
penalty for murder. Ruth Ellis was hanged on 13 July 1955, nine
years before the abolition of hanging, having killed her husband
to end an intolerable situation. For her husband had subjected
her to years of indignity and abuse. A friend showed her how
to use the gun, before he decamped to Australia. She shot the
husband dead outside the Magdala pub near Hampstead Heath,
one of a range of quiet pubs in that area patronised by Rory,
walking over the heath from Muswell Hill. Michael Morrow
had a room up the hill from the Magdala and, if not exactly
witnessing the killing, saw the effects, the husband's brains spread
over the pavement 'like ice-cream'.

Did the sentencing judge, donning the black cap before
pronouncing the dread words, feel that justice had been done?
Did the hangman, putting the hood over Ruth Ellis's head, tell
her that it would be over soon? Did they sit down thereafter to
hearty breakfasts, each satisfied that justice had been done? A pot
of hot tea, kippers, toast and coarse-grain marmalade, kedgeree
or split pulse, onions and condiments served piping hot for the
hangman, and the judge in his chambers.

Did the hangman let her go in silence? Or touch her shoulder,
she already hooded, straighten his bow-tie and murmur, *Be a
brave woman. It'll soon be over*, grunting as he hauled on the switch?
One way or another, he let her go.

Harry the hangman died on 17 August 1992 at the age of
eighty-one.

J. Pierpoint Morgan was seventy-four in the summer of 1911
when he took up with Vita, the illegitimate offspring of the
Honourable Lionel Sackville-West. She was nineteen to his
seventy-four; each had something the other wanted. At Princes
Gate he was chairing a meeting involving a loan to some
Chinese, but when he received her message he quickly left
the boardroom to see her: 'In he came like a whirlwind and
crushed me.'

Rory was fifty-nine years of age when he met his nemesis in

the shapely form of the gentle lady Alannah who was some twenty and more years his junior, divorced wife of Pedro Sanchez of Mexico City, a failed photographer who had ambitions to be an architect.

When Sanchez went up, he went up, when he went down he went down, and carried her with him. After a while she had nothing to say; they separated, she left Mexico City for Cuernavaca (where eighty-four vultures circled over the Rancho Pico, casting slow-wheeling shadows on the lawns, they moved slow as bluebottles over the carcass of the dead horse, sinking down and settling at given intervals and then rising again, joining the flock above, wheeling at different altitudes, their eyes fixed on the corpse) and then left Mexico for London, and returned to Ireland, drifting sideways towards her fate, Rory of the Hills.

Twenty-one years previously, in 1970, you were nineteen years of age, weighing just under eight stone and got up as Juliet Greco with kabuki doll's white face masked in make-up, Nefertitian black eye outline, eyelashes inches long, dark hair down to your waist and a skirt brief as decency would allow, bolero waistcoat with dazzling baubles and Aztec-style pendant earrings. You were certainly 'with it' in the free-for-all fashion of the swinging sixties, living in Mexico City and working as a freelance photo model wedded to Pedro Sanchez.

Together these two fine love-birds, holding hands and exchanging fond looks, called for payment due to them in an advertising agency near Reforma, on the eleventh floor of a modern skyscraper, much of it occupied by other advertising agencies, fashion outlets and film production companies. Still linking, like Siamese twins, they stepped together into an elevator, accompanied by a friend called Juan, who was in the movie business.

A third man stepped quickly into the elevator and stood behind Juan who had his finger on the button for the eleventh floor.

'¿Que piso?' asked Juan politely.

'Cinco, por favor,' said the stranger in a tough gangsterish voice out of the side of the mouth.

The belted beige gabardine gave him an exotic European

touch; leastways it was an unusual mid-morning get-up for Mexico City. He seemed to have no face, only threatening surfaces angled at them. (Was he carrying a piece?)

Even with his back turned to the Sanchez love-birds holding hands, he had presence. The beige gabardine was loosely belted, the epaulettes stood up like wings, the coat collar was upturned, the trilby worn down over the brow, the gangster's voice was as rough as Georg Grosz, that of your habitual cigar smoker, the menacing glint that emanated from the dark sunglasses shadowed by the downturned hat brim, was alarming. This fellow was obviously not to be trifled with, a louche figure from *film noir*.

They rode up together in silence, not exchanging a look, the stranger standing there impassively, not fidgeting, hands in the deep pockets of the gabardine, eyes fixed on the flying digits of the little screen as they rose swiftly.

When the elevator had shuddered to a pneumatic halt on the *piso cinco*, the door slid open and the gangster slipped out. The air vibrated a moment and he was gone, gone to see his money man and producer Oscar Danziger, no doubt.

The elevator gulped air, released its brakes, and sailed upwards. Juan was gobsmacked as one might say, rendered speechless, swallowing his spittle, white-faced as though he had seen an apparition; at all events he said nothing until they reached the eleventh floor. Backing out of the cage he marvelled: *'Subsimos en el elevador con Luis Buñuel, el Maestro de los Maestros del ciné Mexicano, olé!'*

'Luis Buñuel!' chirruped the Sanchez love-birds in unison. 'Luis BUÑUEL!!'

La Voie lactée (The Milky Way) had been released the previous year; now he was preparing *Le charme discret de la bourgeoisie* (1972); ahead lay *Le Fantôme de la liberté* (1974), and *Cet obscur objet du désir* (1977).

Luis Buñuel, at eighty-three, sat in the bare study of his house in Mexico City surrounded by high monastery walls crowned with broken glass.

The great Mexican gasbag Carlos Fuentes, tireless in his pursuit of important connections, 'names', last saw Buñuel in February

15

The Monk in the Cornfield
(Where There Was Nobody)

Beau comme un large champ d'été . . .
Henri Michaux: *L'Espace du Dedons*

S ince there seemed to be nobody about, I crept like a thief into the lamp-room where formerly the Aladdin paraffin lamps had been stored but which was now used by the Dodo as a reference library, generally for sporting matters. Tidy mounds of magazines and newspapers were arranged in alphabetical order along the shelves, a morgue of out-of-date newsprint yellowing and smelly that still retained some things of interest for the Dodo, the rugby and cricket records. Also photographs of English royalty, the little Princesses Elizabeth and Margaret Rose in decorous manner presenting bunches of flowers to other smiling eminences, all that ritual royal bowing and scraping; here an interest that he had inherited from Mumu, always a great admirer of British royalty.

A cat had also found its way into the sanctum, for there under the lowest shelf was an ossified mound of cat-cack that had solidified and grown a stately carapace of heraldic fluff on a crack of the paving stone, awaiting the attention of Lizzy who would come and scrape up the mess with pan and bucket of water and Jeyes fluid.

And here were the London *Daily Mails*, the *Dispatches*, the *Wisdens*, the *Illustrated London News* and *Tatler & Sketch*, the *Irish Times*, *The Field*, *Good Housekeeping*, *Home & Beauty*, *Lilliput*, and *Herald Tribunes* from America, back numbers of the *Evening Herald* and *Evening Mail*, with cricket and rugby teams in their correct club colours and blazers painstakingly rendered in water-colours by the Dodo.

What was of abiding interest to me were the *Lilliputs* on one shelf low down, for they contained photographic studies of nudes in black and white, by Douglas Glass, showing off English models without a stitch, alone on the seashore. Choosing one of these, I ran for the open fields, through the side plantation leading to the big wheatfield towards Griffinrath, to take the model for an outing with an Irish boy after months of being cooped up in the stuffy study.

These Douglas Glass studies of nudes in woods, seashore and field were my *Wald und Weise* movies; in that respect *Lilliput* was as good as a private viewing of blue movies, better than the naturist feature of nudists supposedly enjoying themselves in a camp somewhere in England, seen later at a cinema in Oxford Street, filmed in a very peekaboo manner that contrived not to show any pubics.

What Churchill and his War Cabinet called World War Two and what Dev and his Dáil were calling 'the Emergency', an elusive Irish euphemism if ever there was one, was a time of strict censorship of films coming into the *Saorstát*. Hollywood productions, already prudish and reserved before the Hayes Office, were trimmed further for Irish audiences, who were kept even more in the dark as to what exactly was happening in the world.

Betty Grable might bat her false eyelashes, pout her luscious lips and expose a certain amount of sheer stocking above the knee, but only so far. Rita Hayworth could ruck up her skirt with both hands and twirl about in *Gilda*; but that was about all permitted. The Hayes Office was there to see that she went no further, also the Daughters of the American Revolution and Mother Machree, for wasn't Rita herself half Irish?

Grable was an emblem on the fuselage of a Boeing 707, part of the war effort, like selling war bonds, when Irish bread was getting darker, rationing of a sort was in force. It was a time before such scandalous blockbusters as *The Outlaw*, with Jane Russell sprawled in the straw, or *Duel in the Sun* with

Jennifer Jones darkened up and poured into a towel; before the later permissiveness, of explicit nudity and full frontals, animal grunting in stereo sound not to be heard even at Wimbledon or Flushing Meadow, and the attendant bad manners (McEnroe); all that came later.

What arrived from across the water were Regency romps from Gainsborough Studios, Margaret Lockwood with permanently wet underlip, a beauty spot, the deepest cleavage imaginable and leather gear, brandishing a brace of horse pistols in *The Wicked Lady*, with James Mason offering to horse-whip Phyllis Calvert.

Then there were Celia Johnson and Trevor Howard carrying on in *Brief Encounter*, but forbidden to Irish viewers, because it was deemed to encourage adultery, strictly forbidden by the Irish Episcopal See, though *Spring in Park Lane* (Michael Wilding and Anna Neagle) was considered innocuous enough to be distributed in Ireland.

The young wheat stood a good three or even four feet high in a field of five or six acres protected by some scarecrows leaning sideways at drunken angles, with faces of straw swaying in the breeze as if it was the wind blowing over a body of water into which the randy Rory sank as into blessed surf, a continuation of the rapture that began with the sharply pleasurable experience of the first nude dip in the cattle trough at the ring-pump, when the mossy sides became a substitute for the female pubic parts, obligingly parting, opening for Rory.

Undressed in a trice, Rory spread out the nude model before him in her Cornish wheatfield as a playful sunny companion, and was soon ejaculating for dear life into a pocket handkerchief spread out.

In Killashee they called it 'pulling your wire', and the priest in confession called it 'playing with yourself'. Well, look here will you now, that was how I pleasured her, when she pleasured me in a hidden wheatfield, without a word exchanged, without a touch; without seeming to be in any way loose or wayward, Dorothy Lamour in a sarong led to lewd thoughts; lewd thoughts led to lewd acts. Not with this one. Dance, pretty lady, dance!

Beau, comme un large champ d'été,
Beau l'espoir!

Henri Michaux

This would have been *circa* 1944 or around the time Mussolini had fallen from power and I had turned seventeen, an indifferent scholar in most subjects in the class of Third Syntax in Clongowes Wood College where the wind always blew coldly around the old castle walls and the Dote (in a class above me) and I had come to learn at first hand all those slang terms that had seemed like another unknown language when spoken by our two elder brothers.

On a fine summer's day when none seemed to be about, I stole like a felon into the study and, in the blink of a wink, had made off with her.

It was one of the Dodo's life studies from Kildare Street drawn by that industrious copier, a roll of stiff cartridge paper drawn upon with graphite or a hard pencil to give no smudge effects and held in place with paperclips, one taken from a pile numbered and entitled in a corner.

The blind was rolled down to the limit, casting a strawberry-red light into the narrow room that smelt of oils. A study of 'The Boy with a Rabbit' was propped up on the table, half finished and looking if possible even deader than the original; the flaccid white hand clutching the lettuce leaf was stiff and moribund, the true hand of a cadaver.

Now I was gliding down the stairs with the stolen roll held casually under one arm and making my way across the hallway, down eight steps to ground level and like a redshank past the lamp-room, out the back door and round with me into the yard and via the harness room up the stairs and through two empty lofts until I had reached the third one and pushed open the groaning door.

In two quick spells of bending, I was already naked and had unrolled the cartridge paper to reveal the round and somewhat chubby model quite nude and seated on a rostrum with stiff folds of cloth shadowed in the classical Roman manner, the nude herself without any suggestion of pencil shading, just the outlined white body seated on an Art School rostrum with hands clasped behind her neck to make her breasts stick out (which they certainly did), the back likewise arched to throw them further into prominence (which indeed it did) as likewise the rear cleft, the near foot flexed and its fellow artfully 'at point', like a ballet pose.

The angled pose (difficult to hold for any length of time) served to hide from view the part that was most desired and thought of but most *verboten*; to wit, the twat. The bush of hair betwixt the legs was hidden away; the coy model had also shaved her armpits for the pose.

Moving now with purpose and precision, I had her laid out on an old copy of the *Evening Herald* with four stones at the four corners of the cartridge paper to prevent it from rolling up again, revealing now at close range my abject state of tumescence brought about by the nudity (mine as well as hers), but mostly by her own close proximity.

'Nymph, in thy orisons be all my sins remembered!'

I slid home the wooden bolt to secure privacy and with simian agility mounted the door frame and clung one-handed to the first rafter, then both hands to the second rafter, then the third, until I dangled directly above the nude spread out below. With both hands locked, I began to swing; and it seemed now that she moved with me, bestirring herself a little from her pose (as flick pictures convey an illusion of movement when the pages are clicked); so, in a white blur of apparent participation, she seemed to gather herself and go with me, as I swung gasping above her, my eyes fixed steadfastly upon that lovely nakedness outspread below.

'Oh if'n I haddana . . .' groaned randy Rory. 'If I cuddana . . .' and dropped lightly on to the floor covered in hayseeds and swallow-droppings, and hunkered up alongside her.

'See what you done to me,' I said, and scattered my seed splashily as Onan himself, though careful not to splash her, as if holding a hose.

Now the worst ignominy would be my father calling out from below: 'What's going on up there?'

Dressing myself hurriedly, rolling up the cartridge paper,

clipping it up again, spreading the *Herald* over the semen, I unbolted the door and fled down the stairs into the front yard, and so by the garden gate around the corner of the house and in by the front door, up the front stairs like jack rabbit (spent buck) and back into the study.

I replaced the roll where I'd found it, closed the door, leaving no fingerprints. Dance, daddy-longlegs, dance!

When Rory was twenty-five years old and into single figures as a playing member of Greystones Golf Club among the grey hairs and suffused features of retired British Army officers, Captain Parsons and Captain Pettigrew and Major Stone and Rory's *bêtes noires*, the Right Reverend Riversdale Colthrust and the Honorary Secretary, Colonel Howard Cornwallis Lewis of the Gloucestershire Halberdiers, the last of the bulldog breed, gallant Rory was hotly pursuing tail in the shape of the adorable Philippa Phillips. A Montessori instructress from Leeson Street convent, hotly pursued by the salad-green and inexperienced Rory with a more or less permanent erection, as a knight of old might have brandished an escutcheon, glove or stocking as a lady's favour. But all to no avail.

Rory then took to banging brassie shots from beside the third green over the guarding bunker, off towards the fourth green, besplattering it with Dunlops and Warwicks, lost balls recovered by the caddies and sold again at discount, the practice balls slashed by the irons.

So what's so strange about that? you may ask. Well, on nights of full moon in winter I wore socks and clunky golf shoes with spikes and nothing else, banging the balls away from beside the third green (par 5) behind which I had undressed. That's how I got my only lonely satisfaction, with a hey nonny yea and a hey nonny no, punching wood from semi-rough and all around me the cuckoo spits and the worm casts and the song of the nightingale soaring. *Mi ne frego.*

16

Ah, Those Moonlit Revels!

*T*hwhackk! *Th-thwhackk!* *Th-thwhackkKK!* went Rory the
hammer hurler, fairly laying into them, thumping the
very skins off the Dunlops, all dispatched on a low
trajectory out of the already stiffening clumps (for it had set in
to freeze); with the regularity of a metronome, every contact
in the fat of the wood another sweet shock to the spine,
carried through with a full swing of the hips with stiffened
member standing up rigid as a poker, the arms held high in
the follow-through, the left as though braced against a shield; a
monumental male nude figure emblematic and stark white as on
the Parthenon, besplattering seed like dewfall on the grass and all
the grass glistening and sparkling with the fiery sparkle of quartz
and mica in the frosty night air, with distant objects brought close
and close things far removed; so that the glossy bulk of the hill on
the eleventh seemed to pulsate in the increasing cold, expanding
and contracting.

And the crows, disturbed by something passing below, had
risen up squawking from the rookery above the Delgany road,
stridently aroused, and the moon too was risen up over the hill;
spread and above was the Milky Way and the Plough all around
the hubbub of subatomic invisible insect life and the remote
stars singing in their constellations and small white clouds sailing
along were beginning to disperse themselves (and Rory, out of

sight behind the mound guarding the third green, was hurriedly dressing himself in order to recover twenty Dunlops scattered like mushrooms around the fourth green).

The best shots had felt like cloth tearing, ratteen or stiff canvas. It was perhaps an uncommon way and occasion (a moonlit night with frost in winter) for conducting practice sessions in the nude; but Rory off a three handicap had felt the shock of each shot travel up his forearms and into his teeth as if he was holding ball-bearings in his mouth that became as soft as dissolving snowballs. With every smash-shot that smote the Dunlops away, Rory felt as though he were eating snowballs.

Now, having collected the scattered shots, with brassie under oxter like a gamekeeper, or a poacher leaving a forbidden wood, pockets bulging not with game but with Dunlops, Rory made his way home to Kinlen Road, gliding imperceptibly in by the back way.

17

Roll On, Ye Mighty River, Roll!

I am attempting to find a trail of wet footprints leading from the rectangular cattle trough under the hawthorn where the wank in the tank occurred, the first temptation succumbed to; and find where the wet telltale prints of naked male adolescent are leading; soon to be joined in the dance by a neat naked female print; and so toe to toe and heel to heel leading this way and that with all the formal delicacy of minuets, bourrées, mazurkas and gavottes; whatever about the entangling and entwining intimacy of the tangos so despised by the high and mighty Señor Borges of Buenos Aires, who was blind.

At our first assignation in the cave-like dimness of the bar Montes (now a bank) I had asked Anna: 'Do you find me feminine?'

And she, as though responding to a password, had answered with another question: 'Do you find me masculine?'

I thought her very feminine, despite her tallness, despite the smallness of her bust, of which she was very conscious, coming from the land of Suzanne Brugger and Anna Lindesgaard. What did the size of parts of her matter to me?

Since the time I was bathed in all innocence by my mother, just escaped out of diapers or free of the clutches of Nurse O'Reilly to romp on the gravel in my pelt with the Dote screeching and pissing himself with excitement to feel the air playing over our skin, I have swum and capered and dipped and cavorted and fornicated and frisked, wallowed and soaked and sodomised with a fair few sirens, some of whom would as soon use the back door as the front, some of whom seemed paragons of virtue yet were veritable engineers of lust ('Is it all the way in?') along the lines of insatiable Messalina, hereunder listed provisionally for the benefit of the more lecherous reader, following incandescent signs that speak volumes to him or her in the dark, burning still, burning bright, winking like the red traffic sign that bids you STOP.

When a woman says 'Stop!' she may mean to convey quite the opposite ('Go!') and is so understood by both parties eager to get on with it and not too particular about splitting hairs; but in order to oblige the lady, one must abide by the formalities.

With Anne Marie in the shower at No. 12 Calle Generalissimo Franco (afterwards Calle Pintada) in Nerja, twice or thrice.

With Hannelore on numerous occasions in the showers of various Berlin hotels, a hotel in Michelangelostraat in Amsterdam, many dips in May in the aqueduct above the Fabrica de La Luz on the Rio Chilar (dried up) outside Nerja.

Showered with Harriet at 20 Granite Creek Road, Santa Cruz, California.

Showered with Anastasia at her place on Oakmont Boulevard, Austin, Texas and swam in the Colorado River (leave your guns at the gate).

In the nip with Philippa in the Irish Sea at Kilcoole, County Wicklow (cf. *Dog Days*).

In the nip with Flora in the Lake of the Blind Trout at Pontoon in County Mayo and in a hot bath in Johnny O'Toole's (RIP) modernised thatched cottage later burnt to the ground in a vindictive arson attack; in the nip in the nippy Liffey beyond Straffan Bridge, County Kildare, on one day of a summer long past.

In the nip with Coppera in the pools of Juanero on the logging trail out of Cómpeta that led into the hills.

In the nip with Anna in the Arcadian pools below Canillas beyond the stinking dump you called Gehenna.

Swam with Erika on Playa de Burriana at Nerja and in the

Stambergersee on the opposite shore to where Mad Ludwig drowned with his doctor, in Bavaria.

And what about Hannel? Last seen by Anna (no friend) 'looking haggard', walking through the King's Gardens in Copenhagen. Perhaps she was not the swimming or dipping type, ever plagued and bothered by an irregular menstrual flow.

In the nip with Hannelore in Krumme Lanke and Schlachtensee in Berlin by night in summer and in a hot bath with Mary at 63 Grand Avenue, Muswell Hill, north London; but hold your horses, who is Mary? Why Mary Mildwater, she whom my former wife Fruitcake nicknamed 'Hotwater', was and is a Piscean like myself. Will you ever forget the day you spoke to three men, all of them Visceans, sitting cool as you please about a table at the Alexandra pub near the police station and the flower shop where the sexy girl worked who wore an ankle bracelet? The Alexandra was one of our thirty-six 'locals'. All five of us in the bar were Pisceans and none too sober, least of all Mary Mildwater; which must tell you something revealing about Pisceans.

All five of my heart-scalds have similar names and identical or near identical initials: Harriet, Hannelore, Hannel, Anna and Alannah.

The first time I saw Alannah, she had come from swimming a hundred lengths of Acton's hotel swimming pool and she seemed more otter than woman, with fish scales or drips of water like sparkling jewels in her dark hair. And when she moved, she moved. I had met up with a Norwegian sailor, Sven Johnson, in the bar, who spoke of his father, the trout tickler. He had a bone-crunching handshake; I was given it, and then Alannah, who didn't flinch.

Sailorman Sven, who had sailed the seven seas, had the right hands wrung off us. We went around the corner and into the Shipwreck, aptly named, where we were served up a most unappetising meal. Both the owners have since died in Spain, where they had opened a bar called Dirty Dicks; no apostrophe where none intended.

The name I adopted was Rory of the Hills, the prototypical

homeless one. Some Russian writer took to looking back to find the source or cause of his archetypal Russian sadness, his sad Slavishness; it wasn't his work, nor his wife, nor his previous girls, nor his parents. At a very tender age he was already sad. Why was that? Then he remembered: as a toddler he had ignited a match in his mouth and burnt his tongue so badly that he had howled, and his frightened pappa and mamma, his babushka, had come running.

As a Piscean, my first memories, after the amniotic fluids that laved the unborn and unchristened Rory in Mumu's stomach had drained away, would be watery ones; and, right enough, in 1933 the Liffey flooded the village. I was six, two years before Mussolini's modern Army and Air Force attacked Abyssinia defended by naked warriors carrying spears. The water came up as far as Marlay Abbey, flooding Flynn's bicycle shop. The penny farthing bike that hung outside looked as peculiar as a giraffe standing on dry land surrounded by Zambesi flooding.

My first feeling was one of fear, fear connected with floods and attendant omens presaging watery ends, rampant flooding and even more ominous omens, for hadn't the river Anna Livia, normally the most tractable and easy-going of well-behaved rivers flowing between narrow banks not half a mile from Springfield lodges, burst and overflowed her banks?

Nurse O'Reilly, a headstrong Cavan woman with buck teeth, a great one for laying cautious bets (a shilling each way on Royal Braide in the 4.30 at Fairyhouse) now could lay no bets because the turf accountant was unreachable there opposite the forge, unless of course he was out in a rowing boat collecting bets all over the village.

We tink of Dee . . .

I sang discordantly with the other little lads of my class, the girleens being off to one side of us, singing out of key as always; the gravel was biting savagely into my bare knees and I thought of St Patrick driving the sharp point of his crozier through a convert's bare foot and he, the injured convert, bleeding like a stuck pig, thinking it was part of an initiation ceremony, never said a word. I wore shorts, kneeling with the others at the May altar to the Blessed Virgin on the gravelled driveway before the Holy Faith convent surrounded by young yew trees bending this way and that before the freshening breeze, the nuns holding on to their coifs when genuflecting piously.

> *We tink of Dee*
> *An whaw dow art,*
> *Dye majusteee, Dy stay-ate,*
> *An I keep singing in my hurt*
> *Imma-kul-late, Imma – KUUL – late!*

But I wasn't thinking of any such thing, her beautified and serene self up there above the clouds in a remote and distant Heaven unimaginably far away. I thought rather of the cold roast beef in the larder at Springfield that old Mrs Henry would bring out and slice up and put in front of me on a plate to take well salted with garden peas that tasted even better cold. And old Mrs Henry would ask me how the sodality had gone, and how the girls had sung; and I would reply that all had gone well.

But did I care how the girls sang, the big girls with their chests heaving, smelling of stale sweat trapped inside their frocks, and the excitement of boys with their mouths open, staring at them, getting fresh? Not I.

I thought rather of the Devil who was my true playmate, Señor Satan with all his suave works and pomps, who wandered through the world for the ruin of souls. He was close enough to touch, though himself invisible, like sin itself. Sin was just something you wanted to do, maybe with one of the big girls who sometimes sat with us in the back of the class and put us through our Catechism, and then you would get the girl-smell; the pong of sin. Satan was always urging me to do the bad things I liked doing, such as touching myself; the priest in the darkened confessional told Rory not to touch himself, not to play with himself. And Rory, abasing himself, low as a slug and just as mean, said, 'No, Father' and 'Yes, Father', whichever way it was; because he was always doing something wrong, something that was said to be sinful.

But Satan was very clever and closer to me than my Guardian Angel, who was said (by the nuns) to be always there but invisible, as my constant counsellor and conscience. I named mine Batty.

What do we do here, eh Batty? He never told me anything, but I could feel him invisibly present, his mouth set in a severe line, his brows drawn down in disapproval, for I did much that Batty would have to disapprove of, if he (it?) was a true GA, wherever he was, with his mouth close to my ear, advising me: *Don't do it!*

I had real trouble with the Holy Ghost. He was the third equally divided part of an everlasting confederacy of goodness and holiness and sanctity that betokened a true divinity split three ways, like signposts pointing off in different directions to Birr and Athy and Edenderry; a tripartite divinity that could divide itself into three equal parts without any bother, like Mumu dividing up a Swiss roll into three equal parts for brother Bun, the Dote and myself.

I saw the Holy Ghost only as the wings of God, torn off and put to one side, not part of the divinity at all but floating away light as a feather, apart and still invisible. These, the priest told us and the nuns agreed, were 'revealed truths which we cannot comprehend'. I thought of them as something kept in a special great chest in a sealed room in the Vatican to which only the Pope had access, the key, or keys, for the great chest with the secrets in it was always kept locked and only Pope Pius XII knew what was in it, and his lips were solemnly sealed.

I sang with the others, with more conviction now, the cold beef and peas close enough to smell. I sang with half my heart in it at least. I sang piously in falsetto:

> Deep in dye wounds, Lord
> Hide an shelter mee;
> So shall I nivver,
> Nivver part from Dee!

'Don't you try and get fresh with me, Mister Man,' warned the big girl staring hotly at Rory, who looked as if butter wouldn't melt in his mouth. At Rory who, as a matter of fact, didn't eat butter.

'Don't you *dare!*' warned the fiery girl and her warm breath fanned my face.

When Molly Cushen walked slowly on to the bridge, I watched transfixed by Breen's Hotel. She moved very slowly and then stopped to lean on the arm of the bridge, dissolving in tears.

I had never seen a girl weep her heart out like that; she wept as though she was being torn up inside, and the insides of girls were to me a total mystery.

Nor did she become ugly on that account, crying so bitterly; she became, if that were possible, more beautiful than before, as though by weeping she had drawn closer to me. And I thought to myself: That must be real love; that's the price you must pay for beauty.

She was the prettiest girl in the convent, with her pale oval face almost Chinese, with round cheeks and long black hair and dark eyes, all pupil. She had a low voice and was in the class behind me, so I did not see much of her except in the playground, where she was sedate and moved about by herself, watching the other girls yelling and screeching as they raced about.

It was the voice that got to me, glottal; sooner or later she would have to get her tonsils out. Intimacies confided in that resonant voice would indeed be womanly intimacies; the voice of Molly Cushen seemed to come up out of the ground, not up out of her stomach. Her mother had died and would be buried next day in Donycomper cemetery. The nun told us that we should be kind to poor Molly who had lost her mother. They had been close, the nun said.

Now she was dissolving in tears.

A wind blew downriver from behind the ruined mill and blew strands of black hair across her face as if she wore a mourning veil and she stopped; on the hump of the bridge as if she couldn't go a step further, because it was closer to Donycomper cemetery which was just up the hill on the Lucan road. Now she was racked with tears, weeping convulsively, her shoulders heaving.

This was real crying, those were scalding tears; she wept as though her heart was broken. A shadowy form was holding her, shaking her; that was her mother in a shroud come back from the dead to comfort her daughter. I thought: That then is true love; it must be hard indeed, love.

I remembered the blood-flecked bowl that stood on a table in the changing room where the girls kept their coats. After harsh dentistry for the whole school, called out class by class for extractions, the girls who had had teeth pulled out spat into the bowl and walked about with chalk-white faces, handkerchiefs pressed to their mouths and their white smocks also bloodstained. They walked slowly about, grimacing, as if in purdah, as if by walking slowly about, the pain would go away. That then was real love: the pain that wouldn't go away.

The white suffering face of the young girl on the bridge was a face 'washed by all waters' as the Germans say. A dark-haired, white-faced pretty girl weeping her heart out on a humpbacked bridge, missing her mother who had been dragged away to her death, that too was certain, a token of love, of not forgetting, holding in the heart that which had vanished. Love had to do with a humpbacked bridge with five arches which took the traffic that moved slowly in two directions, coming and going. Horse-drawn carts and turf wagons drawn by little donkeys moved in terrific slow motion over the bridge, up by Gleason's shop and down past Green's open door, the dark maw of their hovel. The shell of a mill long out of use, a breeze blowing downriver, the beginning of love.

Black Bucks Vain of Their Dicks

At the Bray Head end of the North Beach at Greystones, where the trains came out of the tunnel, it was possible to swim nude, far enough from preying eyes on the harbour wall. The nearest humans were the fishermen some way out at sea, pulling off around Bray Head.

One sultry day in August Rory, horny as Pan, sprinted starkers from the cold embrace of the sea and threw himself like a thunderbolt upon the warm inert vaguely female form, compliant, soft and wet, made from the topsoil that had parted company from the cliff above, now supine or prone, featureless with the suggestion of gigantic thighs.

Into this engulfing bride didn't the bold Rory embed his prick as into a steamy big seaside girl with her chubby legs wide apart, and shagged all the shapelessness and seaside silliness out of her, gasping and panting at the size of it, the strength of it. Then he cleaned his member and dressed in a hurry, just shirt, trousers and sandals, hoping that none of the fishermen out in their boats, hauling in and letting out nets, had seen him shagging the mud pile silly, as though it were a big soft lump of a girl. They would stand up and shout something obscene for sure. But none seemed to be interested, concentrating on their tasks, lost out in the haze. The sea was still very cold in August and the mackerel were running.

Half-hearted attempts to pick up girls down from Dublin sunbathing and oiling themselves on the harbour wall came to naught. Rory asked a girl, who was brown as a nut, if she would go swimming with him on the South Beach; he was on his Raleigh with one foot on the railings above the beach near the ice-cream hut and she had appeared alongside him; he had been watching her for weeks. She went about with her mother; walking from her home near the crossroads on the way to Delgany. She was rarely alone. Rory didn't know her name.

'I can't swim,' she said, staring at the sea.

She had brown eyes, with nice hands and hair. She was lovely.

'I'll teach you to swim.'

'Will you?'

Silence. She stared at the sea; Rory stared at her profile. They would lie side by side on bath towels near where the little stream trickled out into the sea. He might suggest Kilcoole beach where one could sunbathe without togs, perhaps together now on one towel. He would urge her to enter the sea naked with him, would teach her the breaststroke. Read Herrick to her, oil her back.

'How you disturb me,' I said.

Meaning: oh I fancy you, brownie.

'Then you should go to the other end of the beach,' she said with invincible female logic.

Kiss your opportunities goodbye. Such chances come rarely. Rory changed into his togs all of a doodah by the rocks and waited for her to appear in the striped costume he had seen on her when sunbathing; but she did not show up. She didn't like his crab-like approach; she had walked off.

One had to make fit submission to the Great Female Principle. And what was that but immersion in the sea, in a state of total nudity in that fulsome embrace, bracing while powerfully and undeniably feminine?

The semeny odours of the foreshore spoke of the male–female union, as did the clams stuck so obstinately fast to their rocks, little sister clams to big brother rocks, as did the rock-pools and bladderwrack, the fishy tang of cunt, the cunty tang of fish, the mackerel gutted and thrown on the beach by the point, flung out of the boats coming from beyond Kilcoole, given away free at dusk, as well as the general shifting about of sand blown by the breeze, the sucking and gushing and sibilant whispering that went on all the time, the sun scudding into the clouds, only to reappear again, and the beach suddenly in shade and then wiped clean as the sun burst forth again; barnacles clipping and kissing and the little waves rolling in on their sinuous rills, every seventh bigger than the preceding six and the mussels puckering up their slobbery drippy lips and all the ceaseless activity that goes on every day on the beach (even when there is nobody there, just the sand castles subsiding and the lost towel and the paddle as signs of former occupancy). It went on anyhow; life as ceaseless agitation.

Could her name be Molly? Hairy Molly, the dark brown one, the *morena*. Mightn't she be Molly? My Molly. Might not she be my *morena*, if only I could shake off the mother? Stranger things have happened.

Water is the great aphrodisiac for Pisceans. Feared at first (forceful ducking), then accepted, then indulged in, then forgotten, as potency waxes and wanes, as the moon goes around.

I have always thought of bodies of water, no matter how big or how small or agitated (Anna) or tranquil (Philippa), whether in perpetual motion (Harriet), as rivers and mountain streams, or at rest (Lough Dan, where Philippa appeared to be decapitated, up to her neck in dark mountain water), as feminine.

The tang of seaweed has always seemed to me a cunty tang ('salt swoll'n cunt') and something to fear; as the chilly embrace of seawater is calculated to shrink the flinching member, first seizing the balls in a sudden rough grip and presently up around the neck; until one casts off buoyantly into another free element (the one we came out of, when we were fish) that bears one up, miraculously on the surface, a female grasp of male matter (the member getting acclimatised to the cold of the underwater and the nibbling minnows). Trust in the female (what Herr Mann calls *der Andere*) is what keeps the apprehensive and wincing male swimmer afloat and free of his own uncertainty, in this supremely female element, the sea.

So Rory, at first a non-swimmer though born half a mile from Anna Liffey, always saw water, whether hot or cold, harbour or open sea, precocious Mediterranean shore or freezing Atlantic, from taps or coming naturally, whether in thermal springs or in spas with noisome emetics, vile concoctions said to be good for you, to be essentially a *female* element, in its chill deeps holding his male member in its frozen grip, a clutch well calculated to unman Rory.

Rory feared fast-flowing rivers with tricky currents and bends with deep holes, around which the current swirled as if to say *Steer clear, me hearties!* There was the sloping gravelled hole down the slope of which the Dote had once stumbled until the water was up to his nose; another inch and he was under, choking, but fortunately for him the pool levelled out and he walked out the other side, watched by myself and Gina Green, gone pale as sheets on the riverbank.

Then Rory feared deep water, the tidal sea, the befouled Liffey with filthy effluents discharged from the city, flowing out under Butt Bridge and off into the snotgreen scrotumtightening sea referred to by Mr Joyce, himself a great water man, that was Dublin Bay where every summer someone drowned.

Rory feared all this just as he feared the ramshackle rusty hulks from foreign parts, *Valparaiso* and the *Straits of Magellan*, that were moored at the dockside there with moody, dirty-looking crewmen lounging about on deck. He sometimes thought of offering his services as a deck-hand, like the young Conrad or Lowry after him; but never did, could never pluck up enough courage to hail one of these lounging lascars. Just as well perhaps. They would have shagged poor Rory overboard as useless cargo somewhere off Rockall. What happened out there was very remote from the boy and girl stuff.

The movies that came my way and seemed to reveal something of that threatening strange life, the life that other people led, the lovers who *went after* each other like carnivores after their victims ('Studio *Vingt Huit* high up on a windy street in Montmartre in the full blasphemy of a freezing Sunday,' wrote

Cyril Connolly of *Un Chien Andalou*, where Pierre Batcheff and his Spanish-looking girl 'patter after each other like stoats in search of blood'), were

> *Un Chien Andalou*
> *Extase*
> *Blood and Sand*
> *Bahama Passage*
> *The Brothers*
> *The Lady from Shanghai*
> *The Outcast of the Islands*
> *Knife in the Water*

Women are not the best judges of women, nor of their special appeal for specific men, those watchful, horny, thorny lads. 'Can't see what you see in that one,' Stella Veronica told Rory. 'The gommy-looking one,' she called her, Rory's nutbrown maid. In those days all Irish girls were virgins; if for no other reason than they never escaped from their vigilant mothers' ever-watchful eyes. They even dressed like their mothers, wore the same make-up, or none at all. Nude sunbathing would have to be done on the sly, for the mother would notice the Bahama complexion.

But, having taken another look at the sunbather on the harbour wall, Stella Veronica was ready to concede that the gommy-looking one wasn't so gommy-looking after all and was in fact a good-looking girl. A real good-looker, if a bit on the dark side.

Some girls are greedy for it already before their time. What about the one in a pack of screeching schoolgirls running out of the sea and sitting on boulders below the Eden Temperance Hotel in the small stony cove blocked with seaweed? She was very red in the face from excitement and sat in such a way that her uniform school skirt of dark blue serge, rode up to reveal her dark declivities, for she wasn't wearing knickers or hadn't bothered to put them on yet and didn't seem to notice Rory, very thoughtful, walking below, getting an eyeful of her charms, as though he had lost something, say his watch (he never wore one), in the shale.

Hannelore had spoken to me of the nudist camp at Bastia in Corsica where she went with her dancing teacher and Dr Hans Borken, and of the black men 'hung like horses' who were very sportful in the surf, showing off what they possessed to the laughing girls. Their members glistened black as ebony and the girls couldn't take their eyes off them.

She and her friend undressed in the hut and walked out into the sea where the black men were shouting and cavorting and ducking one another. It was a small act of female consideration. Dr Borken followed them a little later, a bit shamefaced about his pale white nudity.

Hannelore had always contended that women were stronger than men. The men dressed up as soldiers and went off to war but the women did something more difficult: they stayed at home and fed and cared for the children during the bombing.

Prone on a towel, not yet having 'gone in', waiting for the sun to come out, immersed in the *Essays of Schopenhauer* and apparently impervious to distractions (Monsieur Gool's handsome son, a French Resistance fighter, had that morning walked on his hands into the sea, to the delight of those watching the upside-down legs advancing deeper and deeper into the sea, like the Manx symbol of three whirling legs or Brueghel's Icarus drowning), the pubescent Rory now being treated to the arousing spectacle of a young wife, no doubt sexually voracious, down for the day from Dublin on her own, drying herself after a dip and kicking off her wet clinging togs now itchy with sand, allowing the bath towel to slip from her hands to take the sun (which had come out again) just as she is, giving Rory a chance to fully appreciate her unadorned charms, stood up just the other side of the bathing box by the railway line.

The sun goes in again; she wraps herself in the towel; Rory runs into the sea. Culvert one hundred and sixty yards seaward. Lap dissolve. Iris out.

19

Roryamours 1956–99

Dostoevesky married his stenographer, Anna Grigoryevna Snitkina; he was twenty-five years her senior, a fitful epileptic and survivor of a Siberian labour camp.

In the highlands of Cuernavaca, in the state of Morelos, the air is like wine. At dawn, in the Rancho Pico, the two black and white cocks crow with the bright clarion-call of bugles.

The later, appealling roughneck, Ernest Hemingway, boasted that he had given 'Mr Scrooby' fifty-five times in one month to his fourth wife, Miss Mary.

My former publisher, Calder, boasted to another potential conquest that he had had three hundred women in his time. Rory doubted if he himself had had more than twenty, being a late starter. But why diversity? Five of the twenty he had surely enjoyed more than three hundred times.

You have to begin somewhere and you must end somewhere. Jack Trevor Story boasted that he had but ten loves in his life and his trouble was that he couldn't forget any of them. I, being choosy, have had rather less than ten, and I too cannot forget any of them.

Chronologically then, here they are, sauntering out into the ring: my first wife Coppera Hill, née Anders, was born in King William's Town in the Eastern Cape of South Africa; we lived together as man and wife for twenty years and more and have three sons, one of whom has given me four grandchildren, one a girl (Hi, Yanika, my sweet!): that long union came to an end in an unforeseen manner like a house of cards toppling.

Then there was Mrs Harriet Deck of San Francisco; Hannelore Schmidt of Berlin; Hannel Vang of Copenhagen, a sort of sob-sister to Anna Reiner, also of Copenhagen, that quiet port on Kattegat. And then there was Alannah Buxton-Hopkin, who was born in Singapore of an English father (Dr Denis Buxton-Hopkin, who had been a voluntary POW staying with his patients after the fall of Singapore) and an Irish mother, one of the Foleys of Summercove. We were married on 20 November 1997 in a Dublin register office.

She is my last love, the love of my life. When I hear the toot of the Peugeot on the one-way narrow street below, the horn tells me that she is near, returned from Castletownbere or Castletownshend or even Ballydehob, visiting the cheese people or the English bird couple, the Foxes, or the art people who are everywhere in County Cork; when not out riding in the riding schools she assiduously attends. She has her rituals.

20

The Hoax that Joke Bilked

My brother's unnamed house, even in an unfinished state, was a peculiar domicile for an architect to conceive, let alone design and build for himself and his wife. If your dentist, upon opening wide his mouth exposed horrors, dental decay run riot, rotten roots, missing teeth, wouldn't you be taken aback?

The uncomfortably narrow stairway led upwards to the narrow sleeping quarters, the rat races in the rafters, and down to narrow rooms crowded in upon themselves. The whole dusty ambience was forbidding, veiled in dust; it was like entering a house shut up for years, the air stale, the surfaces dimmed by lack of daylight.

It was as unlike the house that Charles Eames built, afloat on the air at Pacific Palisades, as you could well imagine. My brother would have maintained that pleasure is *not* useful; we were not put on this earth to enjoy ourselves, so why quarrel with beastly circumstances? You would not get the impression (the feeling of a loft with its habitual cobwebs and scuttle of unseen mice and stale trapped air) that my brother was ever touched by the uncommon beauty of common things, which had touched Charles Eames; certainly not by his architectural forays. All I remembered was an uncompleted shell, the narrow bedroom like the set from *The Cabinet of Dr Caligari* with Werner Krauss oozing out of the ply-wood wall.

Brother C. took against me for the way I had portrayed him and his wife and their unfinished house in *Dog Days*, perceiving only jeers and sneers where I had attempted to portray him as a heroic Dostoevsky character, a mixture of Dimitri Karamazov and Prince Mishkin. I had to portray tsarist-style Russian squalor and of course the *dacha* half finished, an oversight, in the face of other more pressing concerns (the soul).

He didn't like it, didn't get the joke, thought I was ridiculing the neighbours, for whom he would always be Pan Hill, the big boss, the Town Planner. Can you see it? Can you beat it? The style of it!

Now it's as if I'd put a curse on the still nameless house finally completed without any flags raised at cornice or roof to announce all was ready for human habitation; and what remain are blackened beams and owls roosting in the now distinctly chilly and uncomfortable bedroom, the cats running wild; everything now in disarray and the voracious growth of weeds proliferating and obscuring the shapes of the deserted habitation.

Frater, Brüder, hermano, it wasn't ever my intent to belittle you. I have nothing but respect for you. Long ago when we were chisslers, I could have injured you badly or broken your neck on the road from Lough Dan going downhill like the hammers of Hell when the front wheel of my heavy Raleigh locked with your back wheel (boy's bike) and pitched us both on to the road.

Once in the loft above the garage some highly combustible film stock caught fire, surrounded by petrol leaks and full tins and lofts full of hay; we could have burnt the place down, might have suffocated, but managed to put it out. Do you remember that? I was the elder one, I should have known not to play about with celluloid and matches.

There were times when I could have blinded you when we played the Wilhelm Tell game and I shot holes with the Daisy air-rifle through the apple balanced on your head – you were the fall guy.

How do brothers survive brothers? And was it some sort of joke you were making, some point you wished to make, by building your own ruin and folly for all to see and admire on this island crammed with ruins and follies, not to forget the hidden graves of those murdered by the Provos in the night and buried in secret places in Wicklow, in this sometimes wholly delightful Vale of Tears? Was that it? I'll die laughing, if so.

One thing is sure: once your mind is made up, it's made up for good. The account is closed; I know that.

The Anaya-Toledos of Mexico City

C arl, my eldest son, split up with his Mexican wife,
Carlota Anaya-Toledo of the Jardin Balbuena, a grandiose name and address that was, like much in Mexico,
disguising a mess. When the marriage didn't work out, the love
didn't work out either. Thanks chiefly to the father, Adolfo
Anaya-Toledo, who, as a Mexican gentleman of means had on
his word of honour promised them a flat and Carl a job and
when neither was forthcoming the marriage was already on the
rocks. Carl couldn't find a job without the official papers Adolfo
had promised to secure. The ignorant wife sent her putative
son-in-law to consult a *bruja*, a soothsayer, or witch.

There was a long and painful parting. Carl left Mexico and
returned to London, was given back his old job in the Odeon
projection box. Carlota threatened to follow, would not agree
to a divorce.

Years later he found love again in Hemel Hempstead when
he took up with a pale girl by the name of Sally, who had
a rough father. By Sally he had the long longed-for child he
never had with Carlota, a daughter whom he dearly loved in
the short span of life allotted her, for she was only granted a few
days in winter.

So, she (Elizabeth they christened her) died and was buried
in a little casket in a wood in Hertfordshire and Grandmother

Cappera read an Emily Dickinson poem in lieu of a prayer. Carl was the romantic who believed in all-out love, like Byron, in the reckless way that the late unlamented Dr Goebbels had believed in total war. Carl was for loving blindly, giving all without any reservations, which is a sure prescription for failure. It was the same terrible medicine that Dr Goebbels had prescribed for the *Volk*, with such disastrous consequences. Carlos was for all-out love. Well, that's unwise. Who was it wrote that 'to love without reservation is to be betrayed'? Djuna Barnes?

The Shapely Flanks of Rita Hayworth
(*The Lady from Shanghai*)

i

November 17 of 1946 was a cloudy day in Acapulco with an oppressively overcast sky holding down the heat. Twenty miles out coxswain and famous cocksman Errol Flynn of 'In like Flynn!' fame, stood at the wheel of his yacht *Zaca* (*Circe* in the movie they were about to shoot, a month after Orson Welles, the director, had begun scouting for locations) in choppy seas, trying to hold her on a steady course.

Lawton the cinematographer held the filter to his right eye, waiting for a break in the clouds. In character and dressed for the part, Welles ('Black' Mike O'Hara, who had throttled a man with his bare hands during the Spanish Civil War) and his former wife, Rita Hayworth (Elsa Bannister, *femme fatale* and murderess, unsatisfied spouse of the famous criminal lawyer Arthur Bannister, crippled in both legs), had rehearsed the opening scene of the shooting on the aft deck and were ready for the cameras to roll.

The Acapulco sun blazed forth, the mixer hollered 'Speed ... Take One! Let em roll!' and Welles, holding a beat, spoke his first line. His Irish accent was priceless; but there again his contact with the noble race had been largely confined to working for the two famous pederasts, Hilton Edwards and

Micheál MacLiammóir at the Gate. It was rich and strange, a veritable verbal purple vestment. The shooting of *The Lady from Shanghai* had begun. It was a movie already doomed to fail on many counts, for Welles, for Harry Cohn, the president of Columbia Pictures who wanted to bend Welles and *The Lady* to his will, laying on the terrible theme song 'Please Don't Kiss Me', which was as corny as they come, and obliging Rita Hayworth to sing it out at sea, adding another $60,000 to an undertaking already costing plenty. And how could she refuse? She was under contract; he had her over a barrel. She was appearing as a favour to Welles, who was slow to pay alimony. Their daughter Rebecca had turned twelve and there were school fees, dental fees, God knows what fees, to be considered. When filming was over, Welles planned to vanish into Europe.

In the meantime (back on the *Circe-Zaca*) one of the camera crew, working without a hat, collapsed and died of a coronary thrombosis; to be sewn up in a duffel bag and thrown overboard. 'Sail on, *Zaca*!' sang out Flynn, whose spirits could not be suppressed. He spoke in a strange clipped English accent to match his wispy moustache, and was in awe of Welles. He must have had his own ideas about Rita Hayworth too. His own wife was heavily pregnant, aboard with the crew and cast; the two lawyers, Bannister (Everett Sloane) and Grisby (Glenn Anders) seemed more like criminals; and O'Hara's sidekicks (one was Bud Schilling) turned out to be half-wits. Even the Judge (Erskine Sanford, the fuddy-duddy old editor of Kane's newspaper in *Citizen Kane* seven years previously) seemed loopy. Well, everybody is somebody's fool. Flynn had his rapacious eye on many things; all that moved and was female was his potential prey. All that was female and good-looking moved him; he was swayed by beauty, always greedy for it.

The location shooting would be extremely arduous, not counting the corpses thrown overboard; Welles was up to his neck in what he preferred to do: show ambition thwarted, women disappointed and turning on their men; evildoers at their evildoing. He had run up a huge bill at the Hotel Reforma in Mexico City; he and Rita Hayworth had been received off their flight like visiting royalty. Flynn was jealous of him, not least because of his apparently effortless success with women. And what women! Hayworth and then Dolores del Rio, whose underclothes must have cost a fortune.

'Rita couldn't take the heat,' they said. She had to make two dives from Morro Rock. Temperatures soared and Rita collapsed on camera. Orson was most solicitous, he couldn't do enough for her. She was carried down into her cool cabin and Orson stood guard.

The shooting went on, using understudies, shooting the back of the head, moving shadows, the shifty ones, the lawyers who acted and looked like bad criminals. The unctuous theme song was poured like molasses over everything by Cohn, still trying to bend the great director to his will. Sharks swam in the lukewarm water. Rita said she was finished. Flynn's eyes were permanently bloodshot; now he had taken up with an Amazonian giantess with teeth missing and not a word of English; she spoke the language of the night, grunting and groaning under Flynn, who was insatiable.

When Cohn saw the rough cut he exploded, offering one grand to anyone who could explain the story to him. There was no plot, there were no close-ups of Rita. He decided to plug 'Please Don't Kiss Me' into every nook and cranny, like Muzak into Macey's, penetrating even into the toilets.

'The only way to stay out of trouble is to grow old,' Cohn said, snipping the end off a huge cigar; quoting from the wunderkind's obnoxious script. And his executives seemed to agree with him. 'Hey, fellas, concentrate on that.' They hooted with hearty laughter by the door. 'If you kiss me, don't take your lips away!' Cohn was in stitches. The studio hack composer, Heinz Roemheld, whose orchestration of the toon had snored away on the strings, was summoned to the office and congratulated by the president on doing a great job. Welles of course had hated the song; a long and abusive memo had come in. Rita sued him for a goodly sum to cover child maintenance; but Orson-Black-Michael-O'Hara-Welles was no longer there.

'He never was,' Cohn said bitterly, unaware that he had made a witty joke. He could kiss his money goodbye, *The Lady from Shanghai* wouldn't make one red cent; Rita could kiss her alimony goodbye too. It was a crying shame, Cohn said, choking on his long Cuban cigar.

'We used Acapulco just as we found it,' the wunderkind had told him. 'No more, no less, Harry.'

ii

She had come a long way since, aged seventeen, she had danced in *Dante's Inferno*. And yet, not so far; for she was ignorant as pay-dirt. 'Orsie' (her pet name for Orson) had her reading Plato, Cervantes and Shakespeare, but all that quick culture went in one ear and out the other; she wasn't made for it. She was a dancer, and when she danced her body spoke volumes and in many languages. She was not in control of it; her beauty escaped her; went out to all the men sitting with hard-ons, silently in the dark, smoking like furnaces; their spouses uneasy beside them, rustling like wheat in the wind, the womenfolk knowing that they had lost their men who had run off after Rita.

And then there was her former co-star Victor Mature, a dense fellow who wore trousers two sizes too large for him, and had the mouth of a carnivore. They had met on the shooting of *My Gal Sal* and the relationship had prospered quickly, so gushed the gossip columnist Hedda Hopper. The coupling of cheesecake and beefcake appealed to the romantically inclined gossips and vulgarians of Hollywood. Hollywood *wanted* this marriage.

But it was not to be; her destiny lay elsewhere. Soon her mad Orsie was sawing her in half for the Mercury Wonder Show and cutting off all her long mane of red hair (Margarita Carmen Cansino had Irish and Spanish blood coursing through her veins) for *The Lady from Shanghai* where she undertook some serious man-killing after all the floss and flicker of *Gilda* and *Cover Girl*.

Cohn was fit to be tied. 'Rita, honey,' he implored, 'you gotta stop doin' this ta me. You gotta listen now. Listen good. We *own* you, sweetie, bag and baggage, body and soul. You're ours. Columbia owns you. There's the contract. Now behave yourself. You ain't gonna work for this nutcase no more.' Or some such palaver; Cohn was incensed.

So Rita came to heel. How could she not? She was a contracted star earning real money; it wasn't peanuts. Her great public adored her, servicemen everywhere wanted to get down on her.

The swell of bust was duplicated behind in the swell of proud calf, noble flank and buttock, on the screen in Technicolor. It flowed in all directions. Her curves duplicated the contour of rich coastlines, of good real estate for the seriously rich from Point Conception to La Jolla on through Baja California along the lines of latitude just above the Equator. These were her outstretched and noble flanks in fishnet stockings and mighty high heels, her dancing kit ripping my dreams, something cruel there, with the flaming tresses the urgent frou frou of skirt lifted in the dance, the big pouty lips red as cherries, the show of brilliantly white teeth – infill condition, *asperges*, plenty, America! Nutrition privilege, dollars, security, blaze USA!

When they saw Hayworth or Betty Grable (an even riper peach) dance, the thoughts of all good red-blooded Americans flew to Belmont Park or Saratoga Springs or Aqueduct, all the racetracks and the great fillies and mares that ran in the fifth and the fourth and the third race; the thoroughbreds pounding by had the bodies of supermodels; at every stride the tipsters cheered and waved them on with race cards, binoculars clenched in their hands.

Betty Grable was of course *all* curves. Single-handed she had won the Battle of the Bulge. Her body on the screen was worth two or three divisions in the field.

Cohn, in a black mood, gnashing his molars and armed with clippers, cut and hacked away at the finished film, trying to make it an acceptable vehicle for the masses, cutting it down to eighty-six minutes, holding up the release for a year, releasing it into the second half of programmes, hoping few would notice it. Few did. Orsie had had his scissors out too; he'd sheared off Rita's lovely long red mane, made a peroxide blonde out of her, filmed her in the San Francisco aquarium, wouldn't even show them (her and Welles) embracing, much less glued together in a *beso*.

iii

It was the one movie I always wanted to see again.

Betty Grable, all lips and legs, was just part of the American war effort on the home front; akin to selling war bonds. Her image was stamped on the fuselage of Flying Fortresses where she exposed as much of herself as the Hayes Office would permit; a low-angle shot of the famous come-on look as though she were lifting or thinking of lifting up her skirt to show what little she had on underneath. Years later this would spawn the shot of Monroe standing astride the grid above the subway, in *The Seven Year Itch*.

The heavily insured legs and horse-like flanks assured the servicemen and flyers that Democracy was indeed worth dying for if Betty Grable, with her skirt torn off by a great wind, represented it.

There was too much strangeness in the Welles movie for Cohn. Try as he might with his scissors and 'Please Don't Kiss Me', he could not eliminate the erotic strangeness. I saw the film first in the Adelphi in Dun Laoghaire, where I had also seen Abraham Polonsky's *Force of Evil* with Philippa. The slagging picnic, the sequence in the aquarium, the clinches that never came, or came and were never seen; the whole movie was full of unsaid things: innuendoes, portents of unspeakable things. It was the sort of movie that Philippa detested, full of 'suggestive' images, a very strong Catholic taboo word in those days.

The wank in the tank led forward through all the years to the dim aquarium where Elsa Bannister (Rita Hayworth) and Black Mike, two killers, do not embrace, absolutely do not embrace each other, though evidently dying to do so.

It led to the revolving barrel of water where she of the luscious underlip, permanently damp, revolves in *Les Enfants du Paradis*. The nude Arletty, who had a Nazi lover, a Luftwaffe colonel no less, during the Occupation, swoons in the tank, as though male arms are urgently reaching out for her. She says impudently, '*J'adore la liberté.*'

It led, after some teasing, to the naked wife crouching on the yacht in *Knife in the Water*, a sight to which we in the dark cinema are privy, with the blond young Polish hitch-hiker, but not the husband.

It led to Madeleine Carroll and Sterling Hayden, two stoats on an island where the sun shines all day under the sea, in *Bahama Passage*.

It led to the permanently drenched native black girl of Carol Reed's *Outcast of the Islands* who can speak no English, and is seen showering; she is half otter, all stoat.

It led to Patricia Roc bursting out of her cleavage in *The Brothers* and swimming naked in the sea somewhere off Scotland.

All led back to Hedy Kiesler (who went to Hollywood and was turned into a waxworks figure) in *Extase*, swimming naked in a Czech lake, after undressing behind a bush as provocatively as Madeleine Carroll had removed her stockings behind a screen, with her stoat Hayden watching, in a skyscraper in New York. And all led back to the cattle tank at the ring-pump at Springfield in the long ago.

PART II:

Foreign Faces and Places

23

Voyage

We plunge over the Equator. Flying fish sink, porpoises rise, and evening after evening the sun goes down in formations of cloud, furnace-like, dramatic as anything in Doré's illustrations of Dante. The approaches to a new continent. Such lovely leewardings! They must lead somewhere.

Undersized dining-room stewards – Malays – traverse the decks banging out the same tune on their dinner gongs. I've grown tired of the repetitive meals, the same dull company – it's a kind of prison.

The passengers for the most part are Dutch, German, or Afrikaners returning to their homeland. One tall Afrikaner – von Lieres – is returning to Vanrhynsdorp in the Cape after several years studying engineering in Germany. He tells me that in some South African families they send their sons into the police force for a year or so to toughen them up before they take up a career. Before they take up a more respectable career? I ask. He gives me a blank look and smiles; we do not make jokes about the police in South Africa. On the first lap of the tour we will run into him again. I share a cabin with two young Germans – also engineers. Going to German South-West Africa. Strategists.

Among the German contingent is a family from Berlin. The

parents sit close together on deck, stoutly perspiring, handkerchiefs over their heads, calling for beer. They have one son of
fourteen; it's mainly on his account that they are going to South
Africa. Germany is not for them any more. Two wars in one
lifetime is too much.

What is it they fear? Communism, militant Communism? The
Tartar tank crews with their slit eyes and Mongolian features,
the strange leather headgear of the Red Army spearheads that
entered Budapest to crush the Hungarian uprising, finished them.
Emanations from a nightmare. It is this they fear. Soviet tanks
manned by Asiatic crews.

So off, then; *pis aller!*

The wife hopes to take up her old profession in Johannesburg:
orthopaedics. The husband too will work. Both have done so all
their lives, worked hard; they are not young any more, but they
will work for the future of their son.

The small *Fräulein* in Coppera's cabin has her wedding dress
and trousseau with her. Though hardly more than a child, she
is going out to German South-West Africa to marry a man she
has never seen except in photographs. She is a war orphan from
Hamburg. It's an arranged match.

The first sight of Africa low on the horizon on the port side,
a dim white skeleton coast; a mirage that goes.

Walvis Bay, in South-West Africa. A barrage of heat. Offal
from the ship's kitchen floating astern. Seagulls squall over it,
their whiteness reflected in a rainbow trail of oil. From the
stagnant greenish waters a stench of putrescence rises, sharp as
sulphuric acid or rotten eggs. A squat white bird, resembling a
penguin, paddles round the stern and one of the crew – an idle
Malay – takes pot-shots at it through a porthole down by the
waterline.

Empty deckchairs, inert in the heat, creak in the sun. The
wan-looking bride-to-be is taken ashore on a tender with some
of the pale young Germans.

Onshore, a collection of shacks faces the sea, the sun shooting
fire on corrugated iron roofs. *Die Waterman* out of Amsterdam, a
decaying wharf with figures of African dock labourers parading on
it, and beyond them, an excessively long rusty-plated terracotta

Russian tanker from the Bering Strait – on these the sun, from almost directly overhead, brings to bear its fierce and implacable rays. Baked littoral and saffron dunes, a reflection of a decayed wharf swimming in mid-air, with figures walking upside down on it – all burn and tremble in the sun.

A local flat-boat comes alongside, and into its capacious and dirty hold black men dressed in rags, with bright-coloured bandannas about their heads, begin offloading cargo, while others wait in the hold. The passengers, laughing, throw them apples and oranges, as if into a bear pit. The oranges explode down in the hold. Some of the remaining sallow-faced young Germans come with jackets under their arms to gape at the coal-black dockers. After a time the flat-boat sails, laden with cargo, grey-black smoke pumping out of its stack. That side of the ship now seems deserted. Leaning over the rail I imagine I can see sand, fathoms deep, and the reflections of a double tier of bored passengers staring down. Their shadows go shuddering into the deeper green of the sea, where a shoal of voracious red cannibal fish, like mullet, swim up out of the stench against our kelpy side. They come in dense, resolute shoals. When a fishing lime, unbaited, touches the water, they take it and one by one are yanked on deck. They lie twitching on the boards where one cannot walk barefoot; quite soon their vivid colour goes.

This desolate place with its heat and smells, the hyena and lion reek of old Africa – this is Walvis Bay. Sidgewick, author of a beginners' book on astronomy, lived for a time with his girl in a cave up in the hills, and died later of coronary thrombosis on a boat on the Seine.

At last this jaunt is nearly over. Tonight we lie to at Walvis Bay.

A storm before Cape Town. All the ports bolted; the woodwork groaning. The Cape rollers begin. Black sea and waves at night. Nausea. We poor sailors turn in early.

In the morning the storm has blown itself out, though the sea is still running high. We are into Table Bay, *Die Waterman* approaching its berth. A blinding glare comes off the sea. During the night one of the vague young Germans, wandering about the ship, fell down a companionway, had a heart attack and died of it. The body lies now in his white cabin. No one knows anything about him. He is to be buried in Cape Town. A collection is started.

Table Mountain looms over us, balancing on its summit a single cloud. It's a hot day in high summer. The passengers crowd the rail. A beauty in a black dress, wearing sunglasses, stands alone on the quayside and waves to someone standing beside me.

Prancing airs of the Cape of Good Hope. It's 20 December 1956.

On 24 December, two engines pull a long line of carriages through the Blaauwberg Mountains, on the Garden Route, travelling from Cape Town to East London in the Eastern Cape. Wheat lands go right up into the lime-blue foothills of the mountains. The horizon seems very far away, bright and luminous. Everything is on a grander scale here – even the swallows are bigger. At Mossel Bay, on an island, a lady in a picture hat paints at an easel.

Blossom, Le Roux, Zebra, Power, George, the Outeniqua Mountains, the beaches of Wilderness, the inland sea of Knysna, the thick green grass of the ostrich farms, an engineless grain train pulled into a siding and Africans in broken sun-hats unloading sugar cane.

For a whole day we travelled through this landscape of grey-blue militant cactus with no other vegetation, no house, the whole face of the land covered with these things, and nothing else as far as the eye could see, scarcely a blade of grass.

24

The Jacaranda Street Nudist

We toured South Africa and both Rhodesias through 1957–58. After outfitting and rehearsing in a theatre in Cape Town, the tour started in somewhere like Paarl or Worcester in the Cape Province, and we toured via Nelspoort as far as Windhoek in South West Africa, and then looped back via the Transkei, Orange Free State and Transvaal until we reached Ladysmith in Natal, then over the Limpopo at Beit Bridge in floods and rain, a delay of two days, on into Southern and Northern Rhodesia, as they were called then with resolute political incorrectness, for the republic had not yet come to pass.

We 'did' Odendaalsrus, Kroonstad, Volksrust, Nylstroom, Warmbad (we swam at night in a pool made by Italian POWs) until we reached Louis Trichardt; and thence to Gwelo or do I mean Gweru before Victoria Falls; and then Wankie, when we were at our last gasp, did us. We rode alongside the driver in the high cabin of a pantechnicon rented out by the National Theatre, Wright made notes, Brink drove, old Madge went ahead and arranged bookings; the puppets and stage were dismantled and packed and had to be reassembled and set up; the African 'boys' were in a hutch at the back; and in this large uncomfortable contraption we travelled thousands of miles over two years and contrived to put aside £200 (old currency) in hard-won savings.

We ended up in Johannesburg.

Coming from the terminus, a merely facultative stop somewhere near Observatory golf course, the No. 11 bowls along Isipingo Street, a pretty street planted with rows of jacaranda trees, stopping just past our flat (Mount Willmar, where the fifth or topmost floor finds us), conveniently enough; and so into town via Netherley House (a home for the indigent old male whites), a fivepenny ride via Gundelfinger & Weinraub, the Ord Tie Factory, Kahn's Pianos and the municipal tennis courts where a bored coach in flannels and a peaked cap lobs brownish tennis balls over the net to an uninspired novice; hence via Long Street to the offices of the J. Walter Thompson advertising agency. That would be after temporary employment at 66 Loveday Street in the Constantia Bookshop; before I found final employment at the junction of Market and Kruis on the sixth floor at Filmlets (SA) under general manager Pax Moran (emphasis on final syllable as in 'also ran').

Consider this. Two queers are quarrelling bitterly on the landing near Ruth Levy's apartment in Hillbrow. It's a bitter business, a lovers' tiff; but before you could invoke the lizard or utter the charmed word 'Bozy', one draws out a gat and plugs the other three times in or about the heart and takes to his heels down the back service hatch used by Africans (*nie Blankes*). Arriving for one of Ruth Levy's drinks parties, Adamczewski is an impassive witness of the consequences. The dying queer crawls along the ground, blood oozing through the back of his shirt, moving his legs slowly sideways, his fingers in the cracks of the cement. He seems to be 'fornicating with the cracks'. Adamczewski hears the footsteps of the murderer escaping down the stairs. It's a day in late November 1958 in Johannesburg.

In the Adamczewski rented quarters at Samedo we play weekend poker on green baize with new-cut decks of cards bought in the Portuguese convenience store on Isipingo Street. Adam, the host, Callus and Crossley from advertising, and Rory; we drink Smirnoff vodka and play for moderate stakes. Mrs Fiona

Adamczewski (née Doran, daughter of a Dublin doctor) had staked out something else on the accommodatingly expansive sofa with the Israeli paratrooper who happened to be passing by. Callus notices a telltale stain on his flies and raises the bidding. The room is as long as a refectory, breezes blow through, the green baize table is far away; around it sit the figures of the avid gamblers. Figure me there.

In this city, which claims the highest suicide rate after West Berlin, forty persons die every week from unnatural causes. One double-locks at night with a deadlock and lies awake listening to the howling of the watch-dogs. It is a city of watch-dogs, howling in unison by night, when the murderers are about.

Simmonds Street, Marshall Street, Hollard Street, Syfret's Trust (Johannesburg Stocks and Shares Brokerage), the Chamber of Mines, Marshall Square know Rory.

The uncertainty of beginning again. Thin high cirrus masks the sun, but soon it's blazing forth; blue skies and warm air of the high Rand, this marvellous winter climate.

Nu-nite Nitewear, Kahn's for pianos, morning haze. Cold mornings on the sixth floor. The dry fug from the electric fire. In the resounding canyon of Kruis Street below us furniture is being dragged across the pavement and into new premises with a harsh grating noise like the roaring of lions. McGraw buffets open the window with the heel of his soft fist to stare out at Mosenthal's clock to check the time again and admit more blasts of cold air.

But who is McGraw?

My workmates, and what strange colleagues, come and go at the whim of Pax Moran's moods. I believe he hires advertising scriptwriters as he would collect freaks, for freakish we surely are: weepy De Wet, anxious McGraw, silent Hill, and the twitchy Bagley. In appearance the Scenario Department resembles some nihilist cell in times of the Tsar, a desperate group sporting Trotsky goatees, all except the clean-shaven McGraw. However there's nothing even vaguely sportful about this department.

'I *think* I'm hip,' says McGraw, 'but I suppose the young people of today would consider me hopelessly square.'

Another prodigiously watery yawn engulfs him and his weak,

red-rimmed eyes fill with tears. He wipes his eyes and nose with the corner of a Kleenex plucked from the extra-large box by his foot; pulling down his albino eyelashes. I am witness to a boredom scarcely to be tolerated, witnessed or endured; I pity the sufferer but he makes me suffer too. McGraw's spongy feet, hacking cough (he coughs for company), damp damp hands, watery stare. He has his eye on the tight rump of the Afrikaans switchboard girl.

'Chaps, do you realise that this time ten years ago I was burning archives in the gardens of the British Embassy at Liège? The tenth of May?' peering myopically at his desk calendar.

McGraw sucks or rather *grinds* boiled sweets throughout the working day, for the good of his nerves, for tyrant Moran is within reach via the intercom on his desk and likes nothing better than upsetting and terrorising the nervous McGraw. He visits the Gents (*Europeans only*) fifteen to twenty times a day, for an incontinent bladder, tiptoeing past the GM's open door, a bunch of Kleenex in his damp hands, dabbing his wet forehead.

O. Rubenstein, J.B. Pain, the Mental Health Society of the Witwatersrand, African Underwear Manufacturers, these names in turn are revealed to me in the rackety old elevator ascending wheezingly to the sixth floor.

The streets, the evening light and heat; then the pleasant bus ride back to Isipingo Street. Evenings on the back balcony with Kensington mine-dumps in the distance. Danish blue cheese and Gordon's gin, what repeal, what peace! Coppera six months pregnant with our first son, to be named Carl Nicolas after her father and Nicolas of Chamford.

Going to work in the morning in drip-dry shirt and tie, tweed jacket from Horton's of Wicklow Street, sauntering along Kruis Street, and whom do I see before me but a familiar bearlike figure shambling along on his spongy feet, progress by locomotor ataxia – McGraw *en route* to further humiliation.

We like to walk from the jacarandas of Isipingo Street to Observatory golf course, for the scents of pine, pepper-gum and eucalyptus all along the way. The wind is warm, the eucalyptus has a dry clean, hygienic scent, wafted through the warm air. A memory of Cavtat in Dalmatia where we began with the puppets. We have a child now, a little boy; he cries out with delight when he notices the eucalyptus branches flowing away before his newly opened and astonished eyes, above the stroller.

On the hillside above the golf course, where Harold Henning is the pro, the African Zionist sects are singing and parading; it's a very energetic religion, they march and counter-march among the trees, appearing and disappearing near the Benoni road. The deep choral chant of the bearded priests comes to us, the deep voices raised in prayer, promises, invocations and objurgation. The female supplicants respond with their thin banshee wail. A canticle of psalms by the brotherhood and sisterhood of the bushes, the voice of Africa at its lamentations.

A multitude of insects rises over the grass. It's evening time, the sun going down over the hill. The insects show up palely luminous and agitated; the golfers are going home.

The singing and the insects rise together, the golfers neither hearing the one nor heeding the other. We drift along with our child, pushing him in the stroller; he brandishes his fists and woollen booties, smitten by some vision, laughing at the departing golfers, the risen insects, the balmy air all around us. We dream of living elsewhere: on St Helena or in the Seychelles. Endless life; endless choice.

The pedigree dogs in the ornate suburban haciendas along Urania Street bark at us, as they must at all intruders. The dark Daughters of Jerusalem are showing off their brown legs. The sprinklers revolve and revolve on the green lawns, widening their skirts of spray. Peaceful days in Johannesburg.

The brunette's morning exercises in the nude still go on; a resplendent bare white figure exposed in the morning sun, a white goddess burning behind glass in an apartment across the way. Juno's loveback and mesial groove; sure I must perish by your charms unless you take me in your arms.

One fine morning, on taking my seat upstairs in the No. 11 bus, I recognised her below the Canterbury-bell-shaped jacaranda blossoms, standing in the queue. Sardines always swim towards the sun, we are told; to catch them you must go to the east of them in the morning and to the west of them in the afternoon.

At the bottom of Jeppe Street a Bantu boy on a butcher's bike cycled alongside us. I looked down into a deep butcher's basket and a severed bullock's head, with goggling eyes and protruding tongue, glared up at me. Bristles stood up about the severe mouth, as if it had known the extremity of pain when being dispatched; the eyes were as though gouged out with a red-hot poker, and what a fury of resignation about the flayed mouth! A striking death's head.

Unsoberly attempting to alight, an old white ('European') man topples off the platform of an outward-bound No. 11 at the stop before Mount Willmar in Isipingo Street, and lies twitching and helpless on the flat of his back, staring up at the blossoms of the jacaranda tree, an assembly of bell-shaped blue flowers. Some of the passengers reach out as if to help him. Those who are alighting make as if to jump over him. He lies there, holding his heart, his chest heaving. He has hurt his head. 'Oh, oh. I have lived too long,' says the old drunk who lies on his back on the pavement, staring up at them. 'Let me die.' He blinks up at them. 'I am too old.'

'Oh no you're not,' says Coppera, extending a helping hand. Coppera's old man, Jonathan Carl Anders, is immensely old, as old as the hills, pale as parchment, deaf as a post; still putting in six and eight hours as a practising lawyer in King William's Town, still shouting out indiscretions, a man with a heart of gold.

The old man gives his name as Mr Allen, a habitué of Netherley House round the corner. He has alighted a stop too far. Seventy-six years old.

They take him there, Coppera and the kind helpful man from the No. 11 bus. The patio of Netherley House is some way back off the road and oldsters can be seen hobbling about in the gloom. Ferns droop from pots, a turkey-cock is scratching its wings on the cement floor.

'It's like looking into an aquarium,' Coppera says.

I too have my aquarium. Every morning of a working week

the sun rises again over the mine-dumps of Bez valley. Regular as clockwork or cockcrow I am already at my post by the window, shaving gear before me, the kettle on the boil, stark naked.

Greenish and brilliantly lit by the risen sun of the high Rand, she drifts into view at the second-floor window opposite across the darkly shadowed intervening ground. Sharply defined morning shadows lie in the gardens separating Mount Willmar from the block across the way.

Morning after morning the sun shines on a second-floor bedroom. Morning after morning a figure appears at the window to exercise in the nude after showering. Dark-haired and pale-skinned, she raises her arms to expose dark axillary hair. The husband, a shadowy figure appears occasionally in the background, standing and watching, dressed in pyjamas.

Irma La Douce is showing at the Brooke Theatre where we rehearsed and set up the show; *Wedding in Springtime* (Princess Margaret and her swain) at the Coliseum. *Killer Ape* showing at the Bio-Café in Rissik Street. The Black Sash ladies assemble outside the town hall.

But one grows weary of the long sameness of the days here; the only variety offered being the tropical storms that recur punctually at five every evening, refilling the swimming pools; but even of these one grows weary.

On endlessly dusty roads the quacks and commercial travellers with their sample cases go in large dusty limousines. Dr Rex Ferris is a specialist in *natuurgenesing*. Beware of:

Swak longe
Breuk
katar
Swak hart
Slegtesukalasie
Abgesakte maag
Stinkasem mangels
Hardlywigheid
Hare watuitval
Blindedermonsteking . . .

all bad things to be afflicted with, in Africa.

As might be expected in a continent so vast, so tightly held
by the rotten system with such extremes of want separating those
who have too much and those who have too little or nothing,
much credence is given to quackery and faith healing and spirit
mediums and the raising up of the dead.

The manufacturers of quack medicines do a roaring trade in
Sloan's Liniment, purity of blood being of prime concern in the
land of apartheid.

When a woman is doing her face in the mirror, she seems to
be narrowly watching herself. Certainly she is coolly observing,
seeing how the new effects work as they are applied, tweezers
to eyebrows, trimming hair, watching fascinated as the Fast
Little Number becomes metamorphosed into *une femme genete*
('troublesome'?), shedding the years.

Watching a woman making herself up in a mirror when she
thinks she is alone, constantly touching unattractive spots and
striking poses to catch herself off guard in the best light, catch
herself unawares, is fascinating. That's one thing; but what of a
woman who, aware of her attractiveness, walks naked about her
dressing room, unaware that she is being observed from across
the way, at the window darkened because the sun is behind it,
flooding into her wide window?

Naked she sits at the mirror, applying unguents where needed,
moisturising cream for body tone; rising and moving out she
begins to dress herself, wearing only a bra as she glides about
the room, soundlessly, light as gossamer.

Clear as an oxygenated well-lit aquarium tank in which swim
fish of all stripes, exotic ones as rare as orchids found high in
the Himalayas, the wide span of window showed the mysterious
depths of the room as a secret chamber, the innermost sanctum
of the pale nudist who moved about there in perfect sang-froid,
towelling her hair, the dark auxiliary parts showing. The naked
woman came and went, at her toilet, as though no one was
watching her; profoundly alone and silent and undisturbed, in
her own time. She passed by in her tank, her clear glass room,
come wet from the shower, undulantly ripe in her movements,

her style; as an exotic fish might swim to and fro in perfect isolation
and silence, neck throbbing, fanning the tail, causing the eyes to
bulge a little; until some stir (husband flushing toilet?) distracted
her and in a whirl of fins and bubbles (seemingly expanding, unless
this was an optical illusion caused by her quick change, or by a
displacement of the water, the uprushing bubbles disturbing the
former perfect composure of the scene set and fixed, the voyeur's
delight) she has suddenly gone. Only to reappear ten beats of the
heart later, come from another side of the tank, moving sedately
into sight again, still stark naked, the dark triangle flaunted: so the
naked brunette strolled to and fro in territory that seemed preciously
close and yet very far off, as though a breath would disturb the
clarity of the tank and frighten off the beautiful fish.

To say that this image (recurring five times a week just before
eight o'clock in the morning, the sun risen on the high Rand
regular as before, lighting up the room as if it were a stage set)
was profoundly disturbing would be putting it mildly; my eyes
were out on stalks. It was the most electrically jolting sexually
charged image I had seen (and watched more of) than any since
Hedy Kiesler took off all her clothes behind a bush somewhere
in Czechoslovakia and the watching camera got an eyeful of her
big bum as she waded into a mountain lake in Gustav Machaty's
disturbing old movie, *Extase*. It was before Hollywood changed
her name to Hedy Lamarr and made her a waxwork figure
of little interest to anybody, young or old. As the sexually
frustrated wife she had been rather chubby with puppy fat; the
coldly embracing water was a masculine embrace for her; it had
always been a feminine embrace for me. Seaweed and seawrack,
the briny tang of the foreshore, the withdrawn foreskin of the
swimmer entering the female sea, the taste and tang of sex.

Was she by any chance the siren Antoinette Botha, a great
attender of art galleries frequently photographed in the Johannesburg
Star? Could that have been the dark-haired one dressed in a smart
black outfit and sunglasses who stood alone on the quayside and
waved to someone (the lover) beside me on D Deck when we
were berthing at Cape Town, sailing from cold Amsterdam on *Die
Waterman* near Christmas some four years previously?

*   *   *

The train went by New Brighton on the Xwartkops river outside Port Elizabeth in the dusk of the evening, the lines and lines of mud hovels gave way to the arid land; an internment camp sprawled featureless in the evening dusk. Destitution is the irreducible minimum, below the breadline. From it nothing can be taken away, an African shanty town made up of line upon line of huts, as forlorn as Belsen or Auschwitz, baked dry by the cruel sun. Through hides and skins hung on poles, lean cattle wander about near open drains, with mangy curs and ghosts, presenting a most mournful aspect. Where the huts ended the barren land began again.

And in the twilight I watched naked children brown as monkeys stretch out monkey paws towards the lighted carriage windows that were gliding slowly by, the dining car festive with Christmas decorations. The kids reached out, chanting, 'Hippy, hippy, hippy!' Happy Christmas in South Africa, grim land of apartheid.

On 25 December 1956, I awoke on the upper berth to find that the long train had been standing motionless for hours out on the veldt. Warm air came through the carriage windows and all along the track the crickets were crackling like wildfire. Then the train began to move again with much banging and colliding of bumpers.

Onward from Hex River, Mossel Bay, Plettenberg Bay, to Port Elizabeth, East London, to the end of the line at King William's Town, Coppera's birthplace under the Amatole Mountains. King, arrived at in the gloaming with her aged parents waiting on the platform for the returning daughter and her newly acquired husband, was like a night scene from Zoltan Korda's *The Four Feathers*, the troops marching to a band, about to embark for the Sudan War. Had no one told them that the war ended years ago? South Africa, and perhaps the whole sleeping continent, was in a time warp. Africans with blankets draped about their shoulders moved about in a dream, stared with dull eyes at the white folks disembarking from the long train.

Death is a silent picture, a dream of the eye; only such vanishing shapes as the mirage throws. We had left Europe (where every grain of sand has passed through innumerable dead bodies killed in wars) four years before with affrighted Germans fleeing after the Hungarian uprising; we would be returning to Europe with affrighted Belgians fleeing the Belgian Congo. We sailed into Table Bay to the lilt of Cole Porter's 'Night and Day' played merrily over the tannoy, and the Rhodesian train-driver, a large beefy man, was still cracking his feeble jokes; and then I spotted the beauty on the quayside, coming closer and closer as the tugs moved in to push us against the quayside.

Was that Antoinette? Ask Achim. Were all the silent sirens we had ever lusted after, whether blonde or brunette, always the same, the one-and-only? The only one for me; but all reducible to a single form, provided she was my type (pretty ones working in flower shops in Durban, frisky *Fräuleins* up ladders in male haberdashery shops in Schwabing). My interest was merely the process of reducing a substance to another (simpler) form. The alchemist's quest and the lecher's keen interest were similar, both intent on turning base metal into gold.

In cookery you reduce by boiling off liquid, turning down the flame in order to intensify the flavour; in much the same way (to mangle the metaphor further) as the conquest or subjugation of a town or fortress is 'reduced', is conquered, so the dream girl is reduced to manageable proportions, becomes seduceable; 'Antoinette Botha', the lovely Afrikaner, waved to someone standing beside me. Naturally it wasn't me she waved to, it was the pretty brunette who had run trippingly in high heels across a Munich street between streams of traffic and threw me a look of unambiguous intent that reduced me to a jelly in the blink of an eyelash. One had to comply with the *visu*, the hot look that subjugates with the finality of a branding iron establishing ownership of a beast.

Apparently my type was the leggy brown-eyed sulky sort of girl who gets you into trouble; trouble before and even more behind.

25

The Sharpeville Massacre, 1960

21 March 1960. Anti-pass law demonstration in Vereeniging. The police, with Saracens in support, fired on and killed 56 African demonstrators, men and women, wounding 162.

24 March. Smell of sickness in the deserted Sundowner Bar. Later the regulars drift in. The subdued brandy drinker orders another Commando from Richard, as he has been doing for months, years, on end. Beginning to show in his face. Soon immersed in his *Rand Daily Mail*.

Of the 162 wounded, 38 are at Vereeniging Hospital and 148 at Baragwanath Hospital; over seventy per cent of the wounds were in the back and so terrible that it was thought dum-dum bullets were used by the police. These wounds were in fact caused by 'tumbling' bullets sprayed from Sten guns firing continuously, without pauses between bursts.

On one of the ominous days after Sharpeville, a time of dire portents when the long-threatened seemed about to come at last, a rumour was circulating to the effect that a mob of Africans was marching from the shanty towns on Johannesburg. The old woman, Anna, our washerwoman from Orlando, I knew was in the flat with Coppera. I decided not to phone, and went back to work.

Moran, who prided himself on his fair treatment of his own African servants, had an automatic pistol out on his desk and some rounds of ammunition. 'If I have to go,' he said, mock-histrionic, 'I'll take some of them with me.' 'Oh, Mr Mor-AN!' pleaded his secretary and scuttled from the office.

The rest of that peculiar day: the feeling that we were on the brink of civil war, that one might perhaps not live beyond tomorrow, that Coppera and Carl would die, lay on my heart like a hand of ice.

After work the city cleared fast, a rapid exodus to the suburbs, leaving the centre of the city deserted. African newspaper boys were flying through the streets on their bicycles and flinging down the late editions at the feet of the remaining white 'European' bus queues, with the swagger of insolent pages come from the enemy lines with bold ultimatums.

But the *Star* reported nothing of an undisciplined horde marching on Johannesburg, no picture of the bloodied head of the Princess de Lamballe stuck on the end of a pike. It reported only common everyday occurrences. The beautiful Miss Antoinette Botha was photographed at the pottery exhibition of Henk Jacobs and Harry Duys.

21 April. A month after Sharpeville, and the bloodstains are still on the road. I ask Lewis Nkose, 'What kind of man is this Colonel Pienaar?' 'Pienaar?' he says. 'He's a butcher. He's got the face of a butcher.'

Nkose speaks of the sweetish smell of blood after the shooting. He was there. The police chief was Colonel D.H. Pienaar.

The air is full of flying mine-dust. I have an inflamed throat and retire to bed before nine, feeling wretched. Mourning air of forgotten childhood mingled with premonitions of one's last end. Evening Benediction begins. Night falls, out of the craters rises the mist. Knowing nothing, believing nothing; live a little longer, if you can. I dream a disturbing dream.

I am flying in the Alps with six others. We are dressed as for skiing. Our arms extended, like gliders we fly about in the rarefied air, our shadows following us below on the virgin snow. High up in the Alps, I am drifting about. Someone calls 'Feel the snow! It's like fire.' I sail down and kick up some with my bare feet. Yes. Like fire. There is a high escarpment that no one can clear. I attempt it, but it is impossible, the face is too steep.

In the Alpine hut one of the party has cut himself by accident. There's not much blood, but nevertheless he says he must return to base. He leaves immediately. A pair of scissors lies on the table. I take them up and cut myself deeply on both wrists. Great clots of blood stain the walls and the snow near the door. I have severed an artery; the blood goes on pumping out. I am weakening; it is I who have done this, yet I seem to be standing outside myself. I watched 'myself' do it: 'him' I take for myself.

Coppera brings in John Wright to see the feverish invalid sitting up in bed reading Spengler's *Decline of the West*.

A Johannesburg *Star* photograph of the 'weapons' used by the African insurgents at Sharpeville. In 40–45 seconds of firing, so many killed, so many wounded, so much blood. A pile of knob-kerries, sticks, stones. Like what? Windfalls in a winter wood.

Nineteen fifty-nine was a dry summer in Jo'burg. Torrential rains came with the autumn and every day the pictures slid a little more off-kilter on the walls, following another fall-in down in the mines. The greatest fall-in occurred in January 1960, the year of Sharpeville, when 435 African miners were buried alive at Coalbrook Mine with six European supervisors or gangers; none was ever recovered.

On 3 March 1960 I was thirty-three years old and beginning to think of myself as a writer, for Calder and Grove Press had contracted to bring out the first stories, *Felo De Se*. In sixteen recently made independent African territories eighty-five million new black citizens had also begun to think differently about themselves.

As and from tomorrow the British flag will be run down and the new flag of the free Republic run up in its stead. The national anthem becomes *Die Stem*. 'Out of the blue sky' sings the massed choir of black and white, or brown and scorched pink.

Seated on a dentist's chair on the sixteenth floor of an office building in the centre of Johannesburg, I command a fine view of flat rooftops and washing blowing on lines, a flagpole with the

Union Jack flying in the breeze that has been blowing since the siege of Mafeking (the tattered original flag is preserved in a glass case in the town hall where we performed with the puppets), and on a distant mine-dump away towards Benoni a white scarf of dust is blowing off the rim.

The telephone rings. Dentist Gavronski's former wife, Nadine Gordimer, is on the line and wishes to know the meaning of 'being on the threshold of pain'. Dentist Gavronski tells her all he knows about the threshold of pain. The air of Johannesburg is a wonderful refining air blowing out of the bluest of pale blue skies; such a pity the system is rotten to the core. The system stinks; and it's not a country one could live in, much less bring up a child in. We toy with the idea of living in the Seychelles, a windy French possession away from the beaten track; or St Helena, a thousand miles into the North Atlantic. An islander whose grandfather sold macaroni to Napoleon, then serving time in Longwood House, advises us against it. We decide to return to Dublin.

26

The Lazy Azores, 1960

21 July 1960. Last day in Johannesburg. Main railway terminal. Train for Blaney and East London. We sail from there on the 28th. I read of ten Africans killed and four injured, three seriously, in a faction fight between Mbonos and Ngulubenis at Maritzburg.

The taciturn soldier in my carriage has little to say; the train passes by Kliptown, Midway, Lenz, the locations out of Johannesburg. A week's holiday in King William's Town lies ahead. Coppera had left ahead three weeks before to show our child to her parents.

Kidd's Beach, Eastern Cape. We rent a house near the beach. The breathing of the cattle at night. Generally deserted beaches. The coloured youths dancing like dervishes naked on the dunes; their swaying stallions' erections. Two African girls coming in their city finery. They all go swimming together. Scrummages in the surf. Their whinnying cries.

The lagoon. Deep coughing of the baboons among the laurels. Days alone there. The dog swimming in the estuary early in the morning. The Bantu girls coming with their fancy-men. Putty-coloured skin of the Cape Malays, with deformed features, like lepers. In the evening we buy brandy, for fifteen shillings a bottle.

Coppera's dream: 'It's a big hotel next to the railway lines. My mother and I have a big room on the second floor. I'm trying to pack but she keeps on emptying the suitcase. She is distracted with worry and moves fretfully from room to room spreading the clothes about.

'On our side of the building and directly in front of the hotel four oil tanks stand, delicate quadrupeds with their four big balls on the top standing about a hundred feet off the ground.

'There's a revolution in the city. The first oil tank is set on fire above our heads. It explodes in flames. There is a great hullabaloo in the hotel, with guests screaming out of windows and running through the rooms. I run to my mother, but she is so petulant she doesn't care. I look everywhere for the suitcase. She's hidden it. I ask her where it is. She says she doesn't know. I hear people running past the hotel and shouts outside. Then I find the suitcase. I begin to pack in a hurry. My mother keeps taking the clothes out and petulantly throwing them on the bed.

'The second oil tank is now on fire. I hear the roaring of the flames and black particles of steel and ash are falling past the windows. Try as I can, the suitcase always remains empty. Outside, we see the flames going straight up. There is a man down there. I knew he was there. I shout to a friend to go and help him. There are two of them after him and I can see him clearly lying on his stomach under the third oil tank, which he is about to set on fire.

'As he reaches up, he is shot from behind through the back of the head. Dying, he goes on making the futile gesture of pulling a lever, but it's someone else who moves his hand.'

28 July 1960, East London docks. The *Warwick Castle* berthed. After an easy Customs check we go to a small cabin, uncomfortably so with a collapsible cot installed. Telegrams from Johannesburg are on the bunk. We will be cooped up here for the next eighteen days, with decaying fruit and damp ammonia-smelling diapers. Sailing via St Helena and Ascension Island to Tilbury, England.

Port Elizabeth. A liner, pearly-grey hull, entering a harbour early in the morning. A seaweed-covered breakwater, a sludge of fog, a liner sounding its horn, and in the dampness on the mole fifty Muslims in red fezzes standing waiting, like diver-birds grouped on a rock. Suddenly handkerchiefs appear in their hands and flutter above their heads. The silence and vastness of the liner making its way slowly into the harbour. Its tiers of deserted decks; chill of the hour, just before daybreak.

Cape Town. The Muslims in full regalia posing patiently for amateur photographers on D Deck in a thin drizzle of rain. The ship's bossy nurse orders them about. They are Cape Coloureds, returning to Cape Town after a nine-month trip to Mecca.

Low cloud over the city, Table Mountain invisible; smoke rising from the business quarter, joined up to low-hanging discoloured clouds – like a city after a bombardment. The persistent thin rain. Two tugs pulling the *Warwick Castle* off its berth. The harbour turns round. The tugs cast off. Music over the ship's loudspeakers; the wake stretches out behind. Now we leave this continent; now the ship sails. Feeling of elation.

A day out and the Cape rollers begin. Vomit on the companionway mats, the dining room half empty, the Belgian Congolese children running wild, yelling: '*Malade! Malade!*'

Two days out and already bored with shipboard life. St Helena in the morning. I wrote to Mr Solomon (or Solomons) there.

St Helena. Volcanic cliffs, then the valley, and Jamestown, with boats coming out. We are to stay here until evening. I see a high waterfall, white water spilling over the rim of rock, and more boats putting out from the island. Festive appearance. The islanders come on board to sell trinkets. I talk to one of the young men. He herds sheep; he brought some from the back of the island at five this morning. His singsong voice. Biblical scene.

The young men are leaving the island, he tells me, to work on the American air base on Ascension. They made an airstrip along the ridge of a volcanic mountain. They can double their wages there, working in radio. The jute factories pay little. Those who stay are attempting to start a trade union movement – the first in the island's history. They load jute into the hold. It has a bad smell. Some of the older islanders are going into domestic service in Scotland. A butler and housekeeper. He is small, scorched black by the sun, his English difficult to follow. He sounds Welsh. Did Welsh missionaries come here?

I go ashore with another passenger – a white-haired, stout,

elderly Chinaman, polite and formal. Mr Johns is courteous, neatly dressed in a blue suit with a white shirt and dark tie, a raincoat over one arm, a rolled umbrella in his hand (tell me, what Chinaman would ever go out without a rolled umbrella?). He carries an expensive attaché case – as an emblem of caste? We introduce ourselves. He tells me that he was born here on St Helena but left it as a young man to seek his fortune in the USA. He worked for fifty years as a traveller in the bible trade, married an American lady from Boston, Mass. and is now retired. He is through with the bible business. He had hoped to spend his last years on the island, but his wife does not care for it – not enough social contact, too many white ants, insufficient refrigeration. They had originally planned to live on the island for three years, in a sort of trial retirement. But his wife couldn't stand it; they are leaving again in the spring. He himself would have preferred to stay, but he will do whatever his wife wants; never would she be happy there. They plan to return to Boston.

I make an arrangement to meet Mr Johns later with Coppera (who has stayed on board with Carl); we are to take a taxi and visit Longwood House. I take leave of him on a small humpback Chinese bridge, surrounded by white blossoms, with the sound of water trickling in the irrigation streams. No sound of human voices in this quiet backward island retreat a thousand miles from anywhere. I take a walk up the valley. The relief of being off the ship, away from the passengers.

The *Warwick Castle*, much diminished, lying offshore about three-quarters of a mile out, seen between two converging cliffs. Terraces sown with peas and beans, warm dry air, hot sunshine, peace. An outdated greeting to Princess Elizabeth and Prince Philip painted on a hillside. A rustic England of the early nineteenth century is perpetuated here with an annual rainfall of 36 inches, a very temperate climate; 1,700 feet above sea level in a temperature of 70 degrees all the year round.

Longwood House in the afternoon. Napoleon's last resting place, a long way from the frozen rivers and corpse-strewn plains of the lost Russian campaign. The cold names of the rivers that flow into the Baltic, Vistula, Niemen. Niemen-on-the-Ice.

Bonaparte getting into a closed carriage with his mameluke at Smorgony, defeated and on his way back to Paris. 'Halted at Jaffa at the western entrance to Asia, and halted at Moscow at the northern gateway to the same continent, he was to go and die among the seas bordering that part of the world where mankind and the sun were born' (Chateaubriand).

In the billiard room, the pockets are rotting from the table, the green baize turning white with age; the billiard balls in their wooden frames rest behind glass in the hall. Chipped antique objects – the Emperor's cannons. I take one in my hand. Napolean used to throw them around; his small hand once touched it. Touching it now, I touch lost history.

The smallness of his bed; its green canopy – a child's bed. His death mask, cast in bronze, stands on a pedestal. Effigies of him in every room and in the hall. Vain as Voltaire.

St Helena lies between the two poles. 'At the extremity of our hemisphere,' says Tacitus, 'one can hear the sound made by the sun sinking in the sea: *sonum insuper immergentis audiri.*' When Napoleon went out, his spirits low, he passed along stony paths lined with aloes and scented broom.

In the narrow valley, known then as Slane or Geranium Valley, and now as Tomb Valley, there is a spring at which Napoleon's Chinese servants, as faithful as Camoens's Javanese, used to fill their pitchers; weeping willows hang over their spring; green grass, studded with champacs, grows all around. ('The champac,' say the Sanskrit poems, 'for all its colour and perfume, is not a sought after flower, because it grows on graves.')

Napoleon liked the willows by the spring, but everything saddened him under a sky beneath which life seemed shorter, the sun remaining three days less in that hemisphere than in ours. Towards the end of February 1821, in his sixth year of exile on the rock, he was obliged to take to his bed ('How low have I fallen! . . . I who have stirred up the whole world, and I cannot lift my eyelids!'), and he did not get up again. He was being systematically poisoned by his English captors and part of the Royal Navy swung off the island, watching and waiting. His end came soon. He died in Longwood on 5 May 1821. 'He sleeps like a hermit or a pariah in a valley, at the end of a deserted pathway,' wrote Chateaubriand.

In 1840 the remains were brought home to France – he had come home to be buried in the grime of Paris. Bonaparte passed through the tomb, as he passed through everything else, without stopping.

Vague feeling that he did live there once; pined away and died there; written of by de Segur, Chateaubriand, latterly Kafka, fascinated by the horrors of the Russian campaign. Suffered from migraine, dysuria (retention of the urine).

Murat, Ney; carnage at Borodino, blood-soaked fields. He had drilled peepholes in the window shutters to spy on the English soldiers going on and off duty. At daybreak here, forgotten. Never forgotten.

The lazy Azores; three miles of sea below us. The English clergyman's anaemic full-grown son in the dining room. 'Oh of course they're not trustworthy as pets.' Finicky English voice – that strange, slight talk which governed the British Empire. 'I never take liberties with an Alsatian.' The English ladies opposite us; their movements, talk, complacency – their security. Lily Briscoe. Walking on the upper deck. Beginning of an overcast day. The jet fighter out from Ascension, island of ashes, a pinpoint, then directly over the mast, then four miles out to sea.

The Canary Islands; Las Palmas. One can smell it approaching: the stench of colonial Spain.

Generalissimo Franco causeway. The taxi ride. In the cathedral the old waxen-faced priest high up in an alcove reading his office – an image from Goya. The confessional stained black about the grille; sins (bad breath?) of generations of humble penitents. An island of bad teeth and halitosis. Smells of cheap Cognac and wine gone sour in the bars. A vegetable market, white colonnades and green trellis, all the charm of Spain.

Fish-tinning factories; the Coca-Cola factory under construction on the hill. An island inundated with Japanese-made merchandise with falsified US trade marks. Populated caves in the dirty hills above the town. The well-dressed tout offering us a

Parker pen made in Osaka; another in the cathedral shows us the manuscript Vulgate of 1614.

Hot idle days. The tourist-class swimming pool with two feet of water, Belgian Congolese children splashing in it, screaming snipe. Shrouded cars on the foredeck with Belgian Congo registration plates. Exodus from the troubled Congo.

Circular intimations of calamity: 'The contemporary of Napoleon conceived his completion of European philosophy as the fulfilment of a primary undeveloped origin: whereas the contemporary of Adolf Hitler conceived the identical history of the European spirit as the gradual epiphany of Nihilism' (Hans Magnus Enzensberger). So what of Father Adam and his teeming billions of posterity? Do not come down the ladder, dreamers, for I have taken it away.

The weather turns foul: heavy seas, troughs of grey waves. A porthole, a stretch of harbour, docks of Las Palmas, a boat loading up alongside the *Warwick Castle*, a view of burnt hills, already only a memory.

Two portholes; slothful slop and wallow of the waves striking the side of the ship; grey-green sea choppy all the way to the horizon. Staring before her with empty eyes. Baby Carl crawls in the playpen, we crowd into our small cabin. Soon it will be over.

The tarpaulin-shrouded cars on deck. Hardly any place to exercise now.

The English Channel.

We reach the mouth of the Thames in the late afternoon, but cannot get into Tilbury. There is a dock strike on (also a printing strike). England is on strike; nothing has changed there.

When we wake up next morning, we're in. Through the portholes we see English bobbies standing about with their hands behind their backs on the wet dockside. It's raining in grey Tilbury. Naturally it is. Naturally so.

PART III:

Nerja in the 1960s

27

Ominous Auguries

A freshening offshore breeze made a kind of inditing on the surface of the water, innumerable diamond-shaped points of light glittered over a wide area, leaving the rest serene. The Mediterranean and its little mirrors, the dance of the little mirrors of the Mediterranean, with everything trembling, constant little tremblings, junctions, disjunctions, nothing still, no, never for a moment still. A calm day out at sea.

Two boats were fishing far out, working well apart, half lost in the haze. On the horizon three or four bigger vessels were hull-down into the glare. I watched the archway – more than my eyes watched it – but there was no sign of her. Instead of Harriet came now a rumble like thunder, but unmistakably not thunder, a long shudder from over the water I felt now under my feet, hard as iron. It passed through the palms, the plaza and on through the village, a pulse, a gust blown in from the sea. Among the wisps of cloud over the ships a puffball of flak appeared, lead-coloured in the centre, turning septic yellow, spreading out innocently enough, as a small white cloud.

I looked up, listening for the sound of aircraft, but none were flying over the area. Nothing in sight at all events, nothing had banged through the sound barrier. Were the ships shelling the clouds to try to disperse them? Was it firing practice? Or had war started? I listened, with more than my ears. Nothing.

Nothing. Only a stirring in the palms, a faint breeze on my face, a voice murmuring *You are done for*, and a few small dun-coloured birds flew away.

Then a second flak ball joined the first at precisely the same altitude. The reverberation rolled in thick and dull, and from over the horizon – a chain reaction – came the spreading rumble of answering fire. Heavy-calibre naval guns were letting go their salvos down near Gibraltar. Baron Gerhar's grim prediction came to mind; the mad Finn thought World War Three was imminent – the final war. Had it started? The last. How could we get back to Ireland, or back to Aran, and would we be safe there? Or, if it came to that, could I give Coppera a 'massive overdose' of sleeping pills? Or would Harriet come to me and say, 'If I have only one more day, one more hour to live, I want to spend it with you.' As I knew I wanted to die embracing her.

My old *amigo*, Harry Calnek was hurrying from the Marisal. The hunched-up figure rapidly crossed the plaza. Hands deep in pockets, caught up in the ardour of narrative construction, Calnek was returning to his trusty typewriter.

No sooner had he left the plaza than a third flak ball appeared alongside the other two. White at first, then turning yellow – and the third ponderous detonation followed; the stiff palm fronds above my head shivered and the last of the dun-coloured birds flew away.

A triple blast of destruction had blown in from the sea. Above me among the palm fronds outstretched like arms, skeleton features grimaced, announcing the opening movements of another war. World War Three had started on the site of the old Peninsular War.

The bell of San Salvador at this precise moment sounded the half-hour: 10.30. a.m. I had not heard the hour strike. The single stroke hung in the hot and luminous air. *You go*, the bell told me sweetly; *I stay*. Half past the hour. A slick of heat on my back. Nothing stirred. A lick of heat, a tongue of flame.

The white puffball with its sickly centre, human pus on cotton wool, hung like a sign in the sky over the motionless ships. I waited for the final blast to blow me off the plaza, off the face of the earth.

The informer was going back into his kiosk, shaking the last drips from the neck of his watering can. Then, always taking me by surprise, the second stroke, like an overtone, sounded calmly from the church. Or from another belfry? But there was only one belfry, one church, one God, one true religion, one winter cinema (but two summer ones to make up a trinity), and fifty tavernas for a population of ten thousand souls, the population of Guernica before the bombing. Iron on iron, hammer on anvil, one questioned, the other replied, and real life was over.

She broke away from our long embrace as if caught up by the wind, with a light step ran quickly down, hearing someone approaching, or so she imagined, someone quickly entering from the street by the open doorway below; perhaps it was her husband or Coppera keeping tabs?

But no one came up. She smiled at me from below. I went down then to embrace her again. A sort of fluid glow emanated from her skin. Everything about her disturbed me, inside and outside, her mouth and unfathomable Nile-blue eyes, the Jewish weight of her sorrowful heavy eyelids, her quickened respiration – I had put my hands over her breasts that rose and subsided with her rapid breathing – the scent of her Sabine-rape blonde hair the colour of wheat.

I was holding another woman in my arms and allowed to intimately touch this forbidden body, hearing voices through the door but unable to make out the words. Calnek and his Canadian girl Sharon Marcus were on the roof above, clinging vine, mimosa spray. We went down and out into the shattering sunshine of no thought, Harriet to their apartment on Calle Generalisimo Franco to 'fix' their lunch, Rory proceeding the other way, towards the bridge. She was to meet me there in an hour's time, to pledge our troth in a cane plantation as the tick-ridden burros hee-hawed, flicking their stumpy tails, tormented by the flies that would eat them. Faith, unfaithful wife kept him falsely true.

John Deck sat on a cane chair on the mezzanine of No. 12 smoking a black cigar. His shirt was open to the navel and he was unshaven; his bare shins showed between rumpled canvas pants and worn canvas sneakers. The cotton pants were tight about the crotch and he seemed all ponderous head, Negroid upper lip and lobeless ears. I sat on the red divan and Harriet stood facing us. She had raised her skirt to expose a discoloured bruise the size of a 50-peseta coin high up on her brown thigh where the panties gripped. Since she sunbathed for two hours every morning in the nude behind screens in their patio, she glowed with health and well-being, a ripe-thighed temple-dancer. She shimmied her hips and looked brazenly at us.

'See here, messmates.'

I looked at my darling's wounded flank but prudently made no comment. Drawing deeply on his cigar John stared at the guilty-looking bruise and then at her face. Was she exposing one of his own love-bites or what?

Who had done this thing to her? What apelike paw had marked her so? Her pose had been a cajoling one, part of a tango that required snapping castanets. One of her most endearing and characteristic movements began as a shudder in those ardently engulfing hips; a beautiful gentleness glowed from her skin. Now, watching her husband, she dropped her skirt.

'What do you make of that?' she challenged him. 'If anything.'

Deck tilted back his chair until it stood on two legs, and allowed cigar smoke to issue from great flanged niggery nostrils.

'Are not health and corruption said to be incompatible? So thought the ancient rhetoricians, and they knew their stuff.'

We had nothing to add to that.

'On a streetcar in Hode, Arkansas,' Deck pontificated in a Negro preacher's almighty drone, 'I glimpsed the exhausted. But, sure, anything's permissible and possible in a world in which no one any longer believes in anything. But don't despair. Study groups among the Pennsylvanian Elks, after extensive Bible poring, revealed that in fact the Second Coming had already occurred, unnoticed by anybody. In 1837, to be exact, with the Kingdom of God established "invisibly" a few years later – let's say about the time that flatulent old bitch Queen Victoria planted her mighty arse on the throne and made herself Empress of all India.'

Harriet laughed a provocative laugh and sailed across the room, very well 'gathered up' as the Spaniards say of horses cantering, *muy recogida*, when tearing along at full speed. Going downstairs now with only the upper part of her body showing with much brown bare back, she called back tauntingly, 'OK, I'll let both you guys do it into my behind!'

Rare, rare, her pierced beauty. The heavy musk of falling hair. In a field of force, the uncoiling honeycomb of forms, the golden wheel of love.

Some nights later I was drinking beer with Calnek in a small bar in Calle Cristo. It was Good Friday and we found ourselves in the middle of a power cut, plunged into darkness, a regular occurrence in those days. Candles were then lit along the bar counter and looked very pretty. The bar was empty but for us.

We heard a scratching sound outside and a whispering in conspiratorial tones and the slap of espadrilles and stood in the open doorway to watch a silent company file past, bearing the semi-naked Saviour covered in veils that rose in a night breeze to expose the braced white chest, the terrible wound in the side caked with dried blood.

The mourners filed silently by, softly as ghosts, hurrying Him off somewhere as if ashamed. We went back soberly to our drinks.

'What do you make of that?' I said.

Calnek looked owlishly at me through his heavy bifocals with his afflicted Jewish eyes.

'That guy wasn't carrying no Cross. He was trying to hold it down.'

Christ's five bleeding wounds (*cinco llagas*) are perpetuated all over Spain, sculpted over church porches like bunches of grapes. St Paul writes somewhere in his Epistles of Jesus as the image of the invisible God, and Alfred Jarry wrote somewhere that God is infinitely small.

> *The world of the Jew*
> *Is the world of the Jew*
> *And yet*
> *And yet . . .*

Colourful expressions of Harry Calnek: 'Old Sharon would talk the scrotum off the statue of David.' And: 'Cold as a gravedigger's arse.'

28

Mrs Harriet Deck

S ome mornings when she came down on to the *paseo* she wore her morning face, having come straight from bed to me. Or, having overslept the hour that we had agreed to meet, had come straight out, her face still marred by sleep, by the sheet, by strands of hair. She brought, as a gift, the face her husband saw every morning when he opened his eyes and she opened her legs for him again. Ah, how sad is the sound of the horn winding in the depths of the wood!

She had come straight to me in this manner: her direct way, from the most distant county there is; brought her brightness unimpaired, even if her voice was slurred, she brought some of her sleep with her, offered something of her secret (wifely) self to Rory of the Hills.

When the brown hand with the symbolic ring of gold made an intensely private gesture, my heart missed a beat and turned over with the movement, as if we were locked together in a kiss and the sheet had fallen off and we were naked, clinging together, hearts beating in unison.

She touched her hair and pouted out her dry lips.

'I must look awful.'

She perched herself on the high bar stool and asked Miguel Rojas for coffee, crossing one leg over the other. I saw the inside of her thigh, that intimate region of give and take, hide and seek, as she spoke of her past, that sure sign of trust, of love, to offer to the new one (Rory) the old one's (Deck's) perquisites. She was travelling towards me now, her hair streaming in the wind. (Deck, who took his conjugal duties seriously, had threatened a Mexican groom who had ridden off with Harriet, coming home an hour too late with buttons undone, covered in dust and sweat. 'I shudda horse-whipped the little Mexican fucker'.)

They had come east on Route 66, from the bottom of California, the legendary coast. At night, tired of the road that never ended, they came to a township in the back of beyond, some Red Indian reservation hardly marked on the map, maybe Winslow in Arizona.

She said she wanted to spend the night there; but her cautious young husband was having none of *that*. 'Those are mean bastards, Dilly. You don't fuck around with Indians. We gotta push on.'

So they pushed on, she staring with a vacuous glare through the windscreen all smeared with the guts of squashed bugs. They sailed out of New York harbour on the SS *Klek*, a Yugoslav freighter bound for Tangier, saw the incoming and outgoing flights circling over Idlewild and landing every three minutes. It made them feel good to be Americans, flying the flag and proud of it.

The ship's doctor was as handsome as they come, dressed in white duck, face the colour of teak. He spoke of Ljubljana in Slovenia where he came from. He was homesick and fancied Mrs Deck something awful.

They walked the decks together at night. John was a poor sailor and spent most of the voyage below, puking his way across the Atlantic.

Dr Vuc Eisen was certainly handsome.

'I guess he fancied me.'

This carefully imparted aside was accompanied by a dip of her knee so that more brown thigh was exposed, tender flesh, as she sipped coffee in a prim ladylike way.

'Did he try anything on, this fresh fucker Eisen?'

'Oh sure' (this was Harriet the Hardboiled City Girl). 'We were after all on the high seas. Every licence allowed.'

I ground my teeth. Miguel busily occupied himself wiping the steaming coffee machine, understanding nothing of what was being said or implied, observing us covertly, for were we not meeting there three or four mornings a week before anyone was about and the *paseo* was deserted. With long travel, smart city girls suffer changes of heart; isn't that true, most times?

'The great romances in life and in literature imitating life, as it's apt to do, have never been between husbands and wives but between husbands and *other* people's wives,' Deck pontificated, at his most mocking and mock-oratorical, 'as I need hardly tell you. Look at Irish and English history from the time of let us say the Norman invasion up to Edward VIII and that American wife so erring in her ways, Mrs Simpson. Consider the known high content of adultery in world literature. Look at Emma Bovary. Where would we be without adultery, I ask you. We'd be where Jacko put his nuts: in somebody else's bed. Think of that gamekeeper, whatshisname buggering Lady Chatterley in the bushes.'

They were awaiting the arrival of Dr Jorge del Bosque who was giving them Spanish lessons. What the suspicious husband meant to convey to erring Rory, who was certainly sending signs to Deck's young wife, was: now I know what you're up to, Mick. And I'll go along with it for form's sake. I'll tolerate it, up to a point. You are, after all, old enough to be her father. I know that Ilium had to burn, as well as Helen, in order to create the *Iliad*, but . . . But. *Don't touch her, she's mine!*

I lifted the knocker and let it fall.

The sudden sound reverberated through the house. It appeared to be empty, with that curious airy emptiness peculiar to Andalucían houses (a window or door was open upstairs), with their bare floors.

I waited for some response, lifted the knocker again, let it fall. The heavy lumpish sound reverberated through the house once more.

I waited, lifted the knocker again, let it fall. Then I pushed the door. It gave inward; I entered. Ferns hung from wire baskets supported by chains under a nondescript chandelier sprouting light bulbs like branched fruit, bunches of grapes. A heavy maroon felt cloth covered the table and in the centre of this lay an air-letter with the chevrons of Old Glory addressed in a swinging female calligraphy to:

> Mr and Mrs John and Harriet Deck
> 12 Calle Pintada
> Nerja
> España

conveyed to Numero 26 Calle de la Cruz by the obliging Correos, no doubt interested in the unfamiliar stamps. I turned it over on its back and learnt that the sender was a certain

> Miss Mimi Fagg
> The Museum
> Nigeria

Well I never. An empty hallway led to the empty stairs of their empty flat. I knocked on their door, knowing there was no one there. No one answered; they were out, perhaps on the beach, or taking a drink on the *paseo* and talking to Miguel in demotic Spanish, swiftly picked up from the ever obliging Dr Jorge del Bosque, who himself (let it be whispered) rather fancied the charming Mrs Harriet Deck. And who did not?

I was alone. Solitude – one knows instinctively that it has benefits which must be more deeply satisfying than other conditions, states of elation aside. I let the knocker fall again, in case the old woman was there. *¡Oyenos!* Quite empty. I walked towards the *paseo*, bore that empty feeling away with me. *¡Oyenos!*

'I'm not gonna help you no more,' John Deck said, avoiding my eye. 'No more pimping.'

He was half turned away from me, leaning on the bar counter, looking sourly into his glass of lukewarm Victoria beer, his shoulders hunched up. His cheeks bulged out like lugs, swelling as though he was suffering from *dolor de muellas*; his lobeless ears gave him a Germanic degenerate look – Himmler's ears.

I swallowed some beer and stared out the door, where the warm wind was blowing the dust along.

'You were helping me. This is news indeed.'

'Sure I was. I was pimping for you. But not any more, buddy. Anyhow, you wouldn't have gotten very far with her unless she'd strewn a few roses in your path.'

The half-demented one went by on his ruined feet, bound for the bar down the Calle; he could imitate the bawling of a burro to the life.

'And Callus?' I said, producing the name as stealthily as if I was soundlessly withdrawing a sword from its scabbard.

'Callus! what the fuck has he got to do with it? You must be mad. Callus means nothing to her. I know her well enough to say that. You need fear nothing from that quarter.'

I said nothing to that (was he pimping for me again?), ordered another beer for him, stealthily.

We were in the Calle de la Cruz in one of the old bars that served lukewarm Victoria beer in bottles and low-grade wine, rough Cognac and anis, *seco* and *dulce*, as favoured by the fishermen.

And who was this Callus, the Troublemaker, not to be confused with Palos, the one who bedded his own mother and invented the saw? Not Philoctetes either; was Callus (born in Malta of a sergeant major in the British Army) related to Talus, who was one of those impetuous and liverish Mediterranean divinities like the freak fire-giant created by Hephaeotus in the story of the Argonauts? Was it he? Maybe it was.

He had a mountain forge at Etna beneath the earth and Minos as guardian and protector of his patch, the Cretan coast. Thrice a day he strode around the island and never stopped for a siesta. If strangers landed, he ran up the hill and jumped into the furnace. Steaming and red-hot, he rushed down upon them, beshitting themselves in their haste to get back into the boats.

None but Medea dared to confront him, one vein filled with liquid fire. That was Callus. Mad as a brush.

The wild man of Borneo was for climbing staircases in Montreal, shinning up the side of a house in Calle Nueva by the wrought-iron window guard, his head appearing at balcony

level to a shrill scream from Sonya Hool, Callus climbing over
the balcony rail and bursting into the room, putting the wind up
the Hools, chatting to an American friend peaceably within.

'*Surprisingly* hairy,' Harriet said.

29

A Child's Funeral

Entre las flores y la nieve ocultarón el Cristo.

A funeral was passing along Calle Pintada (Calle General-issimo Franco), the coffin lid not in place: a little corpse was being carried away in flowers by young boys. I stood on the balcony of No. 12 with Harriet and looked down into the open coffin, and there in the midst of the flowers was the infant's peaceful face upturned to us, a little girl being carried past the wrought-iron dog-heads spewing rainwater, hardly ushered into life before being carted out of it again.

The colour of the dead face was the colour of my dead mother's face on the third day of her dying: off-white clay gone grey putty colour, rock returned with thanks to the hands of her Maker.

The small white coffin was bedecked with flowers, exposing only a section of the *caja-fuerte*; with the lid off to the dead eyes open in the waxen face and that slightly asymmetrical stare peculiar to the very young, an unfocused look directed past us and the dog-heads at a remote Heaven above the clouds.

The boys bore her along at a brisk pace, as if anxious to reach the *cementerio*, followed by a smaller object that was also covered in flowers, a babe perhaps, carried by two other boys. But no. The coffin-lid!

In amongst the flowers a small chromium-plated Christ lay with chest braced against the hard death on the Cross that awaited. Between the snow (winter) and the flowers (spring) they buried Him, hid Him away in the tomb.

Behind this sad entourage walked the stricken father with eyes lowered, hands clasped behind his back, wrapped in sad thought. He was followed by a cortège of little girls dressed in their Sunday finery; and behind them paced the young priest reading from his breviary.

From her deepened breathing, I knew that Harriet, who had a daughter, had been affected; it had affected me, who had no daughter but had three bouncing sons. Suffer us and our offspring not to perish, oh Lord! The grieving padre would return the crucifix to the bereaved *madre* who had mourned at home, as was the custom; no weeping women were allowed at the cemetery. The young hurrying coffin-bearers held the *caja-fuerte* low, like a battering-ram, and all along the way to the *cementerio* women stood in the doorways with folded arms and said *¡Qué guapa!* which was manifestly true: the dead child was beautiful, or death had beautified the clay. The cemetery was outside the town, near the brickworks and the football field on the Maro road.

It was an odd place of some distinction, this home for the dead. 'Deadsville', Trevor Callus named it, quick to invert brand-names and plugs from his years in advertising. 'Endsville'. He liked to stroll about there near the grassless soccer field, hands clasped behind his back, smoking a cheroot to the sound of cheering, the sight of a black and white object being the ball rising above the dead wall and falling back into the field of play.

A narrow short avenue of cypress trees gives on to a high whitewashed wall into which is set a heavy black wrought-iron gate. In the first part of the cemetery lie the well-to-do defunct in ostentatious family vaults, with weighty embossed iron double-doors sunk into a cement bed and held secure against tempests.

This leads into a larger enclosed area beyond the mortuary chapel where banks of coffins rest in the columbarium proper. There are no cypress trees here. The effect is not sombre, however, but functional, along the lines of bakery furnaces. The inscriptions for the rich dead are suitably engraved in marble or stone by Carlos Clu and Co. of Málaga; while the common dead have their names and dates, when born and when expired, cut by inexpert hands on cheaper material like slate. But whether rich or poor, all are dead and can no longer put on airs, and the pleas addressed formally to their Maker are modest and restrained.

The best flowers of the year bloom through October and November as though mindful of the dead ones, and during these two months of the year the cemetery is full of flowers and presents a festive appearance, with chrysanthemums set in the little arched niches. Above the walls the sierras rise, white with snow, in the distance over the river, making a pretty picture. The sierras are the washed-out blue of distemper, a whey-blue haze, Mary's colour.

Children are buried in the centre plot, without headstones. There are no gravediggers as such; the caretaker digs the children's graves, breaks open the white ossuaries with a pickaxe to admit another young cadaver and generally spruce up the place.

At an Andalucian internment there is always the merry sound of hammering and the breaking down of walls for a last look at the petrified face behind a porthole of glass, then more hammering and possibly a burst of song as the coffin lid is nailed down. I liked to walk about there unmolested and address silent prayers to my dear departed mother. Here in a few years' time came the skinny remains of Miguel Lopez Rojas, the tireless *camarero* who worked in the Bar Alhambra from nine in the morning until two and three o'clock the following morning and never had any free time to call his own; he died on 3 December 1964, worn out.

Is it on the night of the *Festival de Todos los Santos* or the *Commemoración de los Fieles Difuntos* that candles of remembrance burn all night in the *cementerio* and visitors behave informally, as if visiting friends, the men smoking and strolling about at their ease, hands in pockets, and the women (never short of something to say) calling out to each other, happy to be there, with all the candles sailing in pans of water and burning down and going out? No kneeling in ostentatious prayer with the lips moving (a most disgusting sight, like lips moving when the finger moves under a line of print) or telling beads; none of that damp Irish mourning, but loud jolly gossiping and the emptying out of dead flowers. Never the deep unfestive gloom of damp cypress ride and Celtic cross awry and mossy ways bemired, matching the hushed and reverential tones deemed suitable by my fellow countrymen on these occasions, which brings the morbidity of their natures to the surface; the women adopting the soothing and mollifying cadences of priests and nuns, those professionals at funeral practices, going about the execution of their sad duties.

The Nerja *cementerio* down its short avenue of evergreens was as unlike Deans Grange as day is to night; of Prospect I cannot speak, where the Protestants were buried near the Botanic Gardens at Glasnevin, where I liked to walk in the curvilinear glasshouses in the subtropical heat. Outside the walls on the riverside there was a dump intended for the bones of those whose term of occupancy had terminated, to be chucked out as *rejecta membra*. It was all done on a very decent human scale.

I stood with Mrs Deck on the little wrought-iron balcony of No. 12 and watched the cortège go on up the hill. A stout woman standing in the doorway opposite stared after the priest. Presently rain began to fall. Mr Deck was out in his espadrilles fetching Bisonte *con filtro*, his wife's preferred brand. Now he was sauntering down the hill in the rain, hands plunged in pockets and shoulders hunched, whistling. Sometimes he acted like the narrator of *Our Town*, kicking imaginary pebbles, a free man in Winesburg, Ohio, or wherever he was in America.

'Here comes the Señor. Let's go in and sit down,' I suggested.

So we went in and sat down.

'They seem to love the dead here,' Harriet Deck said. 'One does, of course. Love the dead, I mean.'

I had nothing to say to that. Was it a Jewish thought? Threads flex, hues meeting and parting in whey-blue haze.

30

Moody, Fenning, Kramer and McCracken

It must have been Christmas Day 1964 when the Decks came dressed formally, as they would have dressed in San Francisco, John in a dark seersucker suit, snowy white shirt, slim Jim necktie and black boots; Harriet very smart indeed in a sort of half-length housecoat and black tights, *Strumpfhosen* that clasped her about the hips. They bore presents with them, flowers and a bottle of JJ from Málaga. We sat about and drank the whiskey. When Coppera pleaded exhaustion and retired for her siesta around two o'clock, we sallied out.

It was a strange day of fierce Andalucían sunlight splashed on whitewashed walls and Nerja seemed deserted. We ran into Exley roaming about and invited him to join us for dinner, drank some *Cuné* in Antonio's bar, spread ourselves out, praised the wine to the jovial patron who moved skittishly on the duckboards behind the service hatch, batted his circumflex eyelashes at us, saying 'Aye, Rory, aye?' without one word of English. And then back unsoberly to the Christmas dinner, to which Harry Calnek was invited.

Adelina had been waiting for us at the top of the stairs, beaming like the Queen Mother. She served up the first course and left. The tougher parts of the chicken were in a *paella*, the tender parts fried in oil with garlic seasoning. Exley did not complain of the toughness of the chicken but threw the bones about, affected by the Jameson. Calnek was subdued, spoke little and left early. We sat around the *brasero* and finished the whiskey. Deck spoke of his time in Korea.

He was second radioman, radio operator and titular gunner on a seaplane, having enrolled in the navy so as not to be drafted into the infantry; he spent a good part of his enlistment in training schools.

'You could buy good whiskey tax free in the NCO Club. I'd gone to an electronics school in Memphis and was assigned to Crew Nine. I learnt Morse Code and was given a chance to fly. It meant extra money and an easy life. Air crewmen stood fewer watches and did less work. Blues, peacoats, winter hats, fall-ins, fall-outs, friction, leaves, pick-ups, occasional women of the looser variety, fuck-ups, that was the Korean War,' Deck said, sprawled at his ease, smoking a thumping big Cuban cigar. 'We were enlisted men. When I was fighting for democracy over there, flying about in old PBMs, stubby-winged and heavy to handle. The bloody things couldn't land on four-foot swells, with none of the grace of the more famous PBYs, we patrolled the east coast of Korea, the Tsushima Strait and the Yellow Sea, in an anti-submarine outfit.

'The port of Wonsan,' Deck intoned. 'Barbershop music and college songs. It was Christmas 1952. The sea was icy. If you dropped into it, you wouldn't survive long. One of the seaplanes came down with thirteen officers and men. None survived.

'Those goddamn kamikazes, feasted and shaven to the pluck, climbed into a kind of flying chicken coop made out of fenceposts, orange crates put together around a bomb, and in these things they'd set out looking for an American destroyer. Some of them never made it. They'd explode somewhere off Wonsan. Desperate men. It was generally known that the Chinese used the Korean War as an extension of cadet training.

'The seaplane ramp,' said the sailor-aviator, warming to his theme. 'We flew out over the strait, a short gravy hop during which we photographed shipping. I was not at all prepared to die.

'The brothels were paper-thin,' said he, puffing like a steamboat. 'The whole joint shook when some of my buddies were hammering a job, polishing their knob. The bar hostesses were perfect. They were human and gentle and they needed us. I have never been around a collection of young, pretty, intelligent girls who needed me – not as a civilian and certainly not as a sailor. It was a blessing, a whiff off a dream, and another eloquent argument against worry. I knew I wasn't going to cream it.'

Leaning back in his chair and puffing on his *puro*, the husband studied his wife. The swollen lip my ardour had given her was back more or less to normal. And what better proof than a cut lip can a woman want, proof positive that a man has her on his mind?

'American service girls seemed a bit coarse in comparison,' Deck said. 'A big perfumed WAVE took me on her capacious thigh as if I were a cigar and she was rolling me. She dandled me up and down but nothing came of it except that I was keenly embarrassed, enough to bring tears to a man's eyes. She explained to me that it was all she could manage, because it was her "difficult" time. A period like lava flow, I should imagine. Glad I didn't have to perform. She'd have swallowed me up.

'You don't fuck around with a shipmate's girl or wife,' John Deck said. 'Jim McCracken, Joe Moody, Pat Fenning, Kramer. Get this: Fenning laid another man's wife and the husband got wind of it, beat the shit out of her, then got *him* drunk one night in a bar, laid him out with a bottle and then began stomping him and kicking the shit out of him good and proper. Sure as hell ruined his good looks. It was the last time he polished his knob there, I can tell you.'

I got the point.

31

The Way She Walked

The way she walked away from me that day, the day of our first assignation, first intimacy, heading for the brickworks and the cemetery, walking with that aura of hers, that short chopping stride, *pasa fina*, with the certainty of being seen and admired. Women feel it in their backs when they are being watched and admired.

The road, the *carretera*, bore her along on its boily back away from La Luna; the conviction of her own allure carried her along. She turned without stopping, sensing me watching her, saw that my eyes still followed her. I was a little below her on the cinder path that went branching off at right angles; it led over the tableland towards the sea, a route for the passage of goats at morning and evening, with much agility leaping across by stepping-stones as the sun came up or went down. Her lemur paw waved. I waved back. Without breaking her stride, she went on. She was my bit of stuff on the road.

Like most women, and all attractive women, she craved the touch of flannel. Was that the last time? If it was, I did not know it then. It was the first time and the last time, the only time, and I was going to establish my alibi. If you are going to tell lies you must be consistent with them, no divergences into the truth. Swimming, dearest. Not waving but drowning. *L'âme adore nager* – what Frog wrote that? I suspect Michaux. The soul adores swimming.

Mrs Harriet Deck was returning with her own no less plausible lies to tell her waiting husband; though what she thought to tell was true enough up to a point; up to the point where the lies began ('Lie in your teeth'), that is. She would not feed him an outright lie but her omissions contained falsehoods, modifications of facts, evasions of the truth; her elisions were masterly. Out walking for two hours, dear, saw a black sheep, spoke to no one, had a cold beer at La Luna.

So she went jauntily down the road, no doubt still feeling me inside her, as I felt her within me, being permeated with her, gripping me deep within. So she knew what it was like to be out of her depth, gliding away, knew the wonderfully dangerous intensification of feeling that comes with lying and cheating in love. There is no prescription against voluntary things, women as forces of nature; it is against *form*.

So she went swaggering away from me down the road and I watched her go, the soldier's girl on her way home. Hers was not the broad prudent seat (*pompi*) of rumpy Gerda Rhodes; nor yet the spare flat deflated seat of Sonya Hool, nor the tresses and hanks of dark hair proper to a Jewess – Gerda's Brillopad thatch, Lilly Lowen's orange golliwog locks – the appearance ineradicably Jewish, an Alexandrian effluvium of torpid female Hebrew flesh. No, she reminded me of none of those ladies. She was my spare-time, fair, loving, Polish-American-Jewish light-of-love.

She had not that narrowly determinable view of her race and the places occupied by that race, the spurious and obsessive concept of nationality that so many Americans have; she was American, sure, but she was surely Jewish too.

Was there something that said *Juden* in those blue eyes of hers? Some knowledge or sadness dredged up from God knows where; or was it merely the power that certain beautiful women have, of suggesting and invoking landscapes? (Cheever called it the dark plains of sexual experience where the buffalo still roams.) Their eyes gaze if not into then at least towards a landscape no man has ever seen, much less penetrated into; that small woman, that Jewy woman who so detested the term 'Jewess'.

When she was depressed and down in the dumps, she was really down; those dumps of hers were profoundly, Jewishly, deep. The guarded look she threw at me then conveyed something along the lines of 'Now am I neither happy nor sad. Now I am what I am.'

I'd think: How well I know you, Harriet, and yet I don't know you at all. You belong to your husband, not to me. I get the scraps.

A sullen wife and a reluctant mother sat all day in silence by the fire. I thought then: This is and is not the Harriet Lipski of Delancey Street that we heard so much about. Was it not profoundly Jewishly Jewish, this dolour, this impenetrable gloom? I can't say, I don't know; maybe it was. Some relative had told her once that she had Jewish eyes 'just like Uncle Ibn's'. But Uncle Ibn ('a loud-mouth with five grown sons in trade') 'definitely had Jewish eyes'. So she preferred not to believe it.

'Look,' said she (standing up close to me and widening her eyes so that I could study them, gaze into them and inhale her Cointreau breath), 'do you believe that I have Jewish eyes?'

'Yes,' I'd say, 'you definitely have Jewish eyes.'

'No, I have Italian eyes.'

'Well then, you have Italian eyes.'

Harriet was honest but in a very feminine way. She came to our apartment in Calle de las Augustias to tell me that she couldn't show up for our very first assignation. 'I can't do it. I wouldn't know what face to wear,' she confessed when Coppera was out of the room.

A partial failure some of the time, semi-successful part of the time, that's how it was for us then. It was passing strange, that winter, and the termination of our intimacy in the spring. Say around May Day.

32

Callus, Alas!

. . . a lover set out with all his equipages and appurtenances.

It was chilly in the Alhambra bar, like a dairy or a morgue, at nine in the morning when Miguel came on and began again tending his coffee machine that no one else was permitted to touch. There was snow along the sierras, cloud on Cuesto del Cielo that Old Parr had climbed with Calnek, Callus and Rory. We were alone there. Miguel diplomatically served us, did not ask of her husband nor of my *esposa*, did not see us, had come to no conclusion about what we were up to but knew we were up to something; else why look so *engaged*? Even transformed; and did we not see each other every day? And why these furtive meetings so early in the day? On these imponderables no doubt Miguel had pondered and no doubt come to some conclusion; but he wasn't telling anybody; mum was the word.

When she crossed one black-stockinged leg over the other my heart turned again with it. I heard a child crying upstairs, or maybe it was in the *retrete* where the *gitanos* cut the throats of the little kids brought there on the carrier of a beaten-up bike. A child was crying, Harriet was sipping black coffee and Cognac. The *retrete* was just a hole in the cement, the stink-sump of Iberia. How did the ladies manage crouching over it in ammonia-reek powerful as chloroform, and be able to rise again? The ladies could manage many difficult things.

Sometimes she dominated me with her eyes, the blue shafts

of her eyes, at other times it was the sight of a brown thigh; but more often than not it was her voice that dominated me, and then again (she seemed abstracted, not knowing how much she was showing) it was the brown thigh that dominated all.

She spoke of the past, the time before she had known me, and Miguel, monkey-faced with the leathery skin of an outdoor worker, served us, '*Si, Señora*', moved away, the paper napkins in the glass like pennants in the breeze, in the morgue we sat in, the *Fundador* warming us.

Miguel saw nothing, heard nothing, said nothing; heard all yet understood nothing. His lips were sealed.

I watched her face, her teeth, eyes, mouth, a touch of apathy, burning lips. She looked at me without saying anything, her eyes somewhat charged.

When she was younger, she had kissed a naked and hairy chest in Chicago. Then that one disappeared out of her life and another took his place, there was always going to be another, because she was a pretty blonde lady and they all wanted her. This one shot squirrels, going about naked with a rifle in the woods; he was a theological student who read Oscar Wilde. Naked in bed together they ate grapes and he read her 'The Nightingale and the Rose'. He gave her a present of *A Shropshire Lad*, because she was his rose-lipt girl. 'Kinda innocent,' she laughed at her lost innocence.

She inhaled Bisonte, remembering the theological student walking about buck-naked in the woods. Then there was another; there would always be another (her Byzantine nose had become more pronounced as she recalled the past, whitening across the bridge), because she was attractive to men. Would she remember all her old lovers? Would I too have that immortality?

I thought of the Albanian wood-cutters, white with the dust of the road, I'd seen passing like princes through a market in Sarajevo carrying Bronze Age saws, come on foot out of Ethiopia. And, by extension, I thought of Trevor Callus, god of misrule, cutting logs in Canada, grunting at each hefty stroke, the axe buried in the wood, a true woodsman, pulling it out again, panting at these exertions.

Callus burning the tyres of his Combi, heading for the Laurentians. He had spoken of a grey period in Montreal. The centre of the city was a cemetery, Mount Royal, where the dead looked down upon the living. Ville Marie was a settlement for missionaries and Place Royale was a fur trading post, and before that again it had been Hochelaga, an Iroquois Indian village.

He had once seen a girl undressing near a lighted window, and he had later accosted her in the street. The turreted roofs and outside stairways of old Montreal were an outright temptation to adventurous libertines like himself; the stairways were useful for assignation purposes since, in many cases, they led directly to bedrooms on upper floors. With a red rose clenched between his teeth and his amber eyes blazing with anticipatory lust, Callus climbed upwards, a lover set out with all his equipages and appurtenances. He liked high game on the edge, good sticky cod from Newfoundland waters; he had whom he pleased.

That was a strange madness of his – to be for ever waking up in an unknown bed. A true *carpe diem* type, his days were filled with vital cravings and satisfactions attempted; all the glut of life available would hardly suffice. Consorting with Montreal whores, he had caught a dose of the clap.

Soon enough he and Harriet would cuckold Rory, for Harriet thought that Rory had seduced Anne Renshaw, a blonde Englishwoman, said to be insatiable: Harriet wanted revenge.

Callus concerns us here. He who enjoyed life as a cannonball enjoys space, blindly travelling as aimed and spreading ruin on the way. He was a true Scorpio, the dangerous ones who kill themselves in a ring of fire. His arms were tattooed with the lime-blue shapes of entwined hearts or vessels in storm, cannons belching fire and smoke. From his army and forestry background came the puce needle diggings. Callus digging with a rutter in Cumberland, grunting down in an open drain, avoided by his fellow workers who feared him, his recklessness and awkwardness, his doomed quality.

'A fast river cuts a deep trench,' he told me. 'A slow river cuts a shallow trench.' Munge was morning-mouth, apen armpits, ullage was something else, and he knew the word for false axillary hair worn by chorus girls, which for the moment escapes me. When we passed an open drain in Calle Carabeo, the stench was enough to make your hair stand up. He inhaled deeply as though smelling flowers.

'Shit, I can't get enough of *that*.'

Not bearing to be quiet, not able to abide still at home. Now abroad, now in the streets, now lying in wait at corners, that was Trevor Callus. 'You dig the soil to get something out of it and you have a woman for much the same reason,' said he. Digging with his thick tool in a trench in Cumberland, he knew he was finished if he stayed there. Another maddened forester flung a hatchet at his head, but he had one of his intuitions and ducked in time. The wet weapon had slipped from the other's grasp, or so he claimed. 'Sorry, mate.'

A perishing wind blew down from the Grampians. He had to get out. Callus struck with the hatchet, pulled it out, hit again, grunting at each blow; sweat poured off him. The bulge at his crotch became pronounced; everything 'turned him on'. No more sickness or excessive evacuation. The sun went down over a hill.

'He's changed,' Coppera said. 'He was different in Johannesburg, steadier. There he was a man.'

'With an excreta phobia,' I said. 'He was never steady. And now here, what is he?'

'Now he has become a chimpanzee.'

Wisdom of Coppera Hill: 'A woman's heart is like a room filled with pitiable stuff. Dancing with another woman is like drowning.'

33

Can After Can . . .

Can After Can . . .

Can After Can . . .

'She sure as hell was white,' said John Deck. 'The winches were white, the anchor chains were white, the covers on the lifeboats were an unsurpassable glossy white; the plates, the hatch covers, all alike were spotlessly white.

'Peer into a vent and the shadow was white. The sand in the fire buckets was as white as the smoke belching from the stacks. Look into the paint locker; can-after-can-after-can-after-can of white paint!

'Sailors in white singlets and officers in spick-and-span white uniforms pace the white decks. It was the whitest, brightest small freighter in maritime history; the SS *Klek* of Yugoslavia. We crossed in her.'

I saw the radiant Harriet walking the decks at night in the company of the ship's doctor, the handsome Dr Vuc Eisen. She told him all about herself. She looked brilliant, indeed dazzling. A mixture of honey and sun, matt skin, burning lips (*and* roving eye).

'Sunset followed sunrise as regular as decanting wine,' said the Deckman lugubriously, giving a flare to his niggery nostrils by taking a deep breath, deepening his voice, really laying the accent on thick. 'The boredom was absolute, man. Changes of current, tidal shifts, the wake of passing vessels, garbage bobbing in the wake, the diver-birds diving, the flying fish doing what flying fish do, the islands, oh God, the *islands*! Where would we be without islands? I can't recall which ones we stopped at. They all looked the same to me. Perhaps we stopped at them all? No matter, the sweet winds were blowing from the horse latitudes to the doldrums.'

'And the ever-attentive Dr Vuc Eisen?' Rory inquired slyly. 'What was he up to?'

'He sure as hell charmed the pants right off her,' Deck agreed. 'Once in our cabin he gave her an injection up the ass.'

She lay facing her husband on her bunk and the handsome ship's doctor prepared the hypodermic. 'This may hurt,' he said. She was ready for him, smiling at her husband, her skirt riding up, she was ready for it, biting her lip.

'Walter Pater spoke of two things which penetrated Leonardo's art and imagination beyond the depth of other impressions – the smiling of women and the motion of great waters,' said Rory the Everready.

'We cut loose,' Deck said, snipping the end off his cigar.

34

Kampen Nact-Strand

'You should see Brigitte Winkler in a bikini,' Coppera said. 'She wore a red one down on Torrecillas today and looked ripe enough to eat. There was a young German chap with her and *he* looked as if he was about to eat her. You'd think you had the whole picture when you see her in a bikini, but not at all. She was showing us some photos of herself taken in the buff at Sylt, where the Berlin nudist girls go, and there she was in all her glory. There was a hairy naked chum crouching in the shallows, devouring her with his eyes, whom she described as a 'good friend'. She really is startling, nude. The female shape undressed is so blatantly avid and sexual, so hungry-looking; I wouldn't like to be a man.'

'Sardine become shark,' I said.

The odours of inlets and creeks. Brigitte Winkler had those great simple limpid eyes that stared at one appealingly. Medea the wife of Jason, leader of the Argonauts, must have stood so in all her beauty alone on the Cretan shore. The good ship *Argo* stood some way out to sea; the Argonauts in it were tired and hungry, fed up following the Golden Fleece.

'What about her golden fleece?'

Private parts tend to become public, if not outrightly pubic, along the shores of the Costa del Sol in season. Franco was hardly cold in his grandiose sarcophagus in the Valley of the Fallen before young *Fräuleins* were diving into the sea in smaller and smaller bikinis, with no tops before King Juan Carlos had well settled onto his throne.

Harriet, who liked to talk horny, asked me what it was like to have one. 'It must be great to feel it there between your legs, to feel the weight of it dangling down.'

Harriet Deck talked dirty like one of the mouthy, fancy-free young wives in Webster or Congreve, a bold reincarnation of Lady Bracegirdle ('I'll let both you guys . . .'). Come-ons were her speciality, her cloak and dagger work, her language as rough as the rasp of a cat's tongue ('lemme talk to the cunt') or loose as a longshoreman; female or not, she wanted to be cock of the walk. Queen of the castle.

'Strewth, Milady, you find yourself in the wrong century and probably the wrong country at the wrong time. Franco's Spain could be puritanical in its own funny Fascist way. In Sir Walter Raleigh's day the gallants bolstered their codpieces with bombast, to make their proudest possession look bulgy and heavier. You'd have me wear a codpiece.'

'Sure.'

She herself preferred sanitary towels to Tampax because they gave her the feeling of an equivalent weight to the missing testicles and tool.

'What about your breasts and hair?' I said. She gave me a look, her eyes somewhat bloodshot from sea-bathing; they had been to Carabeo beach that morning.

'Sure, to feel one's breasts, the weight of them. To let one's hair down, feeling it on one's naked back, that's a good feeling, like slipping nude into bed. That's good too.'

Her own hair was long and oily, as long hair tends to be, particularly in hot places. Oily hair gives a better feeling of abandonment; a hairless Venus would have no power to charm the manly heart.

She'd go for that all right, passionate but a little envious of the male, the ordained taker, the cocksman; and what worse devil hung betwixt their hirsute thighs?

*　　*　　*

'She wants you to come over for supper.' Her husband conveyed the invitation, laying a diplomatic hand on my shoulder. 'Coppera's coming. It's all fixed. She told me to say a place will be laid for you. She's preparing something good for you. So you gonna come, Rory, hey? . . . *¿Que desea usted? ¿Prefiere usted la carne al horno, a la parilla, hervida o guidada?*'

'Thanks. I will,' I said.

Through that other loved body, the other adored flesh that one craves to enjoy, all that is most appealing in that other person is continually fêted, yet continually being withdrawn. Love, that most despairing of grips; the cruel fabled bird that pinches like a crab.

She was all of that for me.

35

Harriet

The potent smell of blood must have assailed Harriet's nostrils where the Decks sat on *tenido*, six rows up above the barrier on the *sol* side, roasting in the afternoon sun near the dark corral, out of which the bulls rushed blindly to their deaths in the arena all watered and raked for them to bravely perform.

'We were sittin' right on the bull-gate,' she boasted. Wherever she sat was *ipso facto* the best seat by the mere fact of her occupying it. When she entered a room, she caused a stir. Wherever she found herself, *that* was the best place to be. She deserved the best seat and special attention; she expected it and got it. The two stout *guardia de noche*, Manolo and Fernando, adored her.

'Queens,' her friend, Anne Marie, said of the Jewesses of San Francisco. 'Jewish queens.' Their besotted husbands saw them as queens and treated them accordingly. It was something that grated very much on the white South African sensibilities of Coppera.

On that Sunday in the Málaga bullring most of the working of the bulls and the subsequent blood-letting took place right in front of the Decks. Even without binoculars I had spotted them across from us on seats lower down nearer the sanded arena which the *monos* in collarless claret-coloured dungarees raked religiously after each kill, dragging the corpses out on litters pulled by mules at a gallop, dragging them away to be butchered under the stands. This was performed as impersonally as zoo attendants might clear up dungy cages.

But soon another fresh black bull came galloping in with tail erect, and shortly after in clanked the picadors with their lances raised, and the whole bloody business was resumed: rush, push, lean over, gore, gore, push; and now the blood pouring in dark gouts from the great hump raised up in fury, for the bullish spirit had to be brought down, lowered considerably before the gadfly could sting him lethally with the razor-sharp curved sword that found its way past the horns and into the lungs and soon had him coughing up his life's blood.

All this Harriet witnessed, with her low blood pressure and her high, bright expectant look, down there in *tenido* that must have reeked of bull blood, after the scuffles, the heavy lancing, the bull wearing himself out in futile rushes, the blood jerking out of him, so that he arrived all weary and bloodied for the *coup de grâce*.

What Frenchman contended that women are not clean because of their menses? It sounds like de Montherlant. But wouldn't the monthly flushing out of impurities make them cleaner than men, so fixated on blood sports, on killing, like Hemingway?

Rory remembered the child Molly Cushen in the schoolyard after the attentions of the barbarous dentist, the bloody spittle she spat out delicately, the blood-smeared hand, and of the disturbing prepubescent beauty of the young Elizabeth Taylor as Jane Eyre's little friend who cuts off her hair and walks in the punishment circle carrying flat-irons in a heavy fall of studio rain, standing by the deathbed with eyes downcast, and her slurred voice with glottal stops, suggestive already of the coming pains of love.

When Rory saw Harriet Deck after a lapse of twenty-one years she looked like a ghost, standing in the arrivals lounge of San Francisco International Airport to meet her old admirer off the internal flight from Houston and drive Rory to Santa Cruz in her powerful car.

She stood among the others waiting, not waving or calling out, just standing there so that I could see her plainly among all the other strangers. The Rubicon of the years had been crossed and some of the bright lights accordingly doused, though enough remained for Rory to see the old flame undiminished; she was much the same as before.

Rory kept his hand on her warm thigh as she drove and she did not object. Out there in the breathing dark was Berkeley's campus. It was December 1986 and they hadn't seen each other since the Decks visited Dublin in 1965.

In the time when we were apart I had written to Harriet for a swatch of her hair, from head, axillary and pubics. Those intimate parts of her were sent by airmail from Copenhagen to Málaga in a stout manila envelope, with the pages of her letter sellotaped inside, and this was carried in a Correos sack by bus in the twisting and ascending road that went around some two hundred curves, climbing into the hills like a medieval messenger on horseback bearing gifts; eventually to be delivered on foot to Calle Rueda by the unreliable and rarely sober postman, Laureano.

Rory had got the idea from reading Byron. The hair on the head of the former beloved, long separated in time and space, that makes a stone of the heart, is no longer thought attractive, smitten by the passing years, by general wear and tear; the living hair dies, becomes dead hair on the head, like animal hair on Hallowe'en masks of monster faces sticky with glue at the back, eye sockets empty, as on a waxwork or a mummy in a dusty coffin; hair found on the horrid masks that were intended to frighten children.

Once on a winter night flight from Seattle to Heathrow the Boeing had picked up passengers from LA. A pretty darkhead took her seat in front of Rory. Then morning light was leaking in through the oval windows and the darkhead now with hair combed and water glistening on strands of hair as she was having her breakfast, and then she was rising up and collecting her stuff and walking before Rory out into the arrivals lounge at Heathrow, moving into a different climate, but all intact, having crossed time zones flying at 33,000 feet above the clouds, the proximity a sort of intimacy, surrogate intimacy, pseudo-intimacy, like seeing Harriet again after a lapse of twenty and one years, and finding that Santa Cruz was another sort of Nerja.

Who was it wrote that love is Time and Space made perceptible to the heart?

The loved one's mere presence transforms the very climate of a place, *her* place in the world around us, the world at large, which falls away from us when the loved one again appears, offers herself to Rory again, saying 'Take me, for I am yours today.'

PART IV:

Berlin Divided, Munich *Mordfest*

36

Im Doll

Rory liked to walk around Im Doll, liked the name, because it was where Hannelore had walked about as a child with Pappa and Mamma Schmidt, until the Red Army sharpshooter drew a bead and shot the horse dead between the shafts. Another was quickly harnessed up and the housekeeper had the foresight to bury a valuable ring in the sugar canister and they left Berlin behind in a hurry and with it her childhood.

Then Berlin fell and the world came to an end for Germans. It was Rossellini's *Germana, Anno Zero* for real, which was very surreal indeed, with the black market and profiteering and the bartering that went on when there was no more money available, the sharp dealings proceeded in whatever valuables desperate men and women could lay their hands on, a cut-throat survival business where only the strong survived and Uncle Hans was pushed to his death from a train and Hannelore had no more use for dolls.

A city of ruins stood there as dire warning after the bombing raids had brought the people to their knees down in the shelters and the sick Führer, in his deep bunker permeated with bad smells, was preparing his last will and testament, getting ready to do away with Eva Braun and himself. Loyal unto death, Eva would be Frau Hitler for only a short time before he shot her,

183

finally wedded to the death she wanted. The nuptial feast would take place in Valhalla, to which neither Goering nor Himmler would be invited; nor would any of Hitler's defeated generals. *Nein!* The death mills had all been closed down; the city laid waste around the Chancellery. His last face, the features of the vegetarian with stomach cramps, was a face of iron, his true face, implacable.

The man of humble beginnings, who had made himself master of Germany and most of Europe, was a strict vegetarian, a sipper of vegetable soup; he blamed the *Wehrmacht* and the *Volk* for letting him down; they had not shown their true German steel, in his view, and forthwith blew himself away.

37

Some Places She Took Me

W hen the Havel froze over, we took to walking on the
ice. She would only consent to go so far in an east-
erly direction because marksmen with long-sighted
rifles were hidden in the bushes on the GDR bank and those
frontier guards had itchy fingers and were quite likely to squeeze
off a round at anyone foolish enough to venture on to Soviet soil,
the reclaimed land won by the Red Army. Trespassing on Soviet
soil was a capital offence, instantly punishable by death, delivered
at long range; and midway across the Havel the DDR ended and
the GDR began; the West, technically speaking, ended out on
the ice, beneath which the Havel still flowed in the direction it
had always flowed; namely, east to west, following the contours
of the land, abiding by the direction decided upon long ago by
the old river.

She did not relish the idea of venturing into the Grünewald
by night, for some couples never came out again, or the girl was
raped and the man was set upon and done in. She would not sit
demurely on the sandy banks of the Schlachtensee or Krumme
Lanke, because dogs befouled the area; nor would she consent
to swim in either of these tributaries of the Havel lakes, because
they were dirty. On moonless nights and even on nights of full
moon, the waters looked very Grimm-like and black, full of
nameless awfulness, among which might be numbered the bones

of the aircrew of a Lancaster bomber that had been shot down in the war.

To none of these excursions would she agree; but soon all resistance was overcome and she succumbed in the fastness of the Grünewald on the blackest of nights and swam naked with Rory in Krumme Lanke and told him he had the face of a fox, a swimming fox heading for the hen coop, that was Rory to a T, as the hen coop was surely the nudist Hannelore laved by the lukewarm waters of Schlachtensee.

Since they were hitting it off so well, she said she was ready to do whatever he wanted. So Rory, having had the fill of her frontwise, and the full enjoyment thereof, asked her to turn over and then had the fill of her backside which was large and shapely and if possible even hotter than her cunt, which was saying something. All this in the depths of the Grünewald where there were none about to see what was going on, what hogs were rooting for what truffles; except in the daytime when a mezzo-soprano from the Opera House, walking in the rides, exercised her voice at the full pitch of her lungs.

For a fact, some of the places where she took Rory were, I suspect, not her own choices, but choices made by previous admirers, of all of whom she spoke frankly, the four or five in her court.

Such a place was a student dive in Wittenburgplatz where we consumed a great quantity of cheap red wine and plates of sardines all standing upright with eyes and mouths open as if they had died of fright. We frequented a Polish bar and were adopted by a queer barman ('How are the young lovers tonight?') who served us vodka in little goblets with ice and snow about the rims, that was like drinking fire; this somewhere near the burnt-out ruins of the Soviet Embassy about which she made the widest circle and never referred to, as if it didn't exist, something shameful standing in Berlin as a monument to what must never happen again. On rare occasions, when in funds, we dined at Hardy's am Oper and drank expensive Hungarian Tokay; but more often it was an Italian restaurant, Rusticana, patronised by off-duty British Army officers in mufti. Hotel Bubec in Mexikoplatz was lovely in the snow, drinking vodka again, and the dome of the S-Bahn very Russian and the place overheated, so that we were reluctant to leave. Then there was a Greek place.

When Germany played in the final of the World Cup, we were the only couple in Berlin who not only weren't even looking at the television screen, but didn't know who was playing whom; the only loving couple in all Germany who had never even heard of Pele, the wonderworker.

38

In a Strange Sort of Time

You'd think to yourself: 'It'll never be the same again. *I'll* never be the same again.' But to be sure nothing essentially changes; as the importance of the other diminishes and falls away as love wanes, you return to yourself once more. You are yourself again; and she presumably returns to herself, too; whoever she may be; the loved one of that time and place, that place in Rory's anxious heart.

You say to yourself: 'One day, a day like today, a day that has become unlike any other day.' And it happens. You asked for it and it's been given to you, and all is changed.

That ferocious Frog Jean Genet, the princeling of language who turned himself into a real toad, wrote of the sheer pleasure of betrayal; betrayal in love, that is. A betrayed man's face is terrible, he says. But isn't it even truer of betrayed women's faces? Look at Picasso's *Woman Weeping*. Dora Maar weeping tears hot as molten lava, becoming wedges of thick, shattered glass, forced out of her eyes at the thought of losing Pablo.

On the days when I escaped from Coppera and the kids, she liked to arrange them in the windows like the heads of a hanging jury, as the mother made abusive catcalls after the fleeing one who had run up a quick omelette by way of lunch and was now hurrying for the train.

I had an assignation with Hannelore at Podbielski station. It was the day Zbigniew Herbert chose to call on us, walking down from his rented mansion at the end of Beskidenstrasse, a cobbled street with a pharmacy and bakery within easy reach.

I crept away unobserved and was soon out of sight at the Joachim Klepper Weg and hurrying across by the sunken meadows, the Rehweise, by what had been an anti-tank gun pillbox during the war, and approaching the station where Albert Speer, coming in his Mercedes from his Wannsee home, had noticed a crowd of Jews on the platform as he flashed by, not giving them a second glance or thought.

Zbigniew Herbert burst his Polish trousers and had to return home to change, but returned to take Coppera and the kids out boating on Krumme Lanke, knowing something was wrong with the Hills.

As I walked past the stalls of the open-air market that was held on a Thursday, the very air changed to match my mood of elation, as if I was a merrymaker in one of Zille's graphics of a beery Berlin in a happier time. I was so happy that happy is not the word, lucky happiness, *Glücklichkeit*, a happiness with a kernel of sadness (for my betrayal of wife and letting my children down) like a curry that is salted, or a gate vaulted or some hard handicap overcome.

I was leaving the zone of duty and faithfulness that belonged to Coppera and entering the zone that was Hannelore's, the free zone where rights no longer applied; the former's rights ended when the doors of the train that swept me to the latter sighed shut, in a strange sort of time that was both melancholy and monochrome, an illustration from Grimm.

39

The Giantess and the Guardsman

Rory had noticed (how could he not?) the truly amazing giantess strolling along the wide plane-tree-lined pavement near the Spanish bar; panther-like she patrolled the area, making it into a jungle clearing.

She had moved serenely past the two Greek *Gastarbeiters* deep in Greekish confabulation, who hadn't even noticed her, hadn't cottoned on, as she threw them a swift, lethal *visu*, clutching at them like a grappling iron seeking purchase, the lovelorn look that entraps and entrances. But they had ignored her.

As soon as she had accosted the tall English grenadier, they understood how the land lay and how the wind blew and came running with their tongues out for it, but already too late.

She could have taken on the pair of them in tandem, sucking off the warty cock of the one while his pal attempted congress from the rear, a Greekish variant very popular in the Levant. Her high posterior proffered invitingly for his gratification, with garter belt and fishnet stockings dragged down, love-knots dangling, stilettos discarded, buckles and bridles hanging loose as from a richly caparisoned charger, a bay mare with hair swinging like a mane or tail raised, miring.

That was surely one stupendous broad. The randy little

Greeks would have had their work cut out to make any impression on her, let alone mount that peerless German mare.

He was exceedingly tall, well over six feet, reared on All-Bran and as tall as an English guardsman on parade, snapping to attention, deploying the swagger-stick, correctly attired with shoulders back and chin in; he carried himself as an officer should.

His elegant light blue linen suit had all the lickety-spit and polish of the parade ground. He was close-shaven, well shod and pomaded, knew a good barber, and was just taking an evening stroll along the Ku'damm.

So was she.

The big whore Karen Schnell, Mistress of SM, was as tall as he; six-inch stilettos gave her a slight advantage. She was an absolute stunner. Her manner was brisk, business was business, she didn't believe in beating about the bush. She was sauntering along the west side of the the Ku'damm, on the lookout for likely clients. Then along came the tall guardsman as if he were strolling in Kensington Gardens. She stopped abruptly as he came opposite her and he stopped too.

'You wenna get laid, big boy? Get inna my pants?' – pronounced 'paints' – 'Or fuck Karen up the ass?'

The guardsman raised his eyebrows: this was sharp talking. Karen Schnell spoke an obsolete American movie slang never heard in brown Bronxville nor Schenectady, in a nasal intonation learnt from Barbara Stanwyck.

'Won't try an' buck you off if you wanna ride. No time like the present. My pad's just round the corner. If you wanna quickie, Karen's hot to trot. Don't care how long you are.'

An elderly sandwichboardman with mouth agape stood at the entrance to a side street, ringing a small handbell to advertise the strip joints. The evening parade of Berlin whores had begun. Traffic roared up and down the Kurfürstendamm. The threatening head of a big Alsatian dog with lolling tongue hung out of the wide-open window of a speeding BMW. The Mercedes-Benz sign revolved over Europe Centre, in a city split in twain, where rigid Russian-style Communism crept along Stalinallee right up to the wall at Potsdamer Platz; this side was committed to hedonism, the good goofing off, getting stuffed and getting laid – life with a zing in it.

Like ball-bearings rattling in oil, the hurdygurdy man began grinding out an old Berliner tune on his antiquated machine (they had stood toe to toe and eye to eye, her breath fanned his face, she thoughtfully fingering his lapel as if to test the quality of the expensive cloth, absently touching the lapel in an intimate gesture as if presenting him with a rose for his buttonhole); at which they turned as one, of one mind, certain of what they wished to do and just how they would set about it.

'You do rather *arouse* me,' the tall guardsman admitted.

They turned as one in the movement of a formal dance, a dance they had danced before, maybe long ago. They linked arms in a familiar manner (as if they had once been intimate but had separated and now had met again in a city where neither of them had dreamed of ever meeting the other, but they had and were overjoyed, and he was looking forward to servicing her again).

She leant forward on her high heels, tipping her head towards his until they almost touched and whispered hotly into his ear some invitation of unambiguous intent, nibbling an earlobe that had gone purple with embarrassment.

'Would you care for a ride, sir? I'm quite free. My place is nearby. Come!'

And then she made that unforgettable gesture: a quick point over his right shoulder, pointing away behind his back the way she had sauntered out, looking for the first client to come within her orbit. A quick dabbing gesture that an archer might make with one gloved right hand as he released an arrow towards its mark, heading for the bull's-eye with all the fierce suck and pull of a powerfully sprung bow behind it. Or the gesture a surgeon might make after a coronary angiogram operation has been successfully performed and he removes surgical gloves preparatory to washing his hands, with a sort of nimble mimed wringing of all the fingers. Or (to strain the simile yet further), say, the perfectly timed punch that only travels a few inches, and catches the opponent flush on the jaw, moving into the blow, and drops him cold, settles his hash.

'You an army man?'

'No, no, nothing particularly like that. I'm an insurance broker, actually. Different racket altogether.'

It was a gesture made in all innocence once, by a young Dublin woman *en route* to her office, by which she had sought to comfort or anyway reassure me, Rory, that is, the father, to her just a face peering out of a narrow window at 47 Charleston Road, hearing the damn gate creak open again, for her to usher in his son, an excitable anxious child of seven, eight or nine at the time, whom she was sending back in again unhurt, after some rough workmen in an irrigation ditch had shouted something at him, shouted obscenities that had alarmed and frightened him, sent him weeping home again. No, he had stood at the bus stop, weeping, and she had seen and heard enough and had brought him back safely home.

The protective maternal gesture was the gesture that Picasso had caught in the painting of his young wife, Jacqueline, and their two children, Paloma and Claude. The figures of children and mother with arms about them are outlined in heavy black, like the lead holding a stained-glass window in place. The protective motherly gesture of enclosing and enfolding the two children was repeated, once more perpetuated. Almost a throwaway gesture, refusing any show of gratitude for a gift made with the heart, a free gift from the heart; the moue she made with her mouth expressed that. *Bah, it's nothing. Forget it!*

But her I couldn't ever forget; neither have I, Rory, forgotten that unsolicited act of kindness.

The Greek and Italian *Gastarbeiters* and the others from poor Balkan countries were cooped up in their compounds and out of touch with what was going on, never bothering to learn the language of their German employers, the *Deutsch* that might have saved them mutilated limbs from machines plastered with safety precautions, all set forth in script like orders barked out; saved them from electrocuting themselves on power lines designated *VERBOTEN! ACHTUNG!*

What did that mean? Free for a few hours they wandered about the city, window-shopping, gaping in blank amazement at the priceless furs in the windows of the fashion shops. No price tags gave fair warning that they shouldn't attempt to enter here; for it was far, far beyond their means. Those who didn't have funds didn't shop here but at Peek & Kloppenburg.

In any case most of their pay cheques went home intact. They seemed lost, wandering about the sinful city, gaping at the rich goods in the windows. Girlie shows proliferated. Nude playmates besported themselves, splashing about in shallow pools surrounded by tables set for dinner. Red candles glowed on the tables and were reflected in the windows; and the silent *Gastarbeiters*, sadly gazing in, saw the waiters moving about briskly, setting places and taking the first orders from stout patrons who seemed to overflow their fragile chairs; saw the nude playmates, narrow-waisted but big-busted and with big behinds, constantly smiling and aglow with health, tugging playfully at the neckties of smiling male customers sitting alone at tables, inviting them to join the other nude playmates in a frolic. Flashbulbs exploded and the *Gastarbeiters* gaped in wonderment at what they were getting up to around, and then in, the pools. Photographs of previous cavortings were on display, set out beside the mouthwatering menus on the triple-glazed windows.

Ah, but who could aspire to all that flash and glitter? The flesh of the nude playmates seemed incandescent, as if they were about to ignite as part of the floor show, the tie-tugging and the wanton invitations and urgings and splashings were a far cry from the paternalistic hardness of their own grim, goaty land, be it Sicily or Sardinia. What was this – bordello or zoo? The Berlin Zoo was near enough; that was about all they could afford.

Did one go out to eat or to be eaten by these female piranha fish? It was most confusing, never was it like that in old Sardinia.

The giggling girls were asking a real brute to get his kit off and join them for a good splash, to get his appetite up. There he was drawing down his trousers and the nudes were clapping. It was a riot of fun.

The *Gastarbeiters* slouched off into the night. They had seen enough. They would order a beer in the Augsburger Keller under the arches of Bahnhof Zoo and return to their compound. They could not stay up all night like these sex fiends cavorting around the pool.

40

Sommerspiele:
September 1972 in Munich

Red of anther, hush of autumn, tread of panther.

Nothing upsets Bavarians more than the Föhn, a devious Italian wind that slips in over the Alps and whistles through the Brenner, whispering Latin things into German ears. Possibly repeating what Court Ciano had told *Il Duce*: that Germans were dangerous because they dreamed collectively.

Be that as it may, when the Föhn blows, surgeons lay down their knives and publishers' readers cast aside typescripts, both knowing their judgement to be impaired. Remote objects, such as church spires, draw closer. The good citizens of Munich – where I happened to find myself in the Black September of 1972 – like nothing better than to sit for hours on window-seats or out on small balconies, staring into the street below, observing life passing.

In Jakob-Klar-Strasse in Schwabing the retired boxer takes up his position early, and is there all day, fortified by mugs of *Bier* handed out to him by an unseen *Frau*, become just a brawny arm.

A positively Latin feeling for blueness prevails. *Lividus* bleached out to the delicate washed-out blue of the Bavarian sky over the Englische Garten, also in the watery eyes of the citizens, in the flag fluttering in a breeze, on Volksbier labels. It's München blue.

Ciao! the better-educated ones cry out on parting; though in the old-style shops the *Grüss Gotts* ring out right merrily. Misha Galle called, then Volker Schlondorff with his wife Margarete von Trotta, for *Tischtennis*.

From Riem Airport into the city the way was festively prepared with huge Olympic flags. My taxi was driven by a woman. I offered Prinzregentenstrasse Fünf as my address, a Freudian slip if ever there was one, and was driven smartly up to Adolf Hitler's old address. I redirected her to a number in Schwabing. The Isar seemed to be flowing the wrong way – a disturbing hallucination.

Once again I began losing my bearings on the wrong side of *Der Friedensengel*, walking my feet off in this city of fine girls and spouting fountains. Greek goddesses with Bavarian thighs, eyes closed against the inevitable, supported on their shoulders heavy pillars pock-marked by bullets fired from afar. The great stone goddesses were protecting the bridges over the Isar, traversed at set intervals by a villainous low-slung black limousine packed with what I assumed were Italian gangsters, who turned out to be Irish government leaders. *Der Friedensengel* balanced precariously on one foot, hopefully extending a palm branch. Across the plinth an activist had squirted in white aerosol LIEBE DEINE TOTEN!

Preparations for the Games had intensified throughout summer, with Police Chief Schreiber's men out in waders cleansing the old Isar of a detergent overflow from a factory. On 28 August the *Süddeutsche Zeitung* reported that sportsmen and politicians were fascinated (*begeistert*) by an opening ceremony without military overtones. Lord Killanin was in control. Aged Avery Brundage had flown in from the United States. The fire, too, had come from afar: Greece. Whether this was a good augury or not, few were willing to predict. The American traveller and cynic Paul Theroux would write later that the Games were of interest because they showed a world war in pantomime.

But something more disturbing than the Föhn (causing double vision) had slipped into Munich with false papers on 4 September when Rory arrived via Air France from West Berlin namely, Al Fatah. Their target: the Olympic Village. More particularly, Israeli coaches and weight-lifters, the heavy innocents stall-fed on milk and T-bone steaks, who were soon to lay down their lives in the German slaughterhouse prepared for them.

Cauldron of Blood was running at the Outpost Cinema for occupying troops whose regimental motto had a threatening ring to it: 'Have Guns Will Travel'. And fuck syntax.

As bubonic plague, the Black Death, entered Europe as a flea on the body of a rat, so lethal international terrorism, late twentieth-century style, entered Germany from the Middle East in the person of Muhammad Daoud Odeh (code-name Abu Daoud), probably travelling on a forged Iraqi passport. He was to remain there, undetected by the police chief Schreiber, throughout the impossible ultimatums – the terrorists tell German officials that more than 200 Palestinian prisoners in Israeli jails must be released by 0900 or all the hostages will die. Arab intermediaries helped to arrange a further extension until 1300. New deadlines were extended to 1500 and 1700. Regard the carnage that followed, the self-immolation, the capture of three terrorists at Fürstenfeldbruck military airport.

It was Föhn weather, Sharpeville weather, the girls out in summer clothes one day, scarves and coats the next. Police and ambulance sirens never stopped in Luitpoldstrasse, the dogs barking after the fox has gone. In a mossy fountain, somewhat magnified in the water, small white eggshells broken in halves seemed to tremble. Shabby men were reading discarded newspapers in a public park protected by high hedges. Trams clanged around the steep corner at Max-Planck-Strasse, clinging to the wall.

The black limousine was back now, strangely flying the Irish colours on bonnet pennants, with CD registration plates, still traversing old Munich. The Irish Taoiseach, Jack Lynch, was conferring with Willy Brandt in the country. Buttercups grew along the grass verge on Thomas-Mann-Allee. A woman wearing leather gloves was gathering red berries. Near the Englischer Garten two sailors asked the way to the archery contest, one of them drawing an imaginary bow. Men in shirtsleeves were out. I walked by the embankments, saw the skyline drawn and painted by Klee and Grosz; two brown beauties in bikinis were sunning themselves near the weir where terns were wading. It was a lovely September day.

Two workmen in blue denim overalls sat silently at a table on which were arranged some empty beer bottles with the remains of their lunch, under trees buffeted by the wind; a most peaceful scene, one would suppose. But on Luitpoldstrasse, leading to and from the Olympic Village, sirens never stopped wailing; it was difficult to distinguish police from ambulances; destination lock-up, hospital or morgue. The call was for law and order; but what is that but disorder with the lid clamped down?

Why was an Irish Embassy car packed with Italian gangsters? Riddles. One handsome terrorist declared that he would have preferred death with his comrades who had blown up victims and themselves with hand grenades flung into the helicopter.

A sombre choral work, then, to be expected in Munich. A style of killing had been set by terrorists who looked more like movie actors than political activists, acted and spoke like them too, in German and broken English, chain-smoking.

The leaves were turning when the killing began. In shop windows now the signs read HALLO HERBST! DU WIRST CHIC. The yellow press yelled MORDORGIE! The headlines screamed MORDFEST! *The Times* put it more diplomatically, more Britishly: 'Storm grows over what went wrong at Munich.' *Der Spiegel* of 11 September stated bluntly: DAS MASSAKER VON MÜNCHEN!

'The XXth Olympic Games resumed yesterday after a 24-hour suspension while Munich mourned the eleven members of the Israeli team who died at the hands of Arab guerrillas.' The sexy songbird, Mireille Mathieu, was driven around the marathon *Sporthalle*, standing in a white open-top Ford Capri, belting out *'Ein Platz an der Sonne fur jung und alt'*. Pope Paul VI, not to be outdone in outrageousness, was photographed in Venice standing precariously upright in what was described as *eine Prunkgondel*, solemnly blessing some Venetian sewage, a clotting of flowers and scum. To the rear of the precarious vessel stood what appeared to be Roman centurions.

The Schwabing flat had been cleaned and the rugs had their

colours renewed. Framed on the walls were strange tortured viscerae, possibly human, in monochrome. A single flower, richly red damask, with streaks of sunflower yellow at its heart, hung in a small blue vase. Red of anther, hush of autumn, tread of panther.

We went swimming in Starnberger See – my Munich friend Erika, her boyfriend Wolfgang, and Rory. Out there in the blue, insane Ludwig had drowned with his physician. The wooded hills rolled away. On Saturday, the *Süddeutsche Zeitung* obituary notices face pages of movie advertising of an unrestrained lewdness. Marie Garibaldi was showing her all in *Amore Nudo*. '*MEIN TREUER LEBENSKAMERAD*', the obituary notice declared with melancholy certitude. The dead could no longer cavort with the lovely Marie Garibaldi. Hitachi advertised, 'I am you', with Oriental guile. It was time for MacBaren's Golden Blend. It was time for *Volksbier*.

Müller, the player with two left feet, had scored again, and was being ardently embraced by his captain Beckenbauer. *Tip-Kick Fussball* brings competitive fever (*Wettkamptstimmung*) into the home. A modern German family was shown in the throes of 'Tip-Kicking'. Charles Bronson was appearing in *Brutale Stadt*, Jerry Lewis elsewhere, a black detective appeared in *Shaft* ('*Der Absolute Super-Krimi!*'). The girls of the DDR ran away with all the track and field events; a splendid example of specialised breeding and expert coaching achieving good results within three decades. An exhibition of early Bavarian folk art was showing at the Staatliches Museum.

Germans togged out for golf are indeed a sight to behold. They go in for overkill, armed with *Golfschläger*, but cannot laugh at themselves, unlike the English, who do it tolerantly all the time. Nor can they endure their own Germanic incompetence. A game without visible opponents disturbs; and at golf you are your own opponent, even in matchplay. How the Germans suffer! They *detest* losing. By the eighteenth hole, none are on speaking terms.

I played with the Wittys and their elderly female friend on a woody links in the Bavarian Alps above Chiemsee. The lake itself was invisible below in the haze. I spent most of the round searching for lost balls among trees; the lovely Hannelore (another Hannelore!) flushed and peeved, saying 'Shit! Shit!' between clenched teeth. Back to Munich by train with two ancient, leathery-faced, well-preserved mountain hikers, man and wife in deerstalker and *Loden*. A relief to be off the *Golfplatz*. Watch them tearing up the rough, cursing blind. It is a game unsuited to their temperament. Back in Munich again, Rory was passing *Oktoberfest* tents and stalls being erected.

Prone to a certain kind of spiritual narcosis with which the entire race is afflicted, and more so than most races, the Germans must *suffer* themselves. Your average Bavarian is a baleful mixture of sentimentalist and brute. Herr Martin Kruger (long absent) had his trouser legs shortened by a Herr von Bismarck, Munich tailor, who asked him on which side he wore his shame.

It sounded grosser in German. Intemperance, fist-fights, puking, in those lovely Ember Days. Stay clean. Tripper and Raptus were on the rampage. Dominguin had been badly gored at Bayonne; the *carneada* is always the fault of the *torero*. Nature abhors a vacuum. *Neu! Ajax mit der doppelbleiche.*

Chelpolizist Schreiber negotiated with a terrorist whose head was covered with a woman's stocking. Itchy-fingered *Sturm-kommandos* were dressed like frogmen in athletic tracksuits; they watched privily from their hiding places. *Omnipotenz, Super-Helden!*

The aneroid temperature registered somewhere between *ver-änderlichkeit* and *verstörung*, or something between distraction and bewilderment. The cover of *Der Stern* displayed a corn-yellow blonde in the act of peeling off a corn-yellow T-shirt, her only article of clothing; stamped most poshlustily on her backside were the joined circles of the Olympic symbol.

Clouds drift over the roofs of Munich; a blue evening falls. The ex-boxer points down into darkening Jakob-Klar-Strasse, amused by something he has seen below. There are moments when I am able to look without any effort through the whole of creation (*Schöpfung*), which is nothing more than an immense exhaustion (*Erschöpfung*), wrote stout Thomas Bernhardt. *Schicksal* all too soon becomes *Schnicksal*, in Germany at least.

Gusty *stürmisch* wind-tossed weather; then a warm sunny day in Munich. The face on the screen, on high hoardings, walks the streets, the violence is let loose. Hands were constantly feeling and touching, groping and tapping. Fingers parted the long hair of a troubled Jesus-double, touched noses, brows, the bearded lips rarely smiled, the looks exchanged were severe or merely sullen. Hands were never for one moment still, compulsively pulling and picking; plucking at the backs of leather seats, tearing paper, agitated, never still, the eyes restless as monkeys in the zoo.

In the capitals of the West the same feature films were released simultaneously: *Little Pig-Man* [*sic*], *My Name is Nobady* [*sic*]. *LIEBE* was sprayed indiscriminately over walls. *Amerika Haus* was riddled with bullets. The riot squads sat in paddy-wagons behind wire mesh and bulletproof glass, parked in back streets near universities, out of sight, played cards, bided their time. A judas grille opened and a baleful eye observed us. In the heated bar the tall lovely unsober teacher Barbara König was swallowing ice cubes, pulling faces, charming the pants off Rory.

Ach ach; tich-tich. We cannot stop even if we want to, have become voyeurs watching atrocious acts. The lies are without end because the hypotheses are without end. It has become suspect to 'think'; all adults occupy the thrilling realm of moral dilemmas (civic inertia), political drama; *Strassentheater*. Dangerous blindness with a dash of singularity. Angels, for the man who cannot avoid thinking about them, wrote the pessimist Cioran, certainly exist. *So sitzt es mir im Gemüt*.

On the large screens of colour TV sets in the windows of banks the Olympic Games went on, in silence, in triplicate. The high pole-vaulter in the briefest of shorts lifted herself on unseen springs, collapsing in slow motion on to a large bolster. The DDR female athletes were pouring over the 100-metre hurdles, elegant as bolting deer fleeing a forest fire. From the rapt, tormented expression of the long-legged high-jumper, one knew that track records were now being broken in the head. The athletes on the podium were crowned with bay, gave clench-fisted salutes as their national flag flew on the mast.

*   *   *

In West Berlin at midnight, in the small white flat of a pregnant Hannelore (the *real* Hannelore), the phone rang, the ringing tone muted. A hidden voice, a Basque voice (not a Berlin accent) whispered into her ear: *'Es wird noch kommen!'* It vill come . . . It still vill come. Out in the Olympic village the twenty-five hostages were still alive. The ultimatum was that one would be killed every two hours, beginning at 15 *Uhr* – 3 p.m. Central European Time.

On Kurfürstendamm, advertising an empty cinema, two enormous Sapphic heads regard each other steadfastly with frantic blue-tinged eyeballs across an illuminated movie façade. Something funny is going on between those two. On high hoardings opposite Marga Schoeller's bookshop, the braced bodies of huge nude females proclaim a stressful poshlust, *luxuriante.* A nude female crawls into a tent, hotly pursued by a nude male on all fours. Above the murderous traffic that runs all night, a cut-out of the slain actress Sharon Tate looks over her shoulder at the human clotting below, as into a temporary camp in a jungle clearing. Pigs! her murderers had scrawled on the Polanski door: Manson's tribe. Disordered thoughts, *Chaos oder Anarchie* in the here and now. Karl Kraus had defined German girls: 'Long legs, obedience'; not any more.

All strove for a dissipated appearance; many achieved it. Sunglasses were worn indoors, even in ill-lit bars in the depths of winter. Insane seers and mad putative leaders sprang up, were applauded, discussed, shot down, wiped from the scene. Graffiti abounded. The young revolutionaries sprayed aerosol everywhere. ANARKI ELLER KAOS!, as though the terms were not synonymous. The garbled message hardly varied. In the La Rouche district of Paris it ran: LIBEREZ HESS!

An underground disco pulses redly: the Mouth of Hell. The pace is set for hedonism, gluttony, the here and now. Frantic with betrayal, two inverts copulate near the Spree in the headlights of a parked car, in the falling snow. The woodcock, wily bird, is said to dress its own wounds. Partridges sleep with one eye open. The Chinese, more observant than most, maintain that the rat changes into a quail, the quail into an oriole. The female muskrat, as everybody knows, is the mother of the entire human race. That is, unless I am thinking of the Umquat's Sedna. Muskrats are barren when born in captivity; if they breed, they devour their young. A young Munich veterinario blamed stress induced by crowded conditions. Or, more likely, the fact of being under constant human observation.

In West Berlin (population 2.2 million) every second citizen is over forty years; more than twenty-five per cent are over sixty-five. Thirty-nine thousand die each year, with thirteen thousand more dying than are being born; every third citizen owns a dog.

Frau Meinhardt likes to curry-comb her two Airedales on the balcony, and curly orange hair floated into our morning coffee. She drove to Malta in a green Karmann Ghia, a nice change of air for the nervous bitches, mother Anya and whelp, a classical allusion. There was no shade in Malta; it was bad for the dogs.

She, the war widow, never referred to her late husband; the fine house in Nikolassee was all that remained of that lost life. The old heart of the city was dead – Unter den Linden. She owned a house in Wiesbaden, let out the Berlin property; demonstrated how to work the vacuum cleaner, a *Walküre* model, adding on tubular parts and a rigid snout. When devouring dirt, the bag swelled, set up a strident whine, began snarling, all snout and stomach. A true German machine.

Tall beauties paraded on Kurfürstendamm, displaying themselves in tight stone-washed jeans, which advertised a worn but not yet threadbare look; that was the fashion. Their manner implied: 'We belong to the streets'; and by analogy – false – 'The streets belong to us'. *Strassentheater.*

Freedom marches followed protest marches, the squatters occupying empty buildings. They were untouchable, in a way. They, too, were in the dream, living the dream. They occupied the streets, seemingly at home there, some living a hand-to-mouth existence, squatting before lines of trinkets, the twisted metalwork. Wearing sandals like gurus and holy men, or going about barefoot; footloose as Rastafarians, Reb stragglers from the American Civil War, fuzzy-wuzzies from Abyssinia, Tibetan monks with shaven polls. The females were even more lightly dressed, as though in perpetual summer ('*La naturale temperature des femmes*' whispers Amyot in a sly Gallic aside, '*est fort humide*'), their extremists more dangerous than the males. Baader-Meinhoff. In West Berlin the Black Cells, the Anarchists, went among the passive resisters like hyenas among zebra.

Insistence on the unique and particular had spawned the microbe Duplication. The face on the screen was in the street. The violence there was let loose here, in the open, the dream gone mad. They were actors and actresses playing bit parts in a continuing series. The face on the hoardings walked the streets. The Individual as such was disappearing, had disappeared; remained in a disordered milieu grown ever grubbier, more dangerous by the minute. The world's capitals had become *pissoirs*.

On the summer evenings, in Málaga and Athens, Copenhagen and Munich, long cinema queues waited to watch a violent surrogate existence run on huge screens, the sound monstrously distorted. 'To learn is to have something done to one.' But why bother about Bach if a saxophone riff gives you some idea of eternity? Their own life had ceased to interest them. Huge hoardings displayed a Red Indian brave naked from the waist up, advertising a brand of shampoo. Rock cellars throbbed, their lurid entrances leading down into an inflamed red throat, out of which screeched and bellowed the *Schlagermusik*. *Schlagermusik* in *Luftwaffe* slang was the staccato rip of machine-gun bullets tearing at the underbelly of a Lancaster or Wellington bomber bound for Berlin.

Hungarian camomile, asafoetida gum, aeroplane grease, cola nuts, Syrian rue, fly agaric, horsetail, skullcap, yohimbine, these were popular. In Absurdia the poor drank the urine of the rich to get their 'high'. Informed heads, *Tagräumer*, trippers, might tell of the so-called Jackson Illusion Pepper, with a hole bored at one end and a cigarette at the other end through which the entire contraption might be smoked to provide colourful and elaborate hallucinations.

Road hippies on endless round trips sold their blood to Kuwait; took overdoses, observed the 'way out' regions inhabited by the teeming poor of the miserable Third World. Lost ones blew their brains out. A huge organ was playing at noon in a department store heavy with controlled artificial air. Shoppers, passive as fish, stunned by pumped Muzak, ascend and descend by escalators. Overpriced commodities were sold by ingenious advertising campaigns in an all-out psychological war not on want but on plenty. Everything was oversold, overstated, over-heated; fraternity too had gone to Hell. The cities were splitting up from within, supermarts and car parks replacing cathedrals and concert halls. On fine summer evenings the long cinema queues waited silently in the north. To flee the world and dream the past was their intent; a sourceless craving now externalised, brought close. For them it would always be *Sperrmüll-Tag*: Throwing-Out Day. Say rather, Throwing-Up Day.

Alcoholic professors taught their own version of history. The students were apprehensive about leaving the campus. In the surrounding woods maniacs prowled all night, whistling. The young kept to their dormitories, debated much on their 'devel-opment', always making schemes. Schedules were drawn up, considered, amended, then abandoned. Believing that life goes in steps, exclusively concerned with drugs of one sort or another, hard politics, India–Buddha teachings, claptrap about 'freedom', their future was grim. But the protesters went marching anyway. They were lost in the dream. Their own parents belonged to an irrecoverable past.

On which side do you wear your shame?

Faina Melnik in athletic hotpants was displaying the Popo look, said to have been imported from Japan. The discus was thrown an unlikely distance by an unlikely-looking female. The huge Israeli weight-lifters were all dead, blown to kingdom come. The Games had gone on. The so-called Day of Mourning had been nothing less than hypocrisy; too much money was invested, too many interests involved; national honour had been at stake. The word had come down that the terrorists were not to leave German soil with their victims. The terrorists themselves had shown less hypocrisy; they were not interested in deals or (even) human life. The *Rheinischer Merkur* had its *Mordorgie*. 'Aroused Prussia' was a lard factory, a *mortadella* mincing machine.

RUSS MAY BEEF UP NAVY IN MED spoke out the *New York Herald Tribune*. BODIES OF SLAIN ATHLETES REACH LODZ, FLOWN

FROM MUNICH (America Speaking). Lodz Airport, soon to receive its own baptism of fire from Japanese kamikaze terrorists. *Falsche Spekulation der Luftpiraten!* Art, 'progress' (towards what?) comes from weaponry, hot from the kitchen. The arms of the footsoldiers, peasant conscripts, were no different in kind from their primitive work tools. Art and progress came with the finely decorated swords and pistols and tooled leatherware of their mounted officers. Horses for courses.

Der Bomber (Müller) scores again.

In the Neue Nationalgalerie in West Berlin hang two paintings commemorating the student uprising of 1968 in Paris: Renato Guttuso's *Studentenumzug mit Fahnen* and *Barrikaden in Paris*. To the sad cliché of the street barricade, the hero with flag unfurled, the brave corpses, must now be added the Faceless Male Terrorist in Female Bodystocking.

Leni Riefenstahl's extraordinary *Fest der Völker* was showing at the Arri (8 Woche). The XIth Olympiad at Berlin in 1936. In the old recruiting documentary, the plumes of smoke swirling densely black around the imperial eagle might have come from Hell itself. Wagner shows me a world that I'm not sure I would wish to enter.

Hermann Goering, the cocaine addict, grossly corpulent, was shaken with helpless laughter. Hitler, leaning forward, rubbed together his cold political hands. Hess, his putative son, all eye-socket and jaw of Teutonic Tollund Man watched Jesse Owens (assuredly no Aryan) run away with all the track events. A cinema full of war widows watched in an uncanny silence. You could hear a pin drop, the projector's whirr, the collective indrawn breath, suspense building for what would come next. What was one to make of the spider in the web, before the credits rolled, and the scalped athletes running stark naked around a Berlin lake, maybe Schlachtersee, through an early morning mist? No symbols where none intended.

Misha Gallé had been permitted an interview when Leni Riefenstahl, who was still a handsome woman, had learnt that Misha's father had been a Nazi judge. She told Misha Gallé that Herr Hitler had been a good man 'led astray by bad companions', The homosexual Röhm? The war widows, all dispersing silently from the Arri, had set their mouths in grim lines and, separating for *Kaffee und Kuchen*, baring their gums, were offering no comments.

Two months later a Lufthansa flight into Munich was hijacked and the three terrorists sprung from three high-security prisons sixty miles apart. Brandt had been obliged to do a deal, otherwise more terrorists were coming back. When interviewed, they chain-smoked, spoke in broken English and were reported to be of 'terrifying' niceness. They had the rugged good looks of Eddie Constantine and justified their actions at length. Deals had been struck; Brandt's hands were tied. Somewhere in the world ravishing girls eagerly awaited their safe return.

In February 1973, Abu Daoud, now passing himself off as a Saudi sheikh, was arrested in central Amman by a Jordanian security patrol. His 'wife' was a fifteen-year-old girl carrying a handgun and ammunition clips, which, on being arrested, she dropped. Abu Daoud's forged passport showed him to be the father of six children. His own father worked in Jerusalem as a labourer for the Israeli City Council.

On the last day of the XXth Olympiad, all the shops were closed and Rory walked through the Schwabing's deserted streets. It was a dead day. Misha Gallé played *Tischtennis* with Wolfgang. On the huge Olympic board the last farewells; AVERY BRANDAGE [*sick & stet*] for all the world to see. Twenty *Grad* of *Bodenfrost* on 28 September. *Das Ende der Saison*.

Meanwhile the super-rat, immune to all poisons, had arrived unannounced in Rio. Six dead. Abu Daoud, where are you now?

41

One Thrust and He Was In

O ne sunny late September or early October day in the fall not long after the *Mordfest*, Rory went walking in the Bavarian Alps with Karen Reece, who translated porno novels from German into English for the Munich branch of the Olympia Press. Erika had departed into Tuscany for a vacation and Rory had a notion to proposition her good friend Karen, a dark-haired beauty who lived in Schwabing not far away from Erika's flat where Rory stayed. Karen had helped him post off eighteen large packages for the University of Victoria in British Columbia: the drafts, notebooks and final typescripts of *Balcony of Europe*, a broken-backed novel he had been working on for eight years and which was now finished, awaiting cutting and editing by John Calder in London.

They had chilled beer in a *Bierstube* and walked up a logging trail, smoking joints and talking of this and that. It was a lovely warm sunny day in Bavaria and lines of tall fir trees blocked out every horizon.

'It's not fair,' Karen Reece said; we were smoking joints far up the logging trail. 'You talked all day. I never got one word in.'

It was the marijuana talking; it made Rory (normally taciturn) garrulous. One thing reminded him of another thing, and so on and so forth. She was a lovely lady, it was a lovely day in Bavaria; the swallows flew low.

Even before he had kissed her, Rory was consumed with jealousy of her former never-seen loves. They came down to a cove by a river in the cool of the evening and stopped in another *Bierstube* before driving back to Schwabing. With some little persuasion Rory was permitted to spend the night with Karen, who drove as recklessly as Erika, one arm out the window.

Later I heard from Erika that Karen had returned to the States, not to her husband, but to join some religious sect; that was the last I heard of her. She was the one who got away, the lost love, the silver trout that escapes the gaff.

Her apartment was also a replica of her friend's in Destouche-strasse, down to the furniture and fitments. Karen was very neat and collected; the only messy thing about her being the fact that she had married an American called Dick Reece and the marriage hadn't worked.

She retired to the bathroom to prepare herself for Rory and bed. On a cleared table stood a large manual office typewriter. In it a sheet of typing paper. She had stopped (to go out with Rory to the post office) working with one line neatly, barefacedly typed on the top line of an otherwise blank page. With eyes narrowed and heart thumping in his chest as though rummaging and examining the variety of her underwear in cupboard or closet, Rory read, aghast: 'One thrust and he was in.'

Rory sprang back as though stung by a bee as Karen emerged from the bathroom looking positively radiant in a silvery shivery robe. Rory, ever the perfect gent, asked permission to use the toilet.

'*Natürlich.*'

When Rory came out of the bathroom, the page was gone from the manual and Karen was in bed, still in her robe. Rory undressed himself and got into bed with her. Rory removed her robe and proceeded to fondle and kiss her.

But that, sad to say, was the end of his progress into uninhibited night-time Schwabing *Liebe* with a lovely and compliant youngish *Frau* with a thick dark bush and complementary herbiage in her armpits. For Rory couldn't make love for all the tea in China, cuckolded by a ghost who had slipped between the blue sheets and, before Rory could well bestir himself, the heavy gross intruder without even an '*Entschuldigung bitte!*' had pushed him aside and boldly mounted.

'If you can't, it doesn't matter . . . just lie by me,' she whispered. Karen Reece was most accommodating. One thrust . . . oh sting-a-ling of salt-lick pan! Oh *pachanga*! Oh peaches and cream! Oh, Lord Rochester!

Meanwhile, hidden amongst the books, the most torrid love-making or rather free-for-all fucking went on apace in the most boggish vernacular German imaginable, in the porno novel that Karen had discreetly put away along with the shameful almost blank last page, the page she had reached in her valiant efforts at translating grunts from German into vernacular English. Almost but not quite so; like a venomous smelly jet of spit from a yak, spat stingingly right into the eye of the beholder peering through the bars of the cage at the yaks grazing in their compound.

The unseen former lovers of Karen, a numerous company of accomplished lechers, were clustered around the bed, making most offensive remarks in guttural German concerning the upstart *Engländer* who couldn't get it up.

In the morning Rory tried again, with no better result. He resigned himself to being just a good *Freund*. That would have to do.

PART V:

Danish Blue

Copenhagen in the mid-1970s

42

On the Rørvig Ferry

Sunday evening
6 July 1975
Copenhagen

My dearest,
Copenhagen is very hot in this weeks. Steffen has taken
care of Petrushka all the weekend, I needed very much
to be alone, have been busy with idiotic things the last
weeks, everything at home was one Big Mess, not a clean
plate, nothing clean cloth. I've been in one of my eternal
recomming depression periods, when it is extra difficult
to pretend effectiv – I'm far-off, cannot get out of my
own figment imagination, the same themes turn and grow
and change but are still the same, a kaleidscope of inner
confusion. Now I am through the outside mess and have
used the rest of the weekend to try to make fair copy of
bewildered notes during the week and it became definitely
bad: a row of high flown inexact words, neither prose nor
poetry, without genuine sensations, a row of old fashioned
assertions which do not hit. I am very depressed. If I never
learn to write properly I cannot nothing in this world. I am
clever to nothing, nothing at all. It is all approats, giving up,
making dreams, useless dreams, hoping a little again . . .

I complain. I promised myself never to complain to you and especialy not about this matter. Now I have done. Now I have been a native woman thrown out of white man's tent because of bad manners.

In a way I remember you so well. Your brightness. Is anything called that? I can't stand to use the dictionary all the time. My only force is to make guess, hope they fit somebody, something. Thinking things over they disappear to me. Intellectual thing at least. They must come as a cut or they vanish as you say. You give me new words, too, I could fall in love in english. Sometimes I'm going to do. When I'm thinking over feelings they don't vanish. Oppersite, they crows. Because you don't think feelings, I guess. How can I live my life? Who is paying for dreams? Why do I need food? Why do I need things? (that damned things). Why do I not live on a greek island? Why is the world so sluggish a material? Down again:

Why can't I make it light?

I am ashame to complain. Will do it again and again. Tell me to shut up.

10/7: You say nothing about I Ching? Nonsense for you? (Old stuff hanging over Anna's head). Steffen always laugh when I absorbed (dictionary) of that kind of matter. But contempt me too, think it is a complicated and childish 'stage-setting' (dictionary) or rather depriving (dictionary) of an obvious reality, understandable for a child of five. Same Steffen get me to laugh so heartily and painfull (in danish: *hjertaligt og smerteligt*, a thorough-fucked-wordpair) the other day when he said; when you feel your thoughts to collect to complaint then beat your head into the wall. I'm beating my head into the wall now. Again. Oh I miss you. Again. Forgive me my love that I miss you so much. Just red your mad letter again, long parts without rest, I think I mean stop, pause, long breath, fading out and starting again, long breath from a love which wants to empty both body and mind. How can you write like that, how can you do it against us, how can you make me suffering that much? Sometimes I'm catched by a great anger to you, to demand, no to give the feeling of present but still you are not here, to prevent me to live here by keeping me there, I am longing and prevented, I am kept in imagination and must drown myself in home-made wine and over-excitement, sometimes I'm catched by a great anger to you. Then it disappears and I must laugh to myself.

[unsigned]

Rørvig

Petrushka and I go to Rørvig about every second weekend. First we take a normal inter-city train, then a little provincial train to Hundested (meaning Place of Dogs) (??) which is a little harbour town on the coast of northzeeland. To get out of the train in Hundested is every time a lovely surprise, the air is clear, the sea as always, the harbour modest.

Then we take a ferry, clumsy as a clog, to Rørvig. I always feel cruising among the Greek islands. Petrushka talks. She always does. In Rørvig my parents are waiting. They are glad to see me, I am glad to see them, Petrushka is very glad. The journey takes a little more than two hours.

We walk home (10 minutes) to the little summerhouse, about forty years old, dark trees, window-boxes even if we are in the middle of nature. ('Im Freien' lovely piano pieces by Bartók.) Rørvig is a Holiday center, lovely nature, victims little butter-hole, the innocence's last chanal to a little reality, a little plants, a little owner-feeling. Very much like my parents are, very well-selected. The beatch still has its wildness, is very beautiful and pure. I use the weekend to wash and iron, wash hair, talk with my parents, sleep, cut the grass for my father, go to the beatch with Petrushka on my father's old high bike (why bar on gentleman-bikes?), look at television in the evening, go for walks with Petrushka and drink a beer at the inn (which is placed by the main road). My parents would die by annoyance because of the extra money, one could drink that beer at home in the garden . . . well, they don't see the pleasure in a polished pub-glass and a perfect temperature of beer and the easiness of being in a public place out of the home, the sacrosant home. I talked very much with my parents, never lie to them, tell them 'everything' but edit my reality.

[unsigned]

44

The Ancient Moats

'Every day in Denmark is different' is a roundabout, not to say tortuous and evasive, way of admitting that one was once infatuated with an enchanting Danish siren.

Or, put another way, 'In the woman who overwhelms us there must be nothing familiar'; a *mot* wrested from a James Salter novel. (Giacomo Meyerbeer frantically attacking the piano keys while Franz Liszt looks helplessly on.)

International airport lounge waiting time, bad-air airborne time, agenbite-of-inwit time, nail-chewing time, doctor's surgery time, railway station time – none of these strange times can be said to be normal time as we know it, in the boredom of living, but time as torture, atrociously stretched to infinity, as if with chewing gum or potent industrial glue, a fixative to fix for good and all.

So too with infatuation time, the most intolerably stretched-out time of all, when you venture with a new inamorata into a new love, into strange terrain; which generally involves *more* airport-waiting, *more* waiting at railway stations and nail-biting and may even involve more of the doctor's surgery. Duration is prolonged and takes on a new keenness when one is subjected to this anxiety, this perplexity. First love, then the *Pharmacia*.

In August 1851 the hirsute gentleman farmer Herman Melville

in his newly acquired house (secured on a loan from his father-in-law) near Pittsfield in the Berkshire Hills of west Massachusetts had completed *Moby-Dick, or The Whale*, full of scattered last-minute revisions.

In London in the autumn of 1889 the thirty-one-year-old Joseph Conrad (born Konrad Korzeniowski in the Ukraine) lived in furnished rooms in Bessborough Gardens on the north bank of the Thames near Vauxhall Bridge, where he was putting together the component parts of his first novel, *Almayer's Folly*.

When the landlady's daughter had cleared away his breakfast things, Conrad noted in his diary the ever-changing colour of the sky over the Surrey docks, where Callus would later moor his canal barge. Conrad wrote:

> Opaline atmosphere, a veiled semi-opaque lustrous day, with fiery points of flashes of red sunlight on the roofs and windows opposite.

In Marseilles Conrad had become apprenticed to the Merchant Marine; had he strode up the gangplank of a French boat instead of an English vessel he might have written his novels in French, and English letters would have been the less for it. He certainly had no high opinion of *Moby-Dick* and declined to introduce a World's Classics edition. 'It struck me as a rather strained rhapsody with whaling for a subject and not a single sincere line in the three vols. of it,' he wrote testily to Sir Humphrey Milford.

Galsworthy of Conrad: 'The first mate is a Pole called Conrad and is a capital chap, though queer to look at.' Who was it described Conrad as 'a certain Pole with a wild look under the skin of his face'? Was it joker Joyce?

Conrad had a poor opinion of people, that was his way.

> I sit down for eight hours every day – and the sitting down is all. In the course of that working day I write three sentences which I erase before leaving the table in despair . . . In the morning I get up with the horror of that powerlessness I must face through a day of vain efforts.
>
> (from a letter to Edward Garnett)

'Words blow away like mist, and like mist they serve only to obscure; they make vague the real shape of one's feelings.'

Conrad must have thought this in Polish, if not French, written out as a precautionary adage to himself in English. Are not our feelings shapeless, sometimes shameless, uncontrollable, not ours at all? In Berlin in March 1930 Cyril Connolly wrote:

> In this stillness I wait for the first sound. In this blackness I wait for the first image – a cough, a motor-horn, the scratching of the dog's leash on the floor. Doors banging in another house, in another country, *Sète*. The dog fidgeting; the wind rising; the image forming. *Sète* at midnight on the way to Spain. The sleepy ride to a hotel near water. (*The Condemned Playground*) The Fascist Curzio Malaparte wrote in Italian The Volga Rises in Europe: another evening we dined by the water in Potsdam. A hot and beautiful night; we had a table by the trees on the edge of the lake . . . The candles lit up the polished table, the dark glow of port, the lighter one of brandy in our glasses. The night-air smelt of lake-water and of smoke from our cigars.

In a collection of essays published as *Myself With Others* (1988), the vain Carlos Fuentes wrote in Spanish:

> It was a hot, calm evening on Lake Zurich, and some wealthy Mexican friends had invited me to dinner at the eleagant Baur-au-Lac Hotel. The summer restaurant was a floating terrace on the lake. You reached it by a gangplank, and it was lighted by paper lanterns and flickering candles. As I unfolded my stiff white napkin amid the soothing tinkle of silver and glass, I raised my eyes and saw the group dining at the next table.

(Three ladies are seated with a man in his seventies whom Señor Fuentes recognises as Thomas Mann.)

> This man was stiff and elegantly dressed in a double-breasted white serge suit and immaculate shirt and tie. His

long, delicate fingers sliced a cold pheasant, almost with daintiness. Yet even in eating he seemed to me unbending, with a ramrod-back, military bearing . . .

I left Thomas Mann sipping his demitasse as midnight approached and the floating restaurant bobbed slightly and the Chinese lanterns quietly flickered out.

Well, in Denmark every day *is* different. You must take Anna's word for it; she was born in Copenhagen, married a Dane who wrote Dada-type short plays and she had a child by him. They lived in a coal-hole infested with rats some years before she met me.

She had changed her name from Olsen to Reiner when she began publishing poetry. When I knew her, she had a rented flat on Østersøgade overlooking what she called 'the ancient moats'. We were separated for four years and during that time she visited Greece.

During that time her sister had also committed suicide by throwing herself from a high place.

Anna ('my' Anne) was standing at the window of her apartment, a sort of attic on the third or topmost floor overlooking the artificial lake, no doubt thinking her own sad thoughts ('Mad of unhappiness') 'glaring out' (she wrote to me) at the ancient moats, as she had stood and looked ('glared') so many times before, at the scene she knew so well, when her sister was alive, that had now changed radically and become another scene in another time; or else something had changed within herself.

She had seen all there was to be seen, when the clouds parted and a sudden spurt of sunlight poured down on a golden church dome which she had never seen before. She was trying not to think of her sister's hard end, how she had flung herself from a high place down to a sudden and terrible death. Most terrible for those who had to clean up. Anna had come 'like a thief in the night' to her parents with the news that she had to break as gently as possible. Her sister had been a Pisces.

I had flown from Seattle to Heathrow where there was an eight-hour delay before the flight to Kastrup, and from there I had taken a taxi to Østersøgade, and found her apartment empty. I entered an empty flat below and looked at some of the notebooks and it wasn't her handwriting; her apartment was the dark attic at the top of the house. When you were in it, it was all windows with a view of the Østersøgade. Her landlady, Mrs Andersen, was half mad, certainly unhinged, and wholly uncooperative.

I kept walking about the streets leading to your flat; at ten o'clock I phoned your number and you answered at once. You had just come back from Helsingør, where Hamlet had chased about after the ghost of his murdered father. I booked out of the hotel and took a taxi around and you were waiting at the door.

45

But Why Kandinsky?

Kandinsky told me that his grandfather had come trotting into Russia on a small steed studded with bells, from one of those enchanted Asian mountains made of porcelain.

Jean Arp, *Kandinsky the Poet* (1912)

People in their local costumes moved about like pictures come to life: their houses were decorated with colourful carvings, and inside on the walls were hung popular prints and icons; furniture and other household objects were painted with large ornamental designs that almost dissolved them into colour. Kandinsky had the impression of moving about inside one of his own pictures.

Will Grohman

As the snail carries its house on its back, so Wassily Kandinsky carried Russia about with him in his heart. By 1909 he had abandoned his legal career in Russia to move to Germany where he lived with the painter Gabriele Münter in a house known as Russenvilla in Murnau. He did not become an art student until he was thirty.

When Kandinsky had left Russia and was living in Germany, looking back he must have seen his lost land as a picture or series of pictures composed and coloured by his own hand; his paintings of Russia, his memories of Russia and he himself a part of the painting, trapped in the paintings. His work shows you that Russia of his childhood in the time of the tsars just before the Revolution; and that dead Russia springs to life again, in the same way that you can hear distinctly an earlier Russia of circus tunes and carnival music and fairground sounds in the work of Stravinsky, in *Firebird* and *Petrushka*, even in simple piano compositions.

You can hear that Russia if you cease thinking of Stravinsky as the experimental modernist of Paris who worked with Nijinsky and Tamara Karsavina for the impresario Diaghilev and composed *Le sacré du printemps* which caused a riot that was the making of Stravinsky. But he was a Russian composer dealing with that folklore before he was anything else. Kandinsky was a superb colourist, as was Paul Klee.

The colours were bleached out in mist and fog. Above the path on the steep slope of the hill among the small olive trees, some animal was struggling in its death throes. It cried out; a sudden screech of terror and then a whole series of gurgles becoming fainter as the predator dug in, dispatching it. It was Monday, 21 April 1980 and 9.30 p.m. in Cómpeta, two thousand kilometres up in the foothills of the sierras. It seemed to be the killing time.

We rose at nine in the evening, having spent the day in bed 'solacing our existence', as Stendhal has it, and sallied out into a clinging mist that had swallowed up the pueblo.

If it was a scene from a French movie, then she was the Danish actress Anna Karina who appears in the inexplicable and dull movies of Godard; or, better still, Elsa Martinelli dressed in black poncho, brown cords, Hungarian riding-britches, pink cheese-cloth shirt with wide leather Russian-style belt, a black high-neck pullover, boots, hair worn long, glistening with mist. I carried a walking stick *and* an umbrella. She (Anna, Nina, Elsa or whatever you care to call her) cried out with delight at the turn of the path by the forge beyond the *cementerio*: 'Uuuuuh, it's a French movie!'

The village had vanished; we were the lost lovers in one of those mysteriously inconclusive French movies by Claude Autant-Lara that seem to lead nowhere.

Well, all women are actresses at heart; I know that, as all men who have mothers know that. Not all women can be Helen, though all women hold Helen in their hearts.

*   *   *

When we walked arm in arm through the Tivoli Gardens late one day in winter, the place was almost deserted. She wore a flannel jacket to the hips and a dashing matelot hat in matching flannel, the clobber which Albertine might have favoured in Danciers. She had strong coarse hands which became delicate when she took something up, a pen or knife or paper or a fruit, as a surgeon's strong hands in protective gloves become delicate when performing some operation successfully. For me she represented the past, a living emanation of that European past, come from the old part of Copenhagen.

We walked through the clinging mist to the Biscuit King's place, the Villa de Chino, to dine there, but found it locked up; and so back down the avenue on to the lower road and past the bus terminus, tall as giraffe or elephant house in the Berlin Zoo, and up the ramp by the concave mirror to help ascending traffic into the plaza and up another ramp and into the Bar el Montes and so to the back room where a long table was set out for the Alcalde's party.

A couple of women with heads close together were gossiping and sipping Schweppes tonic at a table in the window embrasure, which we moved to when they had paid and left. When we sat down we were subjected to a series of hard inquisitive stares from the Alcalde, a bulky man among chatty womenfolk; the hard stares from the Alcalde becoming more persistent, as though he couldn't believe his eyes. Two bananas were brought to us on plates and our order taken; whereupon we patiently waited for more than an hour sipping white wine before the food appeared, two cheese omelettes with fries.

It was raining outside, umbrellas passed by the window going towards the *paseo*; we heard the rain pattering on the plaza. We drank not very good white wine, unchilled, and I was as happy there as ever I could be anywhere, stared at by the Alcalde, subjected to that implacable regard whilst listening to your voice telling me what you wished to say. You told me about your small walk-up apartment in Copenhagen on Østersøgade, the lake that was seventeen feet deep in the middle, and of your unhinged landlady Mrs Andersen. You told of a Russian icon with a bullet hole in it and parts missing, torn from a well during the Russian Revolution; and of a pewter candlestick and a Chinese scroll. You didn't travel about Copenhagen by bus, because of the stinks of the commuters in damp clothes; instead you cycled about on your old trusty bike.

Anna's ex-brother-in-law, the homosexual sea captain, has a flower shop in Copenhagen, where his friends come for beer and arguments. Anna can hold her own there. The apartments of Copenhagen gays are always full of flowers. The sea captain throws out roses just past their prime.

She pleads, 'For Hell, do not!' She takes thirty roses on her antiquated bike, cycles to Østersøgade, barely visible behind the bank of sweet-smelling roses.

She spoke a sort of archaic Tudor English with Teutonic roots that evoked valour and escutcheons and banners flying and the neighing of frightened horses in the hairy olden times; and this was so charming to my ears that I never bothered to correct her. She said: 'The cold of hot countries is absolutely poignant.'

She said: 'I never played little girls' games when I was young and that is my unfortune.'

Unfortune!

She said: 'I talk in showers and then I am sad.'

She said: 'The sounds of the south are louder than those of the north.'

She said: 'The Danish forests are so lovely – they are so leetil compared to real forests. Uuuls aff karse. [Owls of course.] All these are leaf-tree forests of a good standard; they are most beautiful, I think. Most *bee*autiful! The Danish forests are full of flowers and birds and underwood [undergrowth] that in the springtime are nothing less than a pure *dreeem*.'

She said: 'You only have to look at nature to see how amazing nature is. Nature lies under God's protection and the Devil has no power there' (quoting the suicide Swede Edith Sodergram).

'Hell is the Devil's Paradise,' I said, quoting Tomi Ungerer.

46

Borges and I

Borges as a boy in Buenos Aires spent a great deal of time indoors. Little Jorge Luis and his sister Norah invented two imaginary companions, the Windmill and Quilos. 'When they finally bored us, we told our mother they had died.'

One of my own mother's many sisters had lived for most of her life in Buenos Aires, where she and her husband brought up a family. Was that Aunt Ida or Aunt Ada? Rory was unfamiliar with his many relations.

Borges's blindness began to come upon him by 1927, the year I was born, following no fewer than eight eye operations.

One rainy morning in June 1930 Borges met Adolfo Bioy Casares. Between them they invented an imaginary third man Honorio Bustos Domecq who emerged and 'was to take over and rule with a rod of iron'. Between them they created the comic detective saga, *Six Problems for Don Isidro Parodi*.

Borges thought that Copenhagen was among the most unforgettable cities he had seen (with his defective eyesight), along with Santiago de Compestela, Geneva and Edinburgh. Berlin he thought ugly, the ugliest city on earth. He was pro-English, with Northumberland blood on his grandmother's side.

Jorge Guillermo Borges, father of the author, was philosophical anarchist, lawyer, teacher of psychology in the School for

Modern Languages. He gave his courses in English and wrote a novel, *The Caudillo*, published in Majorca in 1921, since lost.

> One night in Salto, Uruguay, with Enrique Amorim, for lack of anything better to do, we went around to the local slaughter-house to watch the cattle being killed. Squatting on the threshold of the long low adobe building was a battered and almost lifeless old man. Amorim asked him, 'Are they killing?' The old man appeared to come to a brief and evil awakening, and answered back in a fierce whisper. 'Yes, they're killing! They're killing!'
>   (J.L. Borges, *Commentary on the Man on the Threshold*, translated from the Spanish by Anthony Kerrigan)

In late May or early June, the swifts return to Kinsale to reoccupy their old nesting places in the eaves opposite the Stony Steps. Clinging with their primitive feet, they launch themselves out and away, hurtling over the rooftops; their screeching announces the arrival of summer; they are the last to come and the first to go.

Swifts are continually on the wing from the moment they leave the nest. In a lifetime of eighteen years they fly four million miles, to the moon and back eight times. They consume twenty thousand insects daily, travel six thousand miles on their migratory courses. The young are much pestered by blood-sucking woodlice in the nest.

Between Alannah and me, joined in matrimony in a Dublin register office in November 1997, there is a yawning gap of twenty-three years. Twenty-four years separated Dostoevsky and Ann Smitkina, twenty-five years separated King James II and his consort, Mary of Modena.

The years pass, flit by; the giddy lad becomes the staid old codger; the nipper has become the very old guy; and both are Rory. But there again, who has not sometimes felt a stranger to themselves?

Henry David Thoreau wrote over two million words in his lifetime, at the rate of ten to fifteen thousand per day. Working fourteen hours a day he completed the thirty-six volumes that were to make up the greatest treatise on natural history ever written; to die at the age of forty-four.

W.B. Yeats at the age of seventy-one wrote to Lady Dorothy Wellesley on 8 November 1936: 'Over my dressing table is a mirror in a slanting light where every morning I discover how old I am. Oh my dear, oh my dear.'

Borges, aged seventy-one, wrote: 'I have even secretly longed to write, under a pen name, a merciless tirade against myself.

'Since our only proof of personal death is statistical, and inasmuch as a new generation of deathless men may be already on the way, I have for years lived in fear of never dying.'

Nevertheless he died of cancer of the liver on 14 June 1986 in Geneva and is buried there under a fine tombstone honouring this gallant Argentinian sceptic, blind as Milton and James Joyce before him, in the rotogravure of time passing, taking all of us away with it.

47

In a Swedish Forest

In Aurelio's dim bar female hands appear at the small serving hatch, extending little plates of *tapes*, *lomo* and *cerdo* cut into cubes and chewy pulpo.

An inflamed sun is going down in the Costa del Sol advertisement, back-lighting the sultry bright face at the end of the long brown neck above a pair of sun-kissed pumpkins fairly bursting from the sea-drenched cotton shirt pulled open to the navel. A very outsplashed lady indeed is Annelise Lundesgaard, the Danish wet dream who adorns this come-on, catch-as-catch-can advertisement.

It was the year when undressed Scandinavian photomodels began to catch on as calendar girls in the dimly lit hill bars, a year after the demise of the prudish or maybe prudent Generalissimo who had once been Señorita Islas Canarias; it was part of the opening up of Spain to the delights of democratic capitalism that would have made Franco pop-eyed, an eyeful of the ripe charms of Annelise Lundesgaard, who they said was yours for the day if you bought whatever it was they were promoting.

Girlie nudist magazines printed in Madrid were passed surreptitiously from hand to hand by pale-faced barmen drained by long hours and self-abuse in Málaga bars near the Alcazaba where the gays went cruising and on San Bou in Menorca an authentic nudist beach was opened in the Catalan stronghold. Viewed with disfavour by the Caudillo, it was taxed accordingly.

My own *potencia* had begun to slip away from me, a leaky old vessel slipping its moorings and drifting out to sea. Hair sprouting in ears and nostrils, withering away from hypogastric regions; sight, hearing and appetite going, insomnia coming on, backaches and various internal disorders, all too clearly announced the outward drift, the downward plunge.

Musil interpreted the waning of the libido as the absence of the will to live; a very Austrian notion, to be sure, for are we not all bound for Deathsville? Heidegger's arduous path of appearances had never looked so arduous.

Anna says: 'The Danes have used up their dreams of power. All Scandinavians believe aff karse [sic] in a well-run world. Not I. The very mean things are just as fine as the finer things. You can love a thing so much that you don't want to disturb it,' referring to *boccoroni*, the little minnows or sprats that had come browned and sizzling off the pan as *tapas*.

From the serving-hatch of the dark kitchen the hands reach out holding the plate imploringly.

The local strumpets have short stumpy legs and the wide hips and big bums of born breeders, with the oval features of Eskimos whom now we must call Innuit or some such name. The Scandinavian calendar girls are their physical opposites, with long legs, sultry expressions, narrow stomachs supporting upthrust bust with nipples already erect, the lips moistful. From the serving-hatch of the dark kitchen the hands reach out. 'I am not yet ready for a middle-aged love,' Anna says, moistfully.

We were in the back room with a wood fire throwing out good heat and the chimneypots vibrating, shaken by the wind blowing down over the high escarpment.

'Uuuuh! The fire has fallen down into the gloams.'

The gloams!

'It's a difficult to think in a forest, the walls of trees keep out the sun. In a Swedish forest there is absolute silence, no singing birds there, even the uuls [owls] are silent. Can you just imagine? Uuuuh, that was a miss for me!

'This was a pine forest, very dark and very heavy, I don't like the Swedish forest much. The Swedish villages were all empty, because all the Swedes were away working, the men and the women. They were working very hard, very industriously, and then driving home very fast in their Volvos. They return in the evening and close their doors and that's it for the day for the Swedes. They don't come out again until the next morning.

'The main tree in the Swedish forest is pine; oak and beech forests would have a different feeling. It's very still there, very quiet. Aff karse you are thinking in a forest but a thought never finds its way to the end, as in the mountains or at the sea, and the silence there is really heavy. The Swedish forest is like a Shakespearian forest, no dead leaves but mossy underfoot, I was walking miserably there.

'Once I came upon an *elg* [elk], a cow, we glared at each other silently and not moving, with only the distance of a bedroom between us. It was a kind of opal grey, like the mountain flower you get here. Then it melted away into the forest without a sound.' She fixed me with her unblinking lynx eyes.

Her favourite colour was lilac, this was the colour of the wood that had frightened Petrushka in Rørvig near her parents' summer place; it was found also in the 'underwood' of Swedish forests. The 'Greekish' islands too had this colour in the evening; Anna loved the lilac Greekish evenings.

There were days when she could be awkward and broke things. She could be tender and she could be fierce. One day she broke, by accident, the blue-and-white eggcup I had found in Málaga, the last of a set. She had left it on the terrace edge and the wind had caught the vines and a branch had swept it over, to be smashed at my feet in the patio below.

'Uuuuuh, not my fault.'

I said nothing, collecting the bits.

'Called you out?'

'Silent as the tomb,' I said.

'Oh.'

In bed that morning after coffee she had threatened to hit me in the face. 'I would like to,' she had admitted, growling in her throat, stretching her strong jaw muscles, narrowing her lynx eyes; lifting her fist as if it held an axe. I saw the gleam of sweat in her axillary hair, and the threat in her green eye.

Sometimes she had a crazy look, had become the dark-complexioned moll of some København dockside hood, the tough face on the expired passport photo taken in her wild non-taxpaying youth before she had taken up with Karr and lived in the coal-hole. Her hands were not soft; she was a big strong Viking woman, most fierce. I held her arm. 'It's not so cold now. Let me just have a sniff on the rouff.' She tore herself free.

48

My Everyday

*The dreams of the night throw long
shadows in the late morning.*

The watch calls half-past seven. Every morning I try not
to fall asleep again but use the time between half-past
seven and eight to get the habit of life again. But
often I'm very tired and fall asleep again anyway and wake up,
confused, five minutes to eight. Petrushka is able to do nearly
anything herself, brush teeth, dress herself (surprising clothes
together, and so much clothes . . . lots of clothes, taken off
again later in the day, brought home from the kindergarten
by me in a big paper bag). We have not really breakfast, none
of us can eat in the morning. I paint my face, arrange myself,
adapt myself so I'm half eat-able for myself and the surroundings.
Without make-up I'm very rough, wild. I feel my own face more
well-known with make-up than naked. In the moderated version
there comes a tenderness which I also have. Indeed.

Then we drive, Petrushka behind on my cycle. When we are
in good time we stop at a certain baker and buy two yogurt, just
across Rosenberg Slot, we have a bench where we eat breakfast.
People pass by, not many, and cars pass by (more) and maybe
think that we don't belong to the slaves of time, but we do
anyway.

Then Petrushka wants me to tell about Rosenberg Slot which
is built by King Christian the Fourth in sixteenhundredsomewhat

(renaissance Castle). He was in love with a hard and beautiful woman called Kirstine Munk, who let him down in his oldness, riding around with a guardsman instead and let the king die alone with dropsy in his legs. Petrushka doesn't mind me telling the same story, but I move longer and longer from the facts which are so unsure anyway. Beside that she will come to school once and have her learning made correct there.

Then I arrive a little too late at my work and drink coffee. The dreams of the night throw long shadows in the late morning. I do not quite awake until later. The post and the nervousity of the day arrive, a dubble nervousity, a real terror for having done – or not done – something irreparable (I neither own general view nor memory, there is lacks in my scratched intelligence) and another kind of nervousity, a secret excitement, an expectation which selden have name and face (but have it now) and which is laying, trembling under everything. The most of my days goes with hiding or re-establish that I'm never quite attentive, not even when I really try, that I always in one way or another are thinking of something else. When I'm working on my own things, other kind of horrors come in, doubt, hopelessness, incapability but never inattention. When I was with you I could sometimes be melancholy but never nervous, there was never this gulf between acting and thinking or what I did and what I ought to do.

I'm the best looking girl here, or rather maybe, that girl with most effect. (About my beauty you are talking: I know of course that I *look* like a beautifull girl, that I *seem* to be clever, but I know too, that . . . well). Because I look like a beautifull girl there is attention around me. That I enjoy in all its craching schizophrenia.

Eleven o'clock I'm mad by thirst and buy a light beer (without alcohol), a buying everybody percieve correct as beginning of alcoholism, still ashamed to be what it is. I'm moving very fast, forget my purse in the canteen and things like that. Half past twelve I eat lunch, sometimes alone at my office if the persons in the canteen look too dull but mostly I stay trying to charm my superior to doubt that I'm so incapable they all the time are just going to discover.

Between four and five o'clock I take my bike and go for

Petrushka in kindergarten. Often we are both rather tired and rather hungry and sit down on a bench on 'Stroget' (the main walking street in Copenhagen) eating ice cream instead of making important buyings or we go to Steffen's terasse and let an hour crumble away. Everything are closing at half past five sharp. Only seldom I'm in time to what I ought, only I am behind in tax, toilet paper, dishing etc. When we are at home about 6 o'clock I make tea, doing house-things, making food. Half past seven we eat, mostly very simple; potatos, salat, sometimes bacon, milk for Petrushka, wine for me (I make the wine myself). In this weeks we are eating strawberry, lots of them, they are expensive but we love them. (Strawberry, oesters and an irish poet and I shouldn't complaint.)

After dinner I make Café con Leche, still missing the goat milk and the 103. In between these things I write to you or myself, it's the same, but Petrushka hates that. She wants to talk. Much banal chattering with surprises in between.

Yesterday she told me that angels had halos in order to find their way in the nighttimes when they are flying in the heavens. Also she told me newly: My mother is dangerous like a crocodile! At nine o'clock a long bed ritual starts, she doesn't sleep before about ten o'clock, had never belonged to the much-sleeping children.

Then I am myself with a daylong need for *wasting the time*. I have a very big need for wasting time. I sit down on my bed, neither read nor write. I'm looking out in the air and dream. The pictures, the situations are pouring in, mostly very banal, difficult to use to anything. I hardly can stop. Late, at 11 o'clock when I ought to be in bed, I'm free and laughing at the pattern I've been running in all the day and which necessarity cannot break only fulfill or not fulfill. In these hours I'm happy, filled with optimism, trustfull and believing in long chains of days of this color. Then I feel young again, that I'm just on the start of all of it, that I in the next moment 'around the next corner will be able to fly'.

That's me, my love. What do you say? – I laugh – No matter what even you (the most precious thing I have in these times) say: the things are like they are. No more than that.

[unsigned]

8 July 1975

For some weeks I cycled a detour while I was on my way to work. Not by the fifth watery quadrilateral, a pond in a park, our bench of the mornings between two churches. Then the old church Vartorv, then the Kanal, Amager Boulevard, the bridge over Stydhavn, cycling close to the water by the flowering chestnut trees, to Islands Brygge quayside. In fact I hadn't time, would be late and was it, but I was a little happy, didn't know why. The way I choosed is ugly: a dusty bypass way a little outside the centre of the town (Artillivej) with little dying factories, football-grass, workships, hutments from the time of war and allotments, insane in their care for flagstaffs and geraniums. The way end in a Clondyke.

Suddenly a miraculous stream of scent come to meet me and up from a high hoarding I saw roses, faint-pink roses, lots of kilograms roses, thirty metres roses hanging climing . . . scented released roses. I felt blessed and plucked three of them and put them in a beer glass on my desk. 10 o'clock a letter arrived, a letter from you, the mad letter, the letter which is one breath.

Since I haven't had time to bike that way, have put it off, thinking of it but not touching it. This day, this morning I turned, without knowing it, to the left and suddenly I was on that road again. The roses scented still more strong than before, many were died, the last ones overbearing. Carefully I took three again, put them in the glass. They scent scent scent and a half time ago your letter arrived, even my instincts you have given back to me.

Sometimes I have that feeling that we are writing or thinking the same things in the same days, that we are in the same moods in the same periods, a lovestory conducted not in fake-german but by somebody else. I feel how the transport of the letters brings a artificial shifting in a congruence (?) which is present. A letter arrived. A answer to my unmailed letter.

[unsigned]

49

On the Beatch with Petrushka

My ambitions groan.

Petrushka is naked, I've very little black bathing drawers, my 12 years old nephew's. I had forgotten bathing suit in Copenhagen, he has forgotten these in Rørvig. I adapt myself to the sand, preparing meeting you. You come slowly with little floating standstill in between. I don't go far into it, people around, Petrushka around, but it is difficult to stop. And difficult to go on to the absolute end. ('We didn't make love enough, far from . . .' didn't refer to something numerically but to the abandonment, the courage.) Petrushka is running around, they fits so beautiful, the sea and her. I try to keep the picture, not making any thinking around it. She is collecting shells in an empty Nescafé glass. She meets a boy. You know how children meet each other and stop, to the extreme watchful, super-animals, sniff with all the senses. Then Petrushka with an abrupt move casts all the shells at his feet and goes away. Sometimes I'm wondering myself, that Petrushka in one hand gives me so much but in the other I could leave her tomorrow, calm, if I knew she was growing well without me.

I went for a walk, alone, went on a narrow high levelled path through sand mountains with pines, brooms and wild roses. I was tempty to go down into the green valley but went on at the narrow path in assurance that something fantastic must be found by the end of it. I went carefully, I'm so clumsy, hidden tree roots under the sand (take care not to dream so you fall, take care not to fall so you must stop dreaming). The air was mild with cold streams plaited in, the bees was humsing; following the less resistance (can I assert that? Like that appeared to me). I felt awake and happy. – And yet I was disturbed by something, somewhat punctured the lovely picture, an unrest which didn't come from myself, and when I came to the end of the road I saw what it was: It was the limitation.

Nearly all over in Denmark you feel the houses with people just beside you, the houses are waiting just around the corner, voices turn up, you don't know from where and when and how many; but you know that only a limit area is preserved, only a quiet limit area have somebody in the city at a meeting decided to preserve – when innocence confuse with an unbroken hymen the point is lost.

I am glad friday evening when I arrive and glad sunday evening when I leave. Rørvig is a lovely place. Exploited, yes, summerhouses close together, but there is still a kind of innocence, a fragile middle-class innocence, open to rape I'm afraid. A holiday-center. A place without necessity, without power of resistance. A hobby. Like my father, so kind in his stupidity and like my mother, so clever in her presentiments and so stupid in her fear, her denying. I love my parents, have tenderness for them. They are innocent.

My Rory – these are lines from the beginning of the sinfonie.

Never more I want to hear who you are fucking at the Third River with the deep smooth vessel. There are so many places in the world – why the Third River? I fling my sorrow back: Your amulet didn't break or turned into a blaze. I took it off. You are trembling by the thought of Coppera with him you call Wittgenstein? I understand that. Poor poor everybody to whom this happen. Was Coppera trembling when you left her?

Sorry you didn't like the pictures. I'm not surprised, they were postcards. An impossible situation with the pictures, so much trouble already, promiscuity in an odd way to hunt love-signs of yourself. Yes, the dark pictures are from the bleu heur at Steffen's terasso. I don't send the naked one.

Strange so often you mention Knud Andersen, your instincts are sure, you remind of him, the same limpid selfishness without any wickedness. He was blond with blue eyes, you are dark with green eyes, it gives the differens.

Your letter scared me. I know that it will scare me lesser in a couple of days when I've red it more times. But I know too, that the sight of you and the dream I dreamt after will be lying, always attentive, in the back of my head. However there is nothing to complaint, I knew it, had expected it, wondering who it came, I saw it in the very second in Pepinos bar. I saw in your eyes that point where longing and fear are meeting each other. Have a meeting.

Strange passionate over-used words. My scribbling is the same for the moment, I have no other words in this weeks, I look at my 'poems' and I'm paralysed by their impossibleness, ridiculousness. 'When they come back often enough they become careless.' You say yes. Like that it is. I presume. I don't know it, never reach that distance, am like a child, in it or out of it, burning or forgetting, absorbed or not caring. My ambitions groan. Oh yes. That also why I lived so well with you: I had no language to force you into my problems. I became only body and soul with you, no spirit. The difference between soul and spirit. 'Old stuff hanging over Anna's head.' I love you. I fear you.

[unsigned].

PS About Wrong placed longings. You say: 'they are not wrong placed for I have them for you too.'

Sweet Rory, a touching misunderstanding. That was exactly what I ment: we have towards each other, and that is maybe the mistake itself. I discovered once that the romantic way of thinking ('to long for each other') started exactly when the religious way of thinking stopped. And therefore maybe all this love feelings among modern feelings are misplaced (religious) feelings . . . do you not understand? How can you hear difference between floating (air) and flowzing (water)???

You can! I just invented a 'z'. but how do you choose?

According to the dictionary, which I love and hate, it is the same. English is to me a very Floating-flowing language. A bee hums and a humsing man does the same (when he sings silently). A nice word-game is lost by taking the consequence immediately and call it the same. Well, english is not floating here – I better stop criticise your language!

[unsigned]

Linguistics

G orm the Old begat Harold Blue-Tooth who begat
Sven Forkbeard who in turn begat Estre who begat
Henning Mortensen who begat – Hold it right there!
Is this by any chance *our* Henning of Calle Laberinto who makes
lethal grog?

'The very man.'

Wisdom of Henning Mortensen:

'We have to make sense out of the pine. Live with the pine,
make a circle of our life.'

'What's this pine, Henning?'

'The pine of living.'

He tells me a story about Jesus who somehow survived
Golgotha and Calvary and fled the Holy Land, settled elsewhere,
married and had a large family, lived to be 108.

He recites

> *Should old acquaintance be forgot*
> *and never brought to mind . . .*

and translates it into Jutlandic, which closely resembles Middle
English and its sounds and rhythms, and the words too.

Anna says that English is a language of the head, a language
without any kind of metaphysical overtones or undertones, a

language from the neck up. 'English novelists are kind old aunts, innocent watchers, unconcerned bystanders, kind people who would never do you any harm, never hurl an insult. And that's the bad side of them, as novelists. They understand in a certain way nothing; a very tolerant people. I like them but I could never trust them.'

Graham Greene, a man of mystery, says the *Listener*, for Hell! Anna insists: 'Graham Greene is not in the *least* mysterious. He's just another old auntie, like William Golding and E.M. Forster and all the other aunties before them, back to Samuel Butler and Edmund Gosse and George Gissing, all the same ilk, all old aunties.

'When the life shrinks, the language must shrink too; one would be tempted to think that, since the available options are few and getting fewer, that it must be so.'

'Trousers' is a very rapid and almost coquettish way of describing this awkward garment. Many of the English sounds have no distinct masculine or feminine roots, as you get in Spanish or French, and might refer either to a man or a woman; no great distinction can be made.

'I heard Gertrude Stein's recorded voice,' said Anna, 'reading some of her stuff. A very clear head-language, I thought. I didn't understand much of what she was saying but there was a bit of smoke and whiskey in the tone of voice that was pleasing. This I suppose is typical old-fashioned high-level speaking. It is one of the most beautiful languages you can get into.

'In German you get the rough stuff, the naked women mud-wrestling. *Lederhosen* really has a filthy sound, a diaphragm tongue for giving orders, *issuing* orders. German is a language of the stomach, a fat language, *svulstig*, as when you have too much fat around the heart.

'Now if English is a language of the head and German a language of the stomach, what is French? French is almost all movement, you might say it's spoken by the hands and arms, all that shrugging they go in for; a very performance language. It is very pleasing to build up the French sounds.

'But wait. Danish more than German is perhaps a true *language of the stomach* – *mauve* is very much a stomach sound. We are after all a nation of farmers and fishers; and Germany has long had its eye on the little Danish butter-ball.'

Anna wrote a fine slapdash cursive dashed off at speed, an unusual mixture of straight lines and cursive, the upstrokes matching the downstrokes. She wrote quickly, always legibly, the letters of her signature squeezed together more than the rest, as though she were hugging herself.

'Uuuh you make me lude! I always seem to have your preek in my mouth when we are in the mountains.'

('It melted away into the forest without a sound.')

It: the elusive elk in the forest that had stared at Anna. She said: 'In Denmark normally they are eating every three hours. My mother is just washing up from the lunch when my father is already boiling water for the teatime.'

Her parents, the Olsens, were small-sized and frugal. This Danish frugality made their daughter into a reckless spendthrift. Her background was Hungarian–Prussian–Pomeranian, an alarming combination. Günter Grass had a Pomeranian granny. Pomerania was somewhere beyond Poland, immensely old, older than Russia, possibly wilder, even rougher. Anna's Pomeranian granny, whom she probably took after, had been tall and austere, a maker of good soups, vegetable soups, nipping off the ends of beans. Anna's mother's maiden name had been Lemm, which means prick, the male member. Once at Christimo's crowded bar she had hissed: 'Unless we leave at wance, I'll lick all the preeks in this bar!'

In the Cómpeta shops she found herself standing amid the tiny and talkative hill-women whom she called the Waggada Waggadas. They had fallen silent when she, the Danish giantess, entered towering over them, to watch her ordering in dumb show, laughing and pointing. She felt herself to be gigantic. But she never held their diminutive size against them: 'The leetle people cannot do anything enormous and ugly.'

She says, 'Beethoven couldn't stand the piano.' When he was dying he reached under his bed, took out the chamber-pot, drank off the contents, saying, '*Zu spät! Zu spät!*' Too late, too late. At his last gasp, Beethoven was a card. It was said of him that nature couldn't have taken another Beethoven; it would have been excessive and intolerable, as two Niagara Falls, or a couple of Grand Canyons.

She said: 'There's never a heavy moment with Mr Mozart.' Sibelius was greedy for the dirty stuff, always stepping into whorehouses. He was an enormous male chauvinist pig. 'I very much like his Violin Concerto – regarded by violinists as the most difficult you could be put into.'

She says that Schubert's *Death and the Maiden* has nothing to do with either death nor any maiden known to Franz Schubert; the title was tagged on afterwards. At the second movement, the second violin is leading, the first often betrayed into over-emotional flights, at which Anna laughs with delight. 'Here comes the bills through Mr Schubert's door.'

51

Such Delightful Copulatives!

Pleaseful, moistful, fleshful are her delightful copulatives; she speaks of 'smashed potatoes'. 'For Hell!' she cried. 'Certainly she perceived me as an uncultured updressed whore, an oldish fucked-up model.' This of Anne Ladegaard, an elderly Danish writer who lived with her brother on the outskirts of Frigiliana near La Molineta; a lady who surely did not perceive her in any such unflattering way.

She is thirty-three years of age, with long legs, a prototype of the photomodel Annelise Lundesgaard in the Costa del Sol advertisement. My fancy is to call her the young whore on the outskirts of a dirty city. Nina, the whore from Singapore.

Cómpeta, two thousand metres up in the foothills of the Sierra Almijara, she thinks of as the past, everybody's past; as when she was young and dressed up in the fashion of the 1950s and went out to display her finery, and on returning home again was noticed by a boy loitering in a doorway. Or perhaps not even noticed, as she sauntered by.

The roof tiles of the north are concave, she says, conduits for rainwater to run off; whereas the roof tiles of the south are convex, like shoulders hunched against the rain.

I asked her to translate a page of Hans Andersen for me. It was about a sliver of glass found on a beach. She translated it from English back into the original Danish and then forward into Swedish; she thought it was better in Swedish.

I asked her how did the Swedes regard the Danes; did they feel superior? She said yes, the Swedes thought of themselves as superior to the Danes.

Once when she had stood between Sven Holm and Rory, Anna in shirt and bikini bottom and sandals, the gaze of Sven and myself was drawn to the line of pubic hair, neat as a clipped hedge or mown lawn. The Danish lawns are so lovely!

Cómpeta (pop. 2,000; alt. 2,000m.)

There are many doubles, or *doppelgänger* as they say in German, of the Caudillo living and working all over Spain, themselves unaware of the resemblance, being versions of the Dictator at various stages of his career. The face on the stamps is powerful; it does not age like the cautious old man with phlebitis.

In Cómpeta too there are some pseudo-Francos. Antonio the former postman, who was sacked but will be reinstated in favour of the alcoholic Laurentio, is one such; with paunch and neatly trimmed moustache and popeyed look, he is a dead ringer for Major Franco Baamonde, the fearless one, who later became Miss Canary Isles, as Rudolf Hell became Fräulein Anna in Nazi days. He had a small grocery shop near the post office with its mountain of undelivered mail and the door always locked.

Antonio, the pseudo-Franco and ex-postman, was a keen chess player. He once sold me a pot of confection purporting to be greengage jam, 400 grams of it marked 'Ciruela'. As he wrapped it up, he favoured me with an antiseptic smile. It was the conspiratorial smirk of the diminutive Generalissimo when just about to assume full power, including the signing of death penalties.

The stuff proved to be tasteless, fibreless and more or less odourless, and I intend to throw it out. The pseudo-Franco with goo-goo eyes and military bearing plays a fast game of chess, swooping on the enemy when least prepared, hissing between his teeth before clearing the board. He runs his small store efficiently and manufactures soda water by night, for Rory heard the pump going in the small hours when he went about the town in the night.

52

A Málaga Morning

A huge rusty freighter in from Odessa was moored to the quayside. A ship's hand in white overalls dwarfed to pygmy size is painting out the blisters on the hull with a long paintbrush dipped in black paint.

Harbour guards in riot helmets with chin-straps, armed with squat automatic rifles, unlock a small green gate that one could skip over, admitting a series of Franco doubles in shabby suiting, who scuttle by carrying briefcases.

Stiff as a ramrod the guard snaps to attention to give a military salute. His sharp eye catches us watching from the window of the seafood restaurant by the harbour. He smacks the rifle butt, marches stiffly away, a broken smile for the lovely foreign girl amused by these soldierly antics. It must be some sort of naval depot towards which the pseudo-Francos are hastening.

At sundown the Spanish flag is ritually lowered, draped and folded, carried indoors by a guard of honour as though it were a baby being put to bed, tucked away for the night with 'taps' blown on a bugle by another stiff soldier.

We are drinking a very good dry white wine from Valencia, port of gesticulating statuary, with *tapas*, little squids. The handsome barman is pretending not to look at you but he notices you all the same, the tall brunette with green eyes from Scandinavia where morals are notoriously lax.

Thousands and even five thousand-denomination peseta notes were being flashed about by the very well-heeled clientele, the fast Málaga set of Scotch whisky drinkers with model girls in tow, puffing Gauloises.

The gorgeous girl with the lynx-green eyes standing so tall at the counter was just casually remarking to her escort, Rory of the Hills: 'I am so witchful when it is hardening up, this egg. And now I can feel it split.' So, no intercourse; the hard business of life must go on.

53

Kronborg

C louds drifted through the September sky as we walked again through Dyrehaven to the hermitage on the hill. The unwalled, unguarded mansion amid a copse of beech was where the widows of dead Danish kings lived out their retirement. No moat or castle keep separated it from citizens who passed on foot, or the horse-riders and pony-trekkers.

A stag was bellowing to its herd of wives near *Tre Pile Stedet*, or the Three Twigs, where a dumpy sweet-faced woman served you coffee and me red wine, calling out for 'Matthew' in an accent that you swore was pure Bornholm. We sat at a table outside. There you had come as a child with your parents. There you had sat as a child, heard the warning bell at the level crossing, saw the little red train rush through. Heard the hoarse stag-bellow at rutting time, felt the air move. There you were young once, an innocent.

In the flower shop run by your stepfather-in-law, a retired sea captain now working as a pimp for male prostitutes, you told a long witty story in Danish, and the pimp shook all over, wiping his eyes.

Copenhagen is a city of uneasy old people, who stay indoors, live on cat food and dog food, rarely venture out, hesitating at street corners, fearful of the wild young, the nudist park, the drug scene. The young are not much in evidence except by night in

Central Station, bumming kroner for more beer, collapsing across loaded tables.

City of phantoms, of tired faces, of sailors on shore leave. Or German students returning from a trip around the harbour. The Master Race, you said, were still after the little Danish butter-hole. Granite port of *Belge brote, somner platte, frikadeller*. Singsong musical voices.

The sleepy Danes are modest in a reserved way; reserve with them being a form of arrogance. A public display of anger only amuses them. The music in the bars is muted. In the San Miguel bar the flamenco music was turned down. There is not too much laughter or high spirits in evidence. These drably dressed citizens of the north are warmly bundled into their lives. Babes with chronically disgruntled old faces peer critically from hooded prams. Headscarves are favoured by the young mothers who move about on high antiquated bikes. The long *Allees* open like yawns.

Elderly couples walk soberly in lime-green *Loden* through the King's Gardens. The males wear pork-pie hats and puff cigars, the tubby wives go sedately in warm little hats with feathers, dragged by a dog on a lead, as like as not. The feeling is of sedate bourgeois Germans in a German provincial town, but don't dare tell that to a Dane.

Flagstaffs are a feature of the island of Rørvig. Narrow Danish house-flags get entangled in the firs. The cellar under your far-sighted father's floorboards yielded up good home-made schnapps made from herbs, very potent. We dismantled two single beds and spread mattresses on the floor for the night. Then went cycling on high old bikes – pedal backwards to stop – from Helleveg, the way to the sea. A three-masted schooner appeared out of the haze, and a swan flew overhead, sawing the air creakily, as I took you in the dunes, in the cold, still feverish, still very feverish, in your heated arms.

One day I went by train on my own to Kronborg, to see the castle where Hamlet had 'run around after the ghost of his father'. There is nothing much to see at Elsinore. Shakespeare had heard about it from his friend John Dowland from Dalkey. A Swedish passenger-craft big as a street seemed to be dragging the houses down along the harbour. Minute passengers crossed over by a glassed-in overpass to the station.

An ashen-faced invalid in a belted raincoat, moving with pain on two arm-crutches, his mouth set in a grim line, closed the train window. Forget the fresh air. Now all the windows were sealed tight, an Airedale stinking of decay, no air all the way to Østerport, in the dog-stink.

I had some words of German, some words of Spanish, but of Danish nothing but *Skaak!* and felt a right Charlie in the shops where no English was spoken, going out in the cold morning, skinned alive at the corner by the North Sea wind, leaving you and little Petrushka together on the mattress trade-marked Sultan under the duvet covers, two pairs of brown eyes watching me from the warmth. I, descending steps into the bakery, tore a ticket from the dispenser, waited for my number to be called. But what did 17 sound like in Danish?

Your language sounds more far-off than it is, its pronunciation is far removed from any known thing, to my ears at least. Your misnomers are charming: 'artist's cocks' (artichokes); 'corny cobs' (corncobs); 'upflung waters' (fountains); 'downburnt buildings' (blitzed London); 'ox' (braised beef); 'outsplashed ladies' (the nude models of Delacroix, with their 'fleshful thighs').

'I am uproared,' you said, meaning miffed. 'I'd jump into bed with Olof Palme.' You left *postillons d'amour* lying around. 'Sweetheart – gone for a little walk. The lunch is set for tomorrow instead of today. Kisses – home again soon. Anna.'

'I look into the mirror sometimes and don't believe what I see' (watching yourself narrowly in the glass). 'I think it's funny to pay the world a gleaming lie' (applying make-up but no lipstick, no scent, no earrings; the scentless perfume was 'Ancient Moose'). Much will have more.

Do you know why witches fly?

You prepared the 'squints' (squid) Bilbao-style in their own ink, following the instructions. Pull the heads off the squids and remove and discard the spines and all the internal organs except the ink sacs, which must be put into a cup and reserved. Cut off the testicles just below the eyes and discard the heads. Wash thoroughly. *Calamares ensu tinta a la bilbaina.*

Conkers split on the cobbles under the chestnut trees near the yacht basin where the 'damned' Little Mermaid poses so coyly naked on her bronze seat on a boulder there, and a plain girl in a loose-fitting blue T-shirt displays big wobbly breasts as she goes laughing by with her pretty friend, and a company of Danish soldiers in sharp uniforms, with long hair and rifles at the port position, go marching by the Lutheran church where your model friend Sweet Anya was wedded to Strong Sven, the translator of Márquez. It was snowing then. Mr Fimbal, the Danish god of hard winters, stumbled by with his single arm.

We passed again by a group of stone women all stark naked, tending one who appeared to be injured or in the toils of childbirth.

'What is this?' I asked.

'The Jewish Memorial.'

Professor Tribini, top-hatted and villainously mustachioed, sporting a red carnation in his buttonhole, flashed his gallant ringmaster's eyes at you, all fire and sexual push, at Peter Lieps in Beaulieu, where the railway tracks lead back to Centrum.

Bakken had come before the Tivoli Gardens, you told me. There was the real rough stuff – randy drunken sailors on the spree and big strong girls wrestling stark naked in mud. It was slightly before your time.

You had been at a Gyldendal publisher's party there, had trouble opening a sealed pat of butter; your dinner partner did it for you. You took him home with you on condition that you rode his tall new bicycle. With skirt rolled about your hips and 'brown all over' and at your most attractive after Naxos, you took him home. It was a time I would never know. You rode slowly home, his hand on the small of your back, through the pre-dawn at Bakken, down the long avenue of trees where we had walked, watched by Professor Tribini, abusing himself behind an oak.

'I was somewhat exalterated,' you said.

'Oh, I am over-lewd!'

You served up an excellent Hungarian soup with sour cream and told me your radio story of Satan in the wood, based on a real lecher, my successor after the time in Spain. You sat opposite me, giving me the eye. You'd certainly been at the Cognac again, a couple of snorters before setting out.

We were in Spain again. You had been going on about 'Paulus of Tarsus'. We were in an olive grove below the logging trail and heard the damnedest noise rising up out of the valley, a strange inconstant murmurous belling, bleating and baaing.

Some time later, over a drink at Viento de Palmas, a herd of over a thousand shorn sheep and lambs went tripping past, with active dogs as outriders and rough-looking shepherds bringing up the rear. The din was stirring – bells, barking, bleating, baaing. The shepherds did not stop for drinks, heading on for new pastures.

Now freezing air leaks into the kitchen and you turn the gas low, open the oven door, light candles. The water in the lavatory bowl becomes agitated, as if we were at sea. Sudden gusts of winter air strike through the interstices of the cramped toilet and the floor seems to shift underfoot. The Danes were all secret sailors, you said.

The spiritual suffering of the Swedes (which knows no bounds) is said to be unmatched in any other European country, their suicide rate the highest in the world. By the end of the first quarter of the next century all Sweden would be in the custody of a few large companies, the suicidal sameness of all Swedish life then complete.

We passed the Jewish Memorial again, the naked women bound together in a lumpish humanitarianism. And once your dotty landlady Mrs Andersen passed us on her witch's black bike, sending a hostile look our way.

I write down the magic names:

Humlebaek	*Hellerup*	*Hundested*
Østerport	*Øster Sogade*	*Ordrup*
Klampenborg	*Kokkedal*	*Kastrup*
Kronborg	*Skodsborg*	*Vedbaek*
Beaulieu	*Rørvig*	*Bakken*

| *Nivå* | *Espergaerde* | *Rungstedlund* |
| *Dyrehaven* | *Helsingør* | *Melby* |

In Denmark every day is different; so the old books say. Blow out the light.

54

Ronda

'I'm a big girl now. I've got a big pussy and I suppose a big *asch* too.'

Anna had all those splendid not-to-be-denied Scandinavian feminine attributes, in spades; and if her bust was a bit on the small side (as indeed it was), it was more than compensated for by the size of her shapely bum.

'Love perfumes all parts,' wrote Robert Herrick, himself ever a lover of wet pussy. The choleric clergyman who had taught his pet pig to down pints of ale like a gent must have been thinking of his Julia whose large breasts bursting out of a lawn chemise he had likened to strawberries half-drown'd in cream.

In the Hotel Polo at Ronda in a lovely quiet blue high-ceilinged double room with long blue drapes drawn from the windows, Anna ordered up breakfast in perfectly accentless English via Room Service, specifying what we wanted and when.

Presently a dark-visaged young *torero*, in a blue tunic and white flannels with razor-sharp creases, bore in a large tray of steaming strong coffee and all the condiments and got an eyeful (one of the undoubted perks of the profession) of the tall brunette in the white robe sitting up in bed saying '*Muchas gracias*' in Spanish that would pass. Soon he was backing out of the the bedroom as though leaving the chamber of the Queen, his eyes steadfastly fixed on the vision in the bed, now pouring out coffee. And my

Anna surely had the face and demeanour of King Juan Carlos's lovely Sofia, ever smiling sweetly on all public occasions.

'Don't move an inch,' I said, and left her arse in air, to fetch a wetted facecloth from the fancy bathroom with its shower stall and faceted mirrors. In whose full-length mirrors she was to see herself nude for the first time since a babe in Copenhagen.

'Uuuuuh! but I'm lewd, aren't I?' I heard her say in the bathroom with its door open. And she had doubtless performed a little skip and dance for the big mirrors and admired her bum, which she had never seen before.

A champagne cork from a previous honeymoon lay behind the radiator. A great yellow building crane straddled a monstrous hole in the ground across from the hotel and its waving palms. We dressed and made ourselves respectable again, preparing to have another look at Ronda, a most pleasing place to be. It reminded me of certain undulating lovely valleys in Yugoslavia near the Austrian border where I had gone with the puppets in a new Bedford truck, just off the assembly line, though the land about Ronda is more like the colour of Africa, pelt of puma.

In an alleyway off a nameless street a bar is crammed with soldiers in green uniforms of Thai-like neatness, bleached out and worn with panache under tasselled forage caps. Ronda is obsessed with green things: lizards, uniforms, oxidised bells. And bullfighting. ¡PENA TAURINA ANTONIO ORDOÑEZ! groans the sign, as if choking to death. I see a line of hanged victims carved in stone.

In the neat pedestrian walks you see the finite gestures of bull-fighters (Ordoñez, the great matador, the first one I saw kill five bulls, was born here), jackets draped over shoulders in matador manner. When the weather permits and the bitter winter sets its teeth into the narrow arses of those brave *toreros*-to-be whose thin shoulder blades protrude like flying buttresses. The pretty Ronda girls are rumpy as *rejoneadores*, flying on blood mares from the bull's horns. Mauve slacks are worn as tight as tight can be. A chess competition takes place in what once must have been a Moorish palace. *Pena: J.M. Bellon. Torneo Social Ajedrez*. For three days the Levant wind blew a half-gale.

'I haven't quite got used to being frustrated yet,' I said. *Todavia no me acostumbro estar frustrado* in the vernacular.

While modern Spain sprawls like a hopeless drunkard along the Mediterranean, busily going to Hell, the new road that grandly ascends to Ronda is as extraordinary as the southern approaches to Barcelona. Cut off from the ongoing sorry mess of the coastal 'development' and deep in the off-season (the only time to travel in style) Ronda (at 850 *metros de altitud*; 32,049 *habitantes*) offers herself as a kind of Sparta. A bullfighters' town; from here came Pedro Romero and the great Ordóñez. Sealed up in the wall of a well on the latter's bull farm, sealed up again in an unmarked blue casket, lie the ashes of Orson Welles, this most secret burying place a last tribute to happy days spent in Spain when he was young.

The coastal stretch from Málaga to Marbella is as ugly as the urban development from Salthill to Costelle Cross on Connemara's frozen Atlantic seaboard, allowing the Spaniards slightly better taste.

Up here in Ronda men with wind-scorched faces speak intently of bulls and the money involved and of bullfighters. They are sage addicts of circles and all shades of green, very partial to chess, with the ingrained habit of contradicting, a Moorish trait. They are half Moorish in their thinking and feeling, wholly Moorish when very drunk. That extraordinary high screech the men emit when in their cups is a modified and secularised version of the muezzin call to prayer. We walk on the windy walls, Seaport Anna and her besotted fancyman Rory of the Hills.

Into Bar Maestro – just wide enough for you to turn around – twitches a grievously afflicted beggar, moaning '¡*Bbbbbooojijii!*' A posse of purposeful men with bursting bellies come roaring for *cerveza* into a long bar overlooking the plaza, to be presently joined by quiet men in expensive suede jackets the colour of jaguars, but with the swarthy faces of Iberian impresarios.

'In Ronda your thoughts fly upwards,' Anna said. 'To live here would be to marry a very strict but beautiful woman.'

A calm nun in a well-cut powder-blue habit is transacting some quiet business at the Banco Central. The waiter with the scorched face above his red jacket is acting in an old Simenon thriller; as is the lovely girl who sold me carbon paper in the *libreria*; as is the contrary old man sitting in the corner. A thin bronze bell is tolling. The bullring is the largest and thus the most dangerous in all Spain. The New Town is as great a mess as Tallaght in Dublin, a sort of Arab shanty town. A ring of towns with peculiar names face Portugal: Arcana, Estepa, Ecija.

'*Una iglesia muy vieja*,' I told the contrary old man seated in a shadowy corner.

'*No, no tan vieja. Solo doscientos años*,' he contradicts me flatly, referring to the *Iglesia Nuestra Señora del Socorro* just across the way.

In the Restaurant Jérez, very Germanic, near the bullring a distinguished grey-haired man arrives with a cane and arming a lady in furs. The noble-looking Frenchman in the neck-brace sits and looks about, hair a sable silvered, pulls up his expensively tweed-clad trouser leg to expose a male calf of corpse-like whiteness to the lady in furs who bends forward as if peering solicitously through a long-handled lorgnette. Slowly removing her sunglasses she exclaims, 'Ouch, *chéri*!'

The squat proprietor, who seems to know Rory, hovers about our table and stares pointedly at me as if at a long-lost son who refuses to acknowledge his own *padre*.

Soon the whole eastern coastline from Estepona near Gibraltar to Gerona near the French border will have gone the way of Marbella and Torremolinos, the Sodom and Gomorrah of the Costa del Sol, and it will be left to hardy souls to move on Ponteverdre or La Coruña. American bombing colonels out from the air base at Moron de Frontera quaff Cognac as if it was beer.

Over Ronda hovers a most Moorish moon and never do I wish to leave it.

'Don't move an inch,' Rory whispered, carefully withdrawing his inflamed member.

'Your cock is afraid of my pussy,' Anna said when I couldn't perform, for she was ever a straight-speaking girl. 'And do you ever take a shit?'

'*Au contraire*, my cock adores your pussy.'

55

Petrushka

[Handwritten] 24 July 1975
Østersogade
My dearest Rory

Yes, my flat faces the lakes. Petrushka and I went down
there tonight, just across the Norre Søgade. She has bread
for the ducks and a letter in a bottle. The time is near to
9.00, the darkness is coming but the lake is still coloured,
the air is misty (hazy?) by heat and smoke – a bird, I don't
know which one, flies by in quiet hurry, the strokes from
wings are regular as morse signals.

I'm happy tonight, have this 20 minutes together with
you. Here are not much people, some few bourgeoises with
dogs and a group of children. The five shout after the sixth;
'Suckling, suckling!' Petrushka is upset. An old man pass by,
stiffly and regular as when you are walking with ski, and
draws an invisible and absolute straight line after him. He
wears a white linen-coat, wide trousers and new-chalked
shoes. His complexion is sickly and sunburned. He reminds
me of an asiat. I follow him with the eyes, turn the head and
talk with Petrushka – about the five which tease the one.
Then I look after the old man again. He is still walking but
on the same spot as before. My reason tells me that he has

stand still in the meantime, but if somebody look sharp on me and said: 'This is not a man but a sign on a Chinese cardemono', I would say: 'Yes, of course.'

[unsigned]

The Floating Trousseau

27 July 1975
Copenhagen,
Thursday night

Mein liebe Liebling, mein Kind und Bruderlein, mein Dichter und Wirklichkeit, mein Angst und Freue, my Rory.

Just received your letter. Sorry to hear about Martin's mother dying. Read my 'epistle' from Bornholm, remember my new name and understand that you have done it again, catched me in my heart, beating me in my stomack, taken the air out from my lungs. You called me Anna Bornholm.

You have done it again. You have seen me again, seen me as I am (can be), you have lighted me through again, you are a seeing person, seeing me anyway. Oh, Gott!

I love every word in your letter, letters. A psychoanalist would tear his hair because of your determining of erotic, your picture of me in this fixing-bath, your Big Tips. I've never met anything like that, you even surpass Knud Andersen. I cannot quite recognize myself but if you see me like that, I may be like that, must turn to be like that.

Your smile made sense to me, help me so much. What a promise – I was never jealous of Hannel, knew all the time that you haven't loved her, that you had tenderness for her but she was a spare-love. Is it cruel to say? I knew she had been the wife of the Pastor and even in separated it hints certain limits in her. For Coppera I have blended feelings. I perceive her, actually, as very sympathetical, beautifull and intelligent too, but obviously wrong for you. As me in my Steffen, apart from that we are through the hate. But I am very jealous of her. You have had your youth together with her, you have been together with her on the impossible beds of your youth and have wished – more fervently than ever since in your life – to make love to her. You (R & C) have had the trust together about you as a famous writer and herself as a beautifull woman in company with gifted men, men who everybody saw was secret in love with her, Coppera Hill. And you have had the kids together. It alarms me that you still quarrel. Then a long way is left before you are mine. Yes, I'm jealous. Jealous so it hurts in my teeth, my teeth turn soft in my mouth of jealous.

When you say that the love for the two H's already disappeared when I was in Competa you are lying indeed, my love. To yourself and to me. I remember so clearly myself asking: When did the lovestory with Hannelore end? And you answered, very fast and with a sharp sidelong look: Who says it is end? I remember that. One remembers when the whip gibes.

But I will not (do not dare) to say something about Hannelore and about what I feel in my bones – Your memories of us are too full of 'unreliablenesses' but mostly more true than the reality. But then again reality stands in no need to be true to life, according to Monsieur Boileau.

That I must type my envelopes shock me directly. If you told Coppera about me then she must know that I'm writing to you? Shall I put on a false name too? I have the address of Martin from a wrong addressed envelope; reserve it because I know you are fond of him in a special way, a voluntary way. It would actually amuse me to be Martin Lindermann (en route to l'Espagne) and then – in out-folded state – Anna again. Like a real fold-out girl as from a pornographic magazine. A picture only for your pleasure, a code which only you know the solution.

If I'm your breath then you are the very mystery behind the breath, you hit me in the middle, fling everything else overboard, I see terrified and delighted the fine trousseau (embrodered with the wrong initials) float on the sea ('the Rough') for a moment and then go down. Disappeared. After real manner of women I think that this anyway was make by fine linen, could be remade for other purpose . . . But you laugh – a bit satanic, quite frankly – against me with the remains of me between your teeth and my objection blows out of my mouth.

With what arrogance you ignore my laborious collected trousseau. Indeed you make me naked. Don't you fear at all my fury that day the love is worn out? I wrote something four weeks ago after reading 30 pages in Rørvig of Böll's *Ansichten eines Clowns* and your stories, indeed, often give me the same kind of thoughts. Try to translate it here (it was actually written for you, – as everything I think).

So many stories is about 'the lust of the flesh and the irreparable loneliness of the souls'. You barely know the quotation, it's from a Swedish female poet from about 1900. Now it is only quoted with becoming ironical distance. So many stories are songs about men's loneliness, men's search for that picture of love which are only given by glimpses. I'm thinking of all the stories (suddenly it seems to me that I never red anything else) about men's effort, their enormous effort in order to give women gifts, to give them their world, builted up through the years of reading and sensations and meditation and coined in stories told in bed in Competa or in a tower in Heidelberg or in a field in Ireland. All this you give away for a kiss.

But when a woman reads these stories she reads them in another direction, sees another message too, she sees your presents (so tempting in their tenderness and beauty) as demands. This gifts demand her 'obliteration', she must follow the man in his world, let her be drowned in presents, follow the man in his dreams, make his dreams alive, turn herself into a dream. And she knows, she expects – from the very first moment in a new love-meeting – your anger and disappointment that day you see that your gifts weren't received in that spirit they were given. She knows your disappointment, turned into contempt in order to be bearable for yourself. Women are stupid, greedy and self-asserting. Stupid because you, the men, have been thinking everything out, have created everything – greedy when they are not happy by that they are given and self-asserting when they demand their own diffuse univers accepted as real (banned into litter and sex as we say in danish, meaning that the ilegitimate children of a king are ennobled). – I'm mourning; for the love (the creating) that cannot endure. After that follows the loneliness only usable for telling at that time when the love was there.

Towards the loneliness (the disappointment, the end) we are leaded, as necessary as the community (the hope, the beginning). This cycle is by most women perceived as created by men, it is him 'to blame', she want to continue the creative of love, prefare to stay in the beginning. A day she sees that his touch was casual, that his gifts are not for her, that the love cannot be thought without its cessation, she understands that the love was a lever for something else, something in himself, not her business, something useful; a new present. From him. As he can give to whom he wish! Then the beloved woman turns into an un-loved woman: a fearfull sight, a fury, a witch or only a tormentor, an envious creature hacking with the rests of her love: the selfishness, the greedyness, the demands. She sees her contribution (the giving up of herself) swallowed, devoured and rised again as *something else*, something outside her. And she is seized by a deadly hate against this giver who used everything, who used her out.

The next time she is offered the love of a man (his world) she first sees the shadows from her dead sisters corpses – and turns into a whore, a suffragette, or very lonely. (Or the most scandalous, the most 'perverse' of all; a woman with the same purposes as a man – a woman excluded from love.)

All this, my dear Rory, I feel in a very strong way in the meeting with you. With Steffen I had not this 'problematic' (what a word); with him there was a kind of cease-fire, a conspiracy, a looking-at-the-world-together. With you there is quite another kind of life. And I want to live, I think I want it so much that I will die for it. I love you. I have decided to love you. You made the decision irresistible.

I know you prefer letters with concrete contents: stories, descriptions (best erotical), you want to fill them out yourself, yes, put colours on. I send you a new cart of Copenhagen with marks and hidden signs which you can follow with the nail of your finger like Job scraped his wounds with a potsherd!

Petrushka is not a bit like me, I'm sorry to say. She is all the family of Steffen. I am not talking always, I'm talking in showers. I like to have letters to my home address. It was not me waiting for hours on the steps, it was the letter.

I haven't the slightest idea of what the postman looks like. I'm waiting everywhere. And not for hours but always. I remember myself standing on the floor in your bedroom, trying to explain you something. I could not and took a pair of dancing-steps in order to show you what I meant. I remember how much it pleased you, this simplicity and joy we had together.

To have few words demands clearness in mind. To have many words demands clearness in heart. You easy grows wild. It struck me that in a foreign language you cannot hear if your words are ridigiously, you can only hear your own thoughts.

I've never met such a absence of barriers from a man before. You must have made your women mad of love when you have been like that to them, too. My Knepp was good, very impersonal, I was thinking of nobody, so natural as washing oneself, a ritual, childish nearly. I fucked with the chap twice, it was the bitterness, the bitter need he took. Then I stopped because he approached to me, approached *your* regions. Do you understand? The fucking only helped me for a very short time. I put on the amulet again immediately of course. How can you think I didn't I only took it off because of delicate reasons.

I meet you in another way than in my former erotic conceptions: lesser touch, more imagination. I tell you Rory, I imagine you so you would die from it if you were here. I feel you, you are with me, you are in me, you are alive in me (slowly and fast) and you die in me, you are flinged up in me, inside me and you stay there and get peace. I tell you, few have been so passionate faithfull to you as I in this months.

And I ... I catch a sweetness so unbearable that I disappear to myself, I dissolve, the top flies off, the bottom out. On Bornholm I found myself on the bed (an afternoon I stealed – stold? – me into my room) laughing against the roof and with my face wet by tears.

It is this I don't dare on the beatch because even the smallest help-from-hand is excluded and any other signs form body. The feeling of love (or the lechery) comes in waves. From the floating flowing standstills the reservoir is filled slowly, the first power from the first wave kept, the next added. Addition. Addition until no more addition is possible.

If I permit you to place me with maximum charm (what a hidden phrase) in the hidden centre of your novel, I permit you everything. And I think you will love most of it. Maybe all. I permit you everything.

Anna

57

Diary, April 1975

I stand at the window of the Bar el Montes commanding a view of the main plaza which presents the usual fucked-up aspect – idlers, straw blown about, the church door open. I did not know what to expect: the second appearance is always different – the sauntering certainly a bluff. Through the window I watch you sail into view. You saunter across the plaza, taking your time, you want to show me yourself advancing. Your tallness surprises, the *nudeness* of your ears, your hair is up. You wear a white linen shirt, a flared skirt of pale colours, you stop outside Luis Perico's bar, bend to look into a parked car, using the glass as a mirror, watchful, tall and self-possessed. The idlers stare. I open the bar door a fraction.

You see the movement, see me watching you, you make no sign. You come on, unsmiling, up the ramp. I open the door just enough to let you through. You come in, the pure fragrance of melilot, the shape that sustains you, the breath that moves. The portable chess set is on the bar counter by my gin and tonic. You ask for the same. Larios gin is made from sugar cane, the cheapest crop in creation, and tastes vaguely of mouse droppings.

You had come from afar, had already spent five days in Cómpeta, were thinking of leaving, the bitch had given you a darkened room, to share with little Petrushka.

'Do you find me masculine?' you asked as if it were a code.

And I answered, 'Do you find me feminine?'

There it began. You had to sit to try and recover. Luis kept close watch from the kitchen, but for us the bar was deserted. You spoke in an accent unfamiliar to me, you were several women simultaneously, come from different directions. It was most disturbing beginning again.

Did I seem real to you, dearest? One day in error I'd call you by a different name, it wouldn't be your name, and all would be over between us. One day you would begin to turn away from me, I turn away from you, you leaving. I know no other life before you. Steffen Karr drinks all evening in a strange hotel. I take you again so that my existence in you can go on. It's a dream, love is invented, we have invented it anew.

Then: the curious long kiss, your head in the clothes. Left behind: the time alone, the dead stillness, bat and lynx faces amongst the cobwebs, stirrings and gnawings in the heat of mid-afternoon, the incessant drone of flies, a small bird suspended on the wire outside. With tight nerves drawn like elastic, I hear the bird fly silently away. The stirrings and gnawings resume.

Against the hill the kiln is fired, thick grey smoke gushes from the pyre, unfurling upwards, then rolling back over Cómpeta. A little girl, self-absorbed and phosphorescent, is dancing in the flames. (We 'was shaking like mads'.) Gunfire sounds over the next hill. We are together at last. Time runs out in a circle.

58

Last Letter

Østersogade 254
8 Julio 1980

My dear

Your letter came one the second of July, a rainy Wednesday
morning, and thank you for that my love. It is Monday
evening now, it is warm, I have all windows open, I am
alone. Petrushka is at Steffen. Sgftfujhklppeoam-bcbcaquapl
– I don't know what to answer. I can tell you about the
beatch yesterday (I was in Rørvig in this weekend the first
of summer's).

The sea was light grey as the sand. There was a vague
wind, not strong enough to create foam but enough for
the sunlight to make small and jumping reflecs, – the
almost unbroken seasurface is colourless, it underlines the
impression of material, – moire.

As so often before when I arrive to the beatch it was
nearly empty. But soon later there are several people – as
usually mostly lonely gentlemen. Where are all their wifes
always hiding? They are not at the beatch. I use your *djelaba*
everywhere now, also at the beatch, I lay on it, take it on
take it off, use it as a pilow and as a tent. It is rarely too cold

270

and never too hot, it makes me feeling home everywhere,
it's a kind of recidense. I am looking forward to the smell
of warm sand when I go to sleep in nights.

Some strand-wanderers pass several times, especialy I
noticed two, loudly talking, not exactly noisy but proud of
the conversation subject (which of the towns of Bornholm
are situated southernmost). There are some people to whom
everything they touch automatically become enviable to
others: Think only to be them . . . and to get those shoes
– and those thoughts, and exactly that colour of hair. They
don't boast to that they are too, nearly royalistic, contented
– I will say they are almost discret comparing to their
contentment.

My father got some of the same, but at him the 'royalistic
contentment' is rather naivite. He still, in the age of 72, gets
astonished that not everybody is like him. But his naivite
has been wounded (or vulnerable?) during the last years
from my mother's knifesharp grief. Now he marvels in
an uncertain way, not in an enthusiastically. (But still he
reads indifferent newspapers aloud even if you keep your
forefinger on the spot in your own book.) I'm vaguely
looking listening to Margot Fonteyn telling about 'The
Magic of the Dance' while I'm writing this. I've discovered
a kind of interest for the ballet during the last years. It is new
to me – like my interest of green plants in my windows.
Both of its spinster-interest (spinster – what a mad word).
But I'm swimming too. And write poems. It is after all
youngish?

I re-read the sentence of the strand. There is something
wrong. How can there be reflecs when the material was
colourless? But there was. Maybe I have told about it in
the wrong order?

I wear a golden chain around the waist, also at the beatch,
also in the night. Try to imagine if you would like the sign.
Feel a little false to wear it when you are not there. Feel
half excited, half shy because of the slavelike in the sign,
the supple. I am attract but know it is all a lie: I am no
slave girl.

Later.

Took my bike, went to my sister's grave (haven't been there since I last wrote to you). The flowers were full of holes because of all the rain, little snails lived in the white petals.

Now it rains again, the windows are open, it is difficult to find out what is the sound of the rain and what of the chestnut leaves.

[unsigned]

PART VI:

Contretemps at
Cranley Gardens

59

Events Leading to the Hill–Anders Divorce, Decree Nisi and Absolute

Berlin,
1 April 1973

My Dearest,

After a long time of silence and then your letter and phone calls now a few lines from me. Today the so-called April-weather started with rain and storm and the sweetness of April seems to have disappeared, but the rain will do nature very well.

Mr Kunoth has died a fortnight ago on a heart attack and Mrs Kunoth dressed in black is doing the garden now in a rather sad manner. I can't write much – my spirits are a bit low, but of my mood sometimes I can't control.

It would of course be lovely if you could come for a weekend but it would not be good for us to be together in my little flat over a longer period as the narrowness would choke us again after a while and we would feel like wild beasts in a cage who can't escape from each other. We have made this experience not only once – on the other hand we would wonderfully live in much more space when

you don't feel bound so strongly to your family any longer.
You see I don't believe it when you say: your family doesn't
mean all that much to you. Once I had this illusion – I mean
once I believed it – but in the meantime I have (and I had
to) learnt the reality. The discovery was hard for me, but
this has re-established my own life and has given me back
at the same time part of my independence.

Nevertheless it has not changed my feelings towards you
and when you think I might be finished with you therefore
I can only tell and reassure you that this will never be the
case (proof of it in September last year) as a considerable
part of my heart belongs to you whatever may happen (in
good and in bad) – something eternal. I hope very much
that you can understand the sense of my words expressed
in such a poor English. I miss you very much, but I had
to learn to live without you and to rely on myself.

Let me hear soon when you will come. *Je t'embrasse
beaucoup*.

Hannelore

Wednesday, 12 April 1972

This morning as I was crossing the hallway I saw 'with fascinated
horror' some sort of long official document being pushed and
forced through the letterbox, for all the world like an elongated
tapeworm being forcefully shat from an anus to fall on the mat
with a plop.

These documents, like lawyers' writs and things that put you
off, can easily attain eighty centimetres and more. Have court
proceedings started in an attempt to expel us from these premises
for non-payment of quarterly rent?

Live at the top of the tree of Tule; excrement to be expected
lower down. The crack in the living-room ceiling extrudes a
foul-smelling caca-like liquid that stinks of urine. The big white
Chinese lantern, so pristine when we bought it in Liberty's of
Regent Street, is now filthy; the air here is bad, petrol fumes

rise from the Broadway below. Five bars of dirt, like tidal wrack, mark the ceiling, painted in black and purple psychedelic stripes by the previous owners, given five or six coats of white emulsion at the start of our tenancy, that for Coppera would last more than thirty years, longer than our marriage.

The books are out of order and uncatalogued, ranged along the dado, leaning at a tilt. No flowers. The wine-stained Staunton chess pieces are ranged in order on the chessboard made by a friend of Hal Rice's.

The crack in the ceiling is before my eyes, the stench remains constant. Outside, a kind of tower, tilted at an angle, ready to fall into the stinking Broadway below.

The refuse has not been collected. A mountain of shiny black plastic bags clots the pavements. The traffic converges from six different directions; double-decker buses wait in their corral below, big as elephants. The stench that rises from the hallway five floors below is formidable. Stench of Chingford Lock. No flowers.

The dark bar across the way has lost the last letter in its name: THE GREE MAN. Here the head-butters assemble, the karate kickers.

Sound of milk bottles being smashed at the dairy at the back, below the fire escape; a way of relieving their feelings? A sudden movement might prove fatal. We are looking at three hundred layers of domestic refuse. No flowers, no air, stink of petrol rises from below. Breathlessness. Reading Conan Doyle: 'The Resident Patient'. He offers a reassuring world, an England that could be controlled. Biddle, Hayward, Moffatt, the hanged man, the merest blind. The black plastic bags glisten in the polluted air, the stench rises up, breathlessness, no flowers. A woodland glade it is not. Like a better past gone rotten.

I used to think that Soho lay underground, populated by criminals and prostitutes. Is it true? Rory, let it be stated, frequents a bleak bar situated just off the disused railway line, now a nature path, patronised by part-time gardeners, long-distance Welsh lorry drivers, tired old sods and other miscellaneous riff-raff, laid-off lathe turners.

Who wrote of 'the confounding melancholy of ordinary

conversation'? A small listless little sod is talking terrible garbage to another sad sod. One is drinking half-pints of Long Life, a disgusting brew, the other shots of Tio Pepe. The genial host grunts as he pulls pints. There is a dart board, of course. A sign says:

> This bar is dedicated to those merry souls who make drinking a pint a pleasure, who reach contentment before capacity and whatever they drink can take it and remain gentlemen.

The name of this quaint hostelry? The Royal Oak. The Weeping Willow might have been a fitter monicker. Rory went there to wallow in its all-pervasive and curiously predictable gloom. An ill-lit place; you see eyes fixed on you in the gloom as you enter. It can be reached via the Dewy Dell along the overgrown railway line.

The stout owner pants like a pug dog, sweats like a pig, likes a game of darts with some of the dart-minded patrons. Drinking Long Life is like sucking off an old tree.

Saturday, 4 August 1979

Fay's birthday, thirty-four today. Rory's presents: two bottles of good German hock, to be shared. A book for her: Hemingway's *To Have and Have Not*. Watney's pub in the evening, in the pub garden under the trees, copper beech, a strong feeling of Berlin, or can it be the love-twinge that colours the place, makes it monochrome, the colour that always augurs happiness for Rory, the sojourner? The premises darken as evening falls. White Shield poured in cunning fashion, rolled cigarettes, speak of this and that, walked back. I cannot say 'home'. Cranley Gardens is her home, not mine, it will be impossible when Terence, her troubled son, returns.

Terence is a disturbed child, the prototypical modern child perhaps, no perhaps about it; the break-up of the marriage upset him and more so than he can well explain, either to his understanding mother with whom he lives, or his less sympathetic father, who lives elsewhere with another woman, to make it all the more complicated.

He wrote Fay a little letter. 'Daer Mummy, I am small like a ant. Kill me. I love you. Good bye.'

He was having trouble in school and in the divided, half-empty home; he had begun stealing, he told lies, seemed confused and unhappy. He stole money from his mother's purse to buy an expensive watch and wore it, flaunted it. Fay made him take it off and told him to jump on it. He did so. No more recriminations, and no more stealing.

The half-Persian cat Medea was crawling with fleas, always savaging its anus, leaving white fluff on the furniture. Fay wore scanty red bra and panties, permitted Rory a glimpse.

'Don't get ideas.'

Rory, clasping himself as though suffering from acute belly-ache, already had ideas. He brought her presents of wine from the wine store, flowers nicked from the gardens around, he came bearing gifts.

'Do you like lamb?'

Fay served him Greek lamb for dinner, much wine, Turkish coffee, Disque Bleu, Jewish bread. She wanted love, would give herself away, she was a most lovable woman.

Fay's severest term of censure was 'Peasant!' hissed between protruding teeth before slamming the door in Rory's face, a meek smile bisected on the mat.

'Dry mouth,' you said, turning away; though not dry below, never dry there, for Rory. 'Eggs make you caustic.'

'But I'm always caustic,' Rory protested.

60

In the Woods

I saw her once hop forty paces in a public street.

i

'If you can't, why do you try?' Her gunmetal blue-black hair unbound, her clothes in disarray, she looked like one of the Sabine women. Rory couldn't let her alone.

An awkwardness with Fay:

'We needn't . . .' (do it), she said, short and defiant. 'We need,' Rory insisted. He was all for it. They did it.

She did not approve of 'cowering indoors', liked to slap on her warpaint, slip into something fetching, go out on the town. Put a brave face on it. Step out.

She came from Plymouth but had little good to say of it; she was of Irish stock on her mother's side, the Foyles of Clifden in remotest Connemara near the bracing Atlantic seaboard backing on the Maamturks where rain poured down incessantly and the cattle bawled in pure misery in the drenched fields. She had graduated from Leeds University with better grades than Henchley the biker, her boyfriend. She was smarter than him; at least smart enough to leave him when their son, Terence, was still a child. She was married at the age of nineteen, too soon and to the wrong man. The chaps in the office did not appeal to her; they were all dead-beats.

She took the Channel ferry to Paris to see some art but found it was a holiday and all the galleries were closed. The captain invited her up to his bridge to admire his instruments, allowed her to drive the ferry. 'It was strange,' she said.

'Oh, you like a bit of strange?'

Evidently.

Coppera, fast as lightning when it came to picking up hints and evasions, detected palpable evidence of misconduct on the very naked body of Rory. Claw-prints and weals on Rory's guilty-looking back and pectorals suggested that he had yielded himself to the wild embraces of some uncontrollable she-beast who had inflicted heavy punishment, had torn, bitten and scratched lumps out of him.

'What are those marks I see?' Coppera inquired most silkily from the bed, watching Rory dressing himself, rapidly, guiltily, evasively.

'Someone was teaching me life-saving methods in the Hampstead Pond,' said the bold Rory most swimmingly. 'The water is very dirty and I bruise easily.'

'You lie easily too, mister,' Coppera said sourly, observing the maulings disappear into a shirt, a belt being resolutely tightened.

'If those are love-bites, then you are in very bad trouble.'

Rory slunk away, looking most abashed.

Hannelore had spoken of the enormous need for compensation that a working life demanded, and the more clerical the work, the more enormous the demand. Panting like a black leopard climbing into a thorn tree to get after an ape she (Fay, in her home in Cranley Gardens) gouged and scratched and tore at Rory's back and squeezed his testicles at the moment of simultaneous climax as if squeezing the bulb of a scent spray that would squirt seed point-blank into her wide open and receptive womb. From these fierce encounters between the sheets Rory emerged all marked and bleeding as though he had barely escaped from the attentions of a cougar or puma and not the rather unrestrained embraces of one of Her Majesty's more able tax inspectoresses in charge of a department in the vicinity of Great Portland Street.

'This mustn't be any hole-and-corner affair,' she told her newest lover. 'I intensely dislike furtiveness.'

Rory's sons had babysat for Terence when his mother was out on the town. When she took a flying leap from the mezzanine into the kitchen, gunmetal blue hair flying, Rory thought he detected something both predatory and feline. Perhaps she was half Persian cat herself? She was in the best of health, unlike the ailing Medea.

She had been a former neighbour on the second floor below, abutting on the Broadway; was to be seen in biker's gear, carrying her helmet. Her husband was Syd Henchley, the biker who left his 'hog' in the hall below. When he rolled it out, Fay jumped on the pillion and off they roared.

Fragments of food adhered to her somewhat prominent incisors, akin to a cougar after the kill. She liked to drink wine, introduced Rory to strong potions in working-class public houses, this brewer's Strong and that brewer's Brown. Rory took her to *Nosferatu* at Notting Hill Gate, where all the freaks in London had converged to see Werner Herzog's unnerving movie. She was a bachelor-girl, having thrown over Syd the biker, struck camp, was 'making out' in Cranley Gardens where Rory came calling with bottles of Rioja and flowers nicked from adjoining gardens. Sometimes she played the piano, to calm Terence before he dropped off to sleep.

She reminded Rory of those scatterbrained and fearless society girls racing about in the early novels of Evelyn Waugh – Agatha Runcible & Co. Crouch End, Finsbury Park and Barnet seemed not quite the places to take Fay Henchley, and certainly not into those pubs there.

The Broadway, Muswell Hill, was a place of broken marriages; the corner block of flats bulked over it like a cliff face with monkeys staring down into the dirty pool below, that was the Broadway with incessantly circling traffic converging from five or six lanes, leading to the West End and out past Barnet into the country, or what passed for countryside there, out Watford way.

Her hair hung down her back to her trim seat, referred to as her 'bureaucratic bum', in the manner of Juliette Gréco. She was petite. Coppera, who detested and despised all rivals, held her in low esteem, dismissed her as a nitwit. Who else but a nitwit would have married Syd Henchley?

Social services, such as baby-sitting and general neighbourliness, had led to sexual services; one thing led to another and before you could say Heloïse and Abelard they were at the game of the two-backed beast, as to the manner born. Lubricity on the sofa and glimpses of red underthings were followed by extended love-bouts in the double bed, commencing just as soon as Terence was down for the night.

Terence was a fair-haired quiet little boy. He had the reserve that the only child has; his parting shots could be devastating. One morning, leaving, he had encountered Rory arriving with stolen flowers and a two-litre bottle of Italian plonk. 'A bit early to start drinking,' Fay's most unsettled offspring remarked, 'Isn't it?' It was 10.30 a.m. Greenwich Mean Time.

She was rounded and ripened, with two of the roundest flanks, from nape to rump hung the longest shank of hair down to the very cleft of her bum; all womanly, of all sirens the most retiring, the moodiest; of all desirables the most modest. 'Nothing is more disgusting than a question'.

No pouting out of lips, no batting of eyes, nor eyelash flutterings, no bust or bum play, no come-hither looks. She was what she was, without deceitful ways.

'You empty me,' Rory (The Mighty Member) expostulated.

'You fill me,' Fay interpolated.

'Finished', pronounced Coppera with relish, ever wont to take wind out of sails, deflate presumptions, a deliverer of grim judgements and prognostications, a facer-up to unpleasant facts that had to be faced. It must have been Jonathan Carl's Calvinistic German blood coursing through her veins, diluted with Welsh pessimism on her mother's side.

There was more Taffy to her than German stoicism and fixity; you couldn't argue with her. Ever try and argue with Balance, the constellation Libra, the seventh sign of the Zodiac? Save your breath to cool your porridge.

We were through with each other, through with our marriage, we were finished with each other, all washed up, for it was impossible to go on. And yet we did go on, after a fashion, for a while longer, anyway.

ii

Anna wrote from Copenhagen:

'I've saved enough money for the journey I think, but the time of the year is wrong, I think; for a long & difficult trip, which Greece always are (is) – it must be spring or early summer, just like it must be morning or early day when you start a difficult work. So I ordered (booked) a room in the monastery in Jutland, I told you about once. I finished the first book there, an extremely calm and beautiful place.

'Again you are so distant even if you are in the middle of my memory. I can never place you in the everyday (in my imagination?) – it's always an island with sun and no money – and no work. I must be bored into the pain before I start to write.

'So, my late love, give sound – tell me constantly where you are and be faithful – as I am.'

I phoned Anna from Fay's place at nine o'clock one night when Fay was out and Petrushka answered in Danish. She had only two or three words of English: 'Actually, Mister Hill'.

Her mother told me what she had to tell me. She would go to Jutland to work on a book from 5 September to 20th and prepare a reading for the Danish Academy in Copenhagen in early October. She would like to fly to Cómpeta for a fortnight. Two weeks was the longest she could allow. Petrushka was in a new school. She had begun that day, she liked it. She (the mother) had to be miserable in order to write. Orslev Kloster, Orsleukloster 7800 Skive, Jutland, would find her.

She was working in a monastery (cloister).

'I have been kicked out of house and home,' Rory told Anna.

'Why?'

'For irregularity. Or do I mean inconsistency?'

'Uuuuuh!'

'Exactly, my thoughts in a nutshell.'

'What will you do?'

'I'll have to find another home.'

'And will you?'

'Who can say?'

After a rapid breakfast of Viennese coffee and Gauloise at Cranley Gardens, which was the only honeymoon that Rory ever had, he took her to a deucedly odd double-feature programme of Werner Herzog movies at the New Electric Cinema in Portobello Road, a 134 bus to Warren Street and a taxi (£2) to the cinema (ticket £3 each) where *La Soupière* (1977) was showing with *Heart of Glass* (1976). The first a documentary about a volcano that never erupted on an island from which 75,000 people were evacuated, the camera tracked and zoomed about an empty city of stray dogs and blinking traffic lights; thousands of snakes had come down from the mountains, alarmed by the ground heat, to drown themselves in the sea. The feature film seemed to be about demented German glass-blowers. Fay sniggered at the deadly seriousness of the amazing Krauts.

Sun under trees. You wanted to. The dogs. Walked to Baker Street Station. Italian coffee place closed. Health food place open. Waited for the Globe to open its doors. Stayed until darkness fell. 27 to Archway, 134 to Cranley Gardens, home not home, not for Rory but for Fay. Port, bed, deep penetration, peaceful night, raining, discussed women's liberation (lower case please) in the kitchen.

In bed you admitted that you had wanted it under the leafy trees, ash or maple in Kensington Gardens, when we kissed, you had wanted more, the whole hog.

The sun in the grass, the dogs cavorting by the pond. Walk by the water, Essex or Sussex Gardens, drops of rain. The night. Back now upstairs. The cats asleep, Terence away.

The moon, scudding cloud, came from behind, you at first passive then passionate, claws. Port and Gauloise before sleep. Intimate odour. Tenderness. Touch. Silence.

'I feel reality is retreating from me', – here Fay glanced quickly with the clouded pupils of a Persian cat at Rory, who was fidgeting. 'Or I'm retreating from reality.'

With shoes off and knees under chin, tucked up in the window-seat, she was watching what was passing outside, a dreamy powder-blue Persian queen cat troubled by something.

Stilly crouches she! Hey, heartache!

Never in his life had Rory forced his attentions on anybody, man, woman or beast. He was in some ways a craven lover, an admirer of fine but *soi-disant* parts, a luster after vanishing tail.

Whenever he expedited a lady's lust (as soon as possible after his attentions have fastened on her), she took a venu under her girdle and swelled upon it. Rory said 'When I touch I then begin for to let affection in,' just like Robert Herrick, the randy divine.

For so had it came to pass for Hannelore, who had conceived with child in the course of a short London break at 29 Chandos Road, Willesden Green, NW2, and had it aborted in the Hague.

Similarly with Fay Foyle: conception in torrid bouts one August in Cranley Gardens, aborted of a five month foetus (a daughter-to-be for Rory who had always wanted one) in a London clinic.

As it had come to pass otherwise for Coppera, who had fruit-fully conceived and brought forth a trio of bouncing boyos.

When Rory had obliged Fay Foyle by staying three nights in a row at her house in Cranley Gardens, in her double bed between her scorching thighs, he had burnt his boats and no error. For by obliging the one he mortally insulted and disobliged the other, her deadly rival, Coppera (Rory's legal spouse for twenty-four years and more); who now had him – *Le Vent Galant* – ostracised from hearth and home, threw the potsherds in his face, told him to push off and never dare darken her door (now it was all hers) again.

Rory of the Hills, the classically homeless wanderer, the lost sojourner heading west, now cravenly begged permission to occupy Coppera's Andalucian *hacienda* in the foothills of the Sierra Almijara, for a year, or for some unspecified space of time. This the very *casa* purchased with Rory's elastic funds, when he was in funds, his time and his signature.

And when his time was up there, on Coppera's sufferance, where would he voyage to? He would see. Time would tell. A way would be revealed unto him. One thing was certain: England was finished for him. Ireland would come to the rescue, and through the good graces furthermore of he who was to be Nobel Prizeman of 1995, Heaney himself, who wrote of Aosdána and Cnuas, all double-Dutch to wandering Rory, now fairly demented with worry, deprived of his family and unable to work, homeless indeed.

'Lies again, always your fancy lies,' snapped Coppera. 'You're telling lies again.'

'What would be the good of telling you the truth?' muttered the devious Rory, blinded with his very own lies, which he deemed to be his truths, the only hope.

'The kids are old enough now to be told the truth.'

Arguing with Coppera was like standing in the doorway and having the door slammed in your face, time and time again.

'I understand you,' Rory told Fay. Whereas even after more than twenty years of co-habitation he didn't understand Coppera. She was as much a mystery to him as the first time he had encountered her, at a party for South Africans in her top-floor room in Belsize Park, London NW3.

'I understand you perfectly,' he told Fay. And he did.

Phoning Fay

Emerging from the depths of Queen's Wood and darting across the road into Highgate Wood (where all the corpses of the Great Plague are buried) and making his way up the disused and overgrown railway track for a service that no longer served Muswell Hill, in the vicinity of Pembridge Garden Villas and the former residence of man-murderer Nielsen who had murdered and then dismembered his eighteen male victims and either flushed them down the drains or buried them in the garden,

Rory presently broke cover to immediately disappear into a public telephone box where he dialled 88 77 44 and he could hear it ringing in Cranley Gardens, close enough to hit with a catapult, and the receiver repeated the number he had just dialled as if uttering the password.

'It's I.'

'You can't come?'

'I can come.'

'Well then come. I'm just out of a shower. Standing here dripping,' she snickered.

'I'm coming as fast as public transport permits.'

'Peasant!'

'More like a pheasant. I do live in the woods, you know, nowadays. Rory of the Hills, blood-brother to Wandering Angus.'

'You're still a peasant.'

iii

The Henchley–Foyle marriage was not made in Heaven, so few marriages are, and had begun to disintegrate as soon as the co-celebrants had shifted ground, come to the big city of London.

Something was wrong; Henchley felt he was losing ground, losing face. When Rory encountered him on the stinking stairs, putting away his hog in the hallway, removing his leather gloves and helmet, flaxen hair plastered to his skull with sweat, no greetings were exchanged. He could already sense the presence of another suitor for his estranged wife here, sniffing around. Henchley wore the cross, disgruntled hot expression that was habitual with him, as though he were worrying about an over-draft, or the hog wasn't performing right, or he hadn't gotten his oats; he was all fired up with resentment; hidden disappointments were devouring him from within. The thought flew through Rory's mind, 'God, she's brave or reckless to lie under this heap of resentment!'

Some hint of this disturbance of heart was in the flushed biker's face as he ascended the stairs to his supper, to more humiliations.

Perhaps she had refused him her favours? Syd was lost without regular nooky. She had told Rory some of their troubles. He had followed her into the child's room after an argument that lasted from midnight until three in the morning, waking up the child with his voice raised in anger, and he had done an ugly act, the child saw it and vomited. He continued to perform the ugly act and the child continued to vomit.

That was the end of Henchley for Fay, the end of their marriage too. He was told to pack and go, take his things with him.

He had given her a last lingering look of pure hatred and stamped downstairs for the last time, hauled out the hog and went farting off through the Broadway. It was good riddance to bad rubbish.

She was a lovely silky lady to be in bed with on a cold night. She liked port for a night-cap and smoked Disque Bleu, liked to play madrigals on the clavichord, seventeenth and eighteenth-century music, Monteverdi's *Ulysses*, read sheet music, which delighted the notoriously unmusical Rory, who preferred Jacqueline Françoise and Billie Holiday. Women do not relish getting old; Fay was afraid of getting into a rut. Change was everything, she said, change was indeed life.

'It's necessary to make a change sometimes. Getting old, being old (Rory was fifty-two), means you can't make it any more.'

It was necessary to make a change, seize the day. Having penetrated into the depths of Queen's Wood with Rory and two bottles of Guinness and found a mossy bank on to which the sunlight filtered, she would sit up and straighten her back, no sluttish compromising positions tolerated. In a little while she sat up; the interrogation was peremptory, peppery: 'Why have you gone all shady on me suddenly?'

In marriage, particularly marriage undertaken rashly at a young and tender age (Fay had been married at the age of nineteen), there is always the strong partner and the weak one. Fay was the strong one and Syd the weak, say the predictable factor, for the failure would be all of his own making. He would make a mess of it. It was only a matter of time before the contracted bonds were broken: they would acrimoniously go their different ways. For he had had something good and now he had lost it. He had only his hog to comfort him, his black leather gear, the lovingly polished Harley Davidson throbbing between his legs when he let her out on the open road, farting like thunder, to show his contempt, to display his waywardness; was he not a biker through and through? He felt tenderly about his hog. Christ, man, he *loved* his hog.

He had settled somewhere far from London, far from Fay, somewhere down the country found other employment out-of-doors where he could display his strength. Terence visited him from time to time. He inquired of Fay, asked how she was, kept in touch, spoke on the phone, the same surly bloke as before. He couldn't help his nature, God had given him that nature, it was what he was, Syd Henchley, late of Leeds.

Fay kept in touch with Rory now, spoke in low adenoidal tones into his ear, a cat-purring, did not identify herself, because Rory at once knew who it was; Fay uttered the code-word for the day, the password for strange places – today it was to be *Winchmore Hill*.

Did Rory know where that was? He did not; but he could find it. Precise instructions were issued. He was to leave immediately, take the 102 to The Cock, then a W4 or 23 or 29 to The Green Dragon on Winchmore Hill, where he would find Fay in the Lounge, sampling the brews.

He went there. And she was there, sitting up like a cat, feeling the fires, purring, a smoky Persian.

She had of course admirers. Pill One and Pill Two and Boris-the-Bad of Yugoslavia were mentioned. 'Pill' and 'pillock' were dismissive terms of contempt. Pill Two took her out to a pub where a fractious drinker had taken offence and wanted to sort him out, hitching up his belt and glaring at Pill Two who had gone white as a sheet.

'Are you a man or a mouse or what are you?'

'No, no, no, I'm a mouse,' Pill Two protested feebly.

Fay was much amused by this frank display of the weak submission of machismo. She tittered when she told Rory that her fine protector had feet of clay. Syd would have sorted him out all right. You don't mill it with a biker. Syd would have beaten the shit out of him, laid him out cold.

Boris-the-Bad had phoned from Yugoslavia. Every so often he liked to phone her in the middle of the night, cracking his whip to make her perform. 'Boris speaking! How is my little perisher?' Love was a dirty business of rape and rapine, women were abject slaves. He was in the carpet business, import and export. Rory saw him as sallow-complexioned, bluff and bossy, with a walrus moustache like Nietzsche. He drank black coffee, smoked thick cigars with the bands on, took no shit from nobody, nobody least of all a woman, least of all a pretty one. Fay was his little London quail whom he adored, in his own way, from a safe distance.

'How do you spell Ljubljana?' she asked Rory.

For some reason or other, nothing to do with reason, she reminded Rory of Molly Cushen. The same long black hair, silken presence, same adenoidal confidential dark tones that inferred some dark conspiracy, talk at a tangent. Fay Henchley-Foyle was the woman Molly Cushen might have become, had she left Celbridge to discover the big outside world for herself. She was also reincarnated in the Dublin brunette Anne Marie, who trimmed Rory's locks and beard in a Cork hairdressing emporium – Ikon, upstairs in Princes Street – the same unsettling presence, same clotted-cream voice, the slurred enunciation suggestive of a Persian cat purring, the same I-know-you look in the eye.

These were to date avatars for Rory, reminding him of the wind blowing dark tresses across a child's chalk-white face on a bridge so long ago.

Rory now found himself standing on what the Danes (they who abhor public rage, calamity, the unforeseen, all manifestations of public and private disorder, for they are an orderly people and without order there is chaos; unless it be Germanic order – *Ordnung* – and then you get a worse chaos) call *Livsfare Jordskred* or unsteady earth, a warning sign on a cliff that beetles o'er its base into the Kattegat.

It was a very bad place for a Dane to be; also for poor Rory, for whom it was Queer Street.

Cranley Gardens would be impossible for Rory when Fay's son returned from the country.

Rory dialled 88 77 44, a most improbable conjunction of

matching numerals and Fay's voice answered, laughing as though she were in the middle of something.

'Rory here.'

'Oh, hello Rory there. Are you coming over? I just had a shower and I'm dripping wet. Why don't you just drop in for tea and trifle?'

'I'm on my way.'

The pubs they frequented were Dick's Bar on the Finchley Road, The Good Shepherd on Archway Road, The Rose and Crown in Highgate, The Woodman by the hill where the 134s turn up for Muswell Hill Broadway between the two woods. She wore a blue tunic, a sleeveless black leather jacket, high heels, an expensive leather shoulder bag full of tenners.

She spoke of a vacation in Simla after Christmas, £2,000 each, with her new husband or man who suffered (on reading her diary) from what she called 'recapitulative jealousy', a bad form of the disease, reading her account of her brief affair with Rory, in and out of the bars and the woods, and the Raoul Dufy exhibition at the Hayward Gallery. Ruddles Best Yorkshire Ale was her preferred tipple.

'Blossom' and 'Sunshine' were her London terms of endearment for Terence, her *muy nervioso*, only son. She was a good mother, concerned for his welfare. 'Sticky' was another of her prohibitive terms.

She was not the early Waugh society girl on a spree, she was not the naughty sixth former looking to lose her virginity in the toolshed with the virile young gardener or the virile handyman or the virile and handsome ice-cream vendor who had his pitch at the school gate, with all three in order of preference; she was rather Cora, the torrid young wife in James M. Cain's *The Postman Always Rings Twice*, having it off with the journeyman who just happened to be passing through.

She had aborted the five-month foetus without a word to the putative father, Rory. She told him later, at what seemed an opportune moment, perhaps in bed, in the dark. 'Did I ever tell you . . .'

She received Rory at the door, hair wet, eyes sparkling, in

loose-fitting housecoat and bare feet, naked under the housecoat, which Rory discovered at the first embrace when the housecoat fell off the wearer of its own accord and with eyes closed she surrendered to the tyranny of love. Was she the deprived child who had grown avaricious for what she wanted? She detested what she called 'routine', by which she meant Missionary-style loving. She wanted the unexpected, close attention to the matter in hand, expected and would get, sexual dynamics; that aroused her to ecstatic states when she capitulated to the attentions of a persistent brute who would take her just as he wanted her, the way she craved to be taken, now receiving Rory (the timid caller transformed) with a new ardour that was mutual, raking his back with her claws, for her claws were out for it, as he took her deeper and deeper, she in a kind of sexual stupor, whispering 'Sorrysorrysorry,' hardly knowing what she was saying or doing. She was Cora, drawing blood.

'Now you can go whistling back across the fields.' Talking was part of the loving and giving that might begin at 11 and end at 4 a.m. with the birds beginning to twitter. It had started on the window-seat with Fay, listening to the revellers going home from The Woodman, and then the long-drawn-out loving, whispering sorrysorrysorry.

> A shudder in the loins engenders there
> The broken wall and tower and Agamemnon dead.

'Don't force me to do something I don't want to do,'
She knew a thing or two about love.
She scratched and panted in the toils of love as if in the clutches of a predator, whereas it was she who was the bloodthirsty one, growling in her throat, her jaw jutting fiercely, blue-black hair tossed, masking a face that had grown longer, hungry now; she was showing her sharp teeth.

Love had liberated her. In her Cora-mood from *The Postman Always Rings Twice* she would have eaten the postman coming with a package. Instead it was Rory, who had crossed from the heath to pass through Highgate Wood and Queen's Wood visiting the off-licence at the foot of the hill, plucking flowers from

suburban gardens, who appeared at the door laden with rhodo-
dendrons. Fay drew him in with one prehensile claw. Terence
was away with friends; they had the house to themselves.

'I wanna be penetrated,' she said in the provocative nasal
whine of Gloria Graham in the movie *Crossfire*. 'I want you to
penetrate me.'

She could not be more explicit. She wanted to be carved up
on the kitchen table like venison. Pyrotechnics were needed
here. She wanted to devour and be devoured, to accept pain
and to inflict it with her bared claws on the groaning beast, the
god Pan, half-beast, half-man, all god who lived in the woods and
was about to start humping her good and proper, running with
her to the bed and throwing her down. She wanted the works.

Pan-Rory pounded her liver as though her pelvic parts so
tender and open were the mortar which his pestle or mighty
member so assiduously pounded; as her breath deepened, her
nostrils flared, exposing the stricken whites of her narrow cat's
eyes, opening wide as if stricken with *petit mal*, blazed up
at Rory.

'Hey, heartache, I'm just slipping away, slipping away.'

Once Rory had returned from Gatwick Airport, having left his
wallet behind in the kitchen of Cranley Gardens, only to find a
soft-spoken innocuous-looking *succubi* or rival already ensconced
in the kitchen, sipping coffee.

'This is Gussy.'

'Oh, howdy Guss!'

The disgruntled Rory spent an uncomfortable night in a
friend's pad near Wandsworth Prison and was away early on
a Málaga flight, put to the expense of buying a further one-way
ticket. Such was life in a pig's eye.

iv

Now Rory would have to begin thinking of 252 and environs
in the past tense, for his life had finished there. In summer the
Broadway had reeked of sickening petrol fumes and the stale

stink of uncollected garbage. When the stand of sycamores was cut down in the Patch, the cemented area where the kids played, there was that much less shade; soon it would all be cement and the United Dairy would close.

The kids, ours and others, played in the Patch below, calling out 'Last one up the fire escape is a lesbian!' Thieves crept up it by night and nicked clothes and football gear off the wire clothesline. The apartments were a place of broken marriages.

The front door of the decaying block of flats gave immediately on to the Broadway, very murky in winter, very steamy in summer when the tarmac melted. But summer and winter, fall and spring, the place was petrol-fumed as though a lit match would ignite it, send it all up. All the double-decker buses would explode behind the public toilets where the dark youths practised karate chops and high kicks. On the top or fifth floor of the cold water walk-up apartment, Coppera heated water on the stove, filled a bath half-full and bathed the kids, all three in the bath at once, little seals in a rock pool.

In Cranley Gardens just down the hill before Crouch End cricket pitches, the O'Neills were next-door neighbours to Fay Foyle. They had a mongoloid son who wandered about the garden with an air-rifle and took pot-shots at a bottle. At night we heard the manic laughter and the *ping* of hits. The mother was up and about early, hanging washing on the line. The apple tree had a bumper crop. The neighbour beyond the O'Neills hated cats and children. His name was Anthony William Snapes. People can be strange, there's no accounting for some. Mumu would have described them as a low lot, common as dishwater. Perhaps they were; perhaps not; people were just people.

On Saturday 11 August 1975, some twenty-four years after the nuptials in the little RC Church of St Thomas More in London N10, the phone went unanswered at No. 22 Cranley Gardens, until, in exasperation, Fay lifted up the receiver.

'It's for you.'

'Who is it?'

'Coppera.'

Rory strode to the phone like the brave hero in the Dickens novel ascending the scaffold.

'Your things are being sent around in a cab. That's it.'

She rang off. Brief and brutal. Would women make good hangmen? Or should we say 'hangwomen'?

A morose, coloured cab-person came pealing the bell.

'Darby Hall?'

'I believe you're looking for me, Rory Hill, a common misunderstanding. I understand that you have my effects.'

'The lady up there said I was to bring your clobber down 'ere.'

We'd planned to walk across the Heath to see Billy Wilder's *Fedora* at the Hampstead Everyman, but hadn't the heart for it. Went instead to the Ruth Ellis pub in the wood, the Magdala of infamous repute. Walked back across the heath in the dark after a session in The White Polar Bear. A bird never flew on one wing. Bought bottle of Schluck at wine store and so home hand-in-hand via the woods. Consumed Schluck in kitchen. Nothing to eat all day. Not hungry. Curiously stunned state, as if struck on head with club. Told to leave home. Fucked Fay silly. Darkness, deep breathing. Ending, ending here.

Without her clothes Fay was more mare than cat. The glossy pelt on her, the dimpled rump, the mane of blue-black hair that reached to the small of her back, the way her nostrils flared. Are you glad to see me? Will you miss me when you're in Dublin? Will you think of me there?

Rory promised that he would. Soon he would be phoning her from airports, flying about, looking for a place to land, a home-base.

The Fay Foyle affair was the straw that broke the camel's back for Coppera Hill. 'You've done it this time. You've let us down too often. You can stay in my place in Cómpeta but I think you should pay some of the bills here. That's only fair.'

When Coppera spoke of fairness and fair play, it meant that she was up to something, scheming; feminine wiles had come into play, or so Rory's naturally suspicious nature informed him. When she brought the children into any dispute and thrust them into the firing-line, it meant the gloves were off and the claws out. Coppera's claws served a very different purpose to Fay's. But all claws were the same when they scratched and drew blood and all women's natures were much the same, particularly when it came to defending their interests, with the weapons they were supplied with, the savvy and the savagery, modified to suit the occasion, or the man for whom allowances would have to be made. If you can't, why do you try? Do you like lamb? Will you miss me? I can I can I can, I do I do I do, I will I will I will I will!

Brace up.

PART VII:

Down Mexico Way

Mexico City, Cuernavaca, Acapulco
February 1998

61

Blood and Sand

I n a handsome park in Acapulco stands a heraldic bronze male figure set up high on a granite pedestal and what is more wearing nothing but Bermuda shorts and sandals, brown-skinned as a medlar but bald as a snooker ball, his brow furrowed as if in deep thought, troubled by matters of state, mouth set in a grim line, the great hooded eyes partly closed. Can it be ennui or boredom or the tedium of office or just constipation? The statue is called 'He's Got the Whole World in His Hands'.

It is none other than Don Señor Alfredo Calles, grandson of the General and President of all Mexico in the troubled decade 1924–34.

There can be no other kind of time in Mexico but troubled time; no time there in that grim goaty land can be other than troubled. The lovely engulfing air trembles as though the spirits of the superstitious Aztecs, fear-crazed and given to making placatory sacrifices to the sun on their blood-soaked altars, on a daily basis, virgins and children not excluded, still breathed in the living air that blew from Cuernavaca and in through the Cortés window of the Rancho Pico set most prettily in the uplands of the state of Morelos, setting the wind-chimes atinkle.

The trembling air was Aztec air, like the brown prehensile begging hands of the women who begged around the

Cuernavaca Cathedral steps; begging, forever begging, their hands outstretched for baksheesh. The twin volcanoes were standing guard fifty miles off; across the undulating valley all was shivery Aztec air, just as much Mexico as the eighty-two (Rory looked up and counted them) buzzards that arrived from nowhere one bright morning to circle slowly in a funeral pyre dance over the Rancho Pico, their shadows moving slow and sedately across the lawn and over the swimming pool, glaring down at the lone nudist doing lengths, Rory looking up at them, numerous as bluebottles and circling, silently, going down one by one to feed on the corpse of the horse killed by another horse in a fit of jealous rage, involving a foal and a kick that killed; where else could it happen but in Mexico, in the state of Morelos?

The expiring breath of the innocents hung in the air. The buzzards were descending one by one or in twos and threes, an inbred courtesy perhaps, the courtesy of the air, the good manners of the buzzards who had flown from God knows where, far away anyway, sensing or knowing of the kill. But how? Their sight was said to be phenomenal; by smell, then? But would the pong of death carry that far? Yes, in Mexico it would.

We came upon them feeding in the dried-up marsh by the soccer field; a preliminary rustling like old papers being disturbed by a wind or an umbrella blowing itself inside-out announced their presence and then three of them came stumbling out, bloated with bloodied beaks they use for slashing open cadavers that they fancy. Getting airborne again with some difficulty, coming out of the long grass where the mare was decomposing, they brought with them the stench.

The stench was brutal. More than all the bad things that had ever happened in Mexico since the execution of Maximilian; a stench more terrible than words can describe. Blood had been spilt lavishly everywhere; it was a fecundating agent, like sulphate of soda, quicklime, petrol to clear weeds.

Rory's fastidious nostrils were assailed by a smell that would make a sickroom seem sweet, a lingering smell of dissolution that seemed to collect bulk and breathing body of all the vileness ever ejected from sick bodies, from middens, from the open holes of Mexican toilets where women crouched to discharge menstrual filth. And it was more than that; it was the stink of a Mexican battlefield, with the buzzards having a banquet. The smell made the hair of his head rise up of its own accord and he was back in a flick sixty-five years to Springfield again and was six years old and standing by the dead sheep that the dogs had opened up in their savagery and now the maggots were busily having a go at the black and purple interior of corruption with a scarcely perceptible yet insistent activity, like cancer eating one up from inside as it had taken Dado. The sheep lay on her side against the wall of Mangan's field where she had come to die or been chased into the corner by the dogs, who had her cornered then, as the maggots had her now and were working on her with a will, poor thing. She was theirs. Is that what the Bard meant by 'progressing through the guts of a beggar'?

And I thought again of Molly Cushen, who had been my first love even if I had never touched her. She had shown me what love was, standing on the bridge with the wind blowing, weeping as though her heart had broken, as it probably had, for her mother had died on her and, who knows, maybe in pain; love was weeping on a humpbacked bridge. Sorrow was eating out her heart, as they say.

I thought too of Harriet seated with her husband above the hot sand of the bullring in Málaga, just like the old movie *Blood and Sand* with Rita Hayworth and Tyrone Power as the stoats pattering after blood. Tyrone Power had to swim across a river and in the blue moonlight of day-for-night photography fight a bull, so that he could ascend to the castle where Rita slept, and climb up the side of the creeper and enter, to find her preparing for bed, her wide mouth decorated with a slash of lipstick like blood, as if she were a vampire, which was all extremely exciting and mysterious when I saw it at the age of fourteen at the Savoy Cinema in Dublin. It was the movie that made a matador of John Fulton, born Fulton John Short, his Italian father, a house-painter, having changed his name from Schoccitti to Short, which Spaniards couldn't pronounce. He killed his first bull in Mexico in 1953, Rita's bleeding mouth no doubt still vividly in his mind when he (aged twelve) had first seen her and knew he wanted to be a bullfighter. She had made a man of him.

It was a day in April when the great Ordoñez dispatched with much valour and panache the five great beasts he had been contracted to slaughter, four black as tar and one the colour of a puma, not disposed to fight, least of all fight Antonio Ordoñez. I had been unfaithful to Coppera in the spare bed in the *casa* Harriet's husband, my good friend John, had rented in Nerja; the downward slide had begun. Harriet lied about the fat lip I had given her; she said a pumpkin had dropped from the patio roof. Her policy was to lie in your teeth until found out and then give in with as much grace as possible.

The smell of blood must have wafted up to her; but weren't women inured to blood and blood-letting, their own at least? They had to grow accustomed to it from the alarm of their first menses. It was in their nature, as love was too, submitting or desiring what you had to have, the chosen one, all that giving and taking; it made me sad to take Harriet, for it meant unhappiness for others whom I liked. That was the price of love, the result of cheating.

The statue of the bronze figure aloft on its pedestal stopped passers-by dead in their tracks. It 'got' to them, as the morons say today. A plaque set into the block of granite informed the inquisitive that the figure aloft was not a military man, but Humanoid Erectus Mexicanitis, Alfredo Alfonso Juan Calles, born in Acapulco and grandson of the brave General.

Known habitat: Mexico City, Cuernavaca, Acapulco. Carnivore and user of tobacco and other euphoria-inducing substances known to science. Under it the rubric:

> He's got you and me, brother;
> He's got you and me, sister;
> HE'S GOT THE WHOLE WORLD
> IN HIS HANDS!

Not a quotation form the Koran, the book without camels, that authenticated it as from the very hand of the Prophet, as some aver; no, these the freewheeling and outspoken lyrics of an old number that climbed the charts in the early 1960s in the time of

Haight-Ashbury and Dr Timothy Leary and pot-smoking when such ill-considered dreams (and dreams they were) of racial equality and freedom for all had got rid of Martin Luther ('I have a dream') King as they had got rid of Medgar Evers, leader of the Civil Rights movement, shot by a sniper using a high-powered 1917 Enfield rifle in Guynes Street, Jackson, Mississippi. His dying words were 'Turn me loose.'

Such notions were being freely and flagrantly bandied about; it was in the air; for ideology is not acquired by faith, but by breathing the tainted air.

The statue was saying something; the pose was referential, enigmatic, almost lugubrious; an outflung imperious arm would not have looked amiss. Big Alf had a distinct look of Professor Tribini the Copenhagen ringmaster and impresario villainously top-hatted, striding about the ring in top-boots, cracking a bull-whip to make the lions growl. Or could he be the master of ceremonies in a bordello?

There was a twin in London: not in Kensington Gardens but in Madame Tussaud's waxworks just off Baker Street, home of Sherlock Holmes. Pablo Picasso was dressed casually in loose drawers and nothing else but the flip-flops that he had favoured at La California. His suntanned body was as dark as undressed teak; he scowled at the loungers who had come to stare at famous dead men.

Other waxen imagery of the famous *defuncti* posed, stuck in one attitude for all eternity or at least until this dead one went out of favour or the unthinkable happened and Madame Tussaud's waxworks closed. Famous politicians dressed in authentic but ill-cut Savile Row suits long out of fashion stood uncomfortably around, waiting for Churchill to say something grandiose and bombastic, so that they could laugh and move away, take a quick smoke outside. Constricted in their stiff collars and neckties, they held their heads high as if being garrotted, strangled in the Spanish manner, jutting their waxen jaws; they looked most uneasy.

Lord Nelson was there too, dying for all time on the deck of his ship, the ship that will never sail again, become part of the great waxworks that had been the British Empire; on whom, it was thought then, the sun would never set. But set it did. And then it was finished, had to be cleared away so that others could live, get out of their bondage; make way for a new and even more terrible England.

Like much that was pleasing in the land, the village green and mince pies, the national game had gone out of favour; no more sticky dog wickets, no more Hobbs.

The game was played at night now, as with other criminal activities, on a floodlit pitch with a black sightscreen and a white ball, the players dressed in lurid pyjamas with draw-strings; it was halfway to being American baseball in a ballpark in Pittsburgh; but played in a determined but joyless way in the chill English air. Next they would be playing games down in the empty mines. But in the meantime there was this nightmare game of cricket, by Jove! Spooky wicket.

62

The Aztec Look

C ertainly he was a singular-looking geek, there could be no two ways about that. He appeared to be a little taller than he actually was, and however he managed that trick I cannot say, because frankly I don't know. He had the look of a despot.

Possibly he was a magician controlling optical illusions, using himself as a subject as he strolled along, shrinking only to become gigantic again, like Marcel Marceau ducking behind a prop to re-emerge on the Olympia stage now tall and elongated as Goliath, now shrunken to the dimensions of little David with his slingshot, looking chastened. (Not that Alfredo ever looked chastened, God forbid.) The master mime from Limoges changed sizes at will as you might don and doff clothes.

The great hooded eyes (armadillo or lizard, certainly reptilian) were unnerving: more so than before the operation, for they seemed to have only one expression, or maybe none at all, except haughty indifference. The stare or eye-probe went right through you and out the other side, without any cognisance of the party perceived; one (Rory) had become a thing; and *that* was unnerving.

As he buttered his toast at the breakfast table he liked to chivvy and bullyrag the little Greek who owned a chain of cinemas through Connecticut and was vendor for all the popcorn machines that supplied the movie buffs.

He had brokered some chair at Harvard, was a little sweet on Roxy; he was a very rich old Greek, very, who went in for long rambling inconclusive yarns as such academics are prone to do.

'Connecticut my arse,' Alfredo drawled with the weary lack of forbearance of a dictator signing another death warrant, and the great prohibitive blinds came clattering down.

Roxy batted her oynx-and-opal eyes at her former lord and master whose overbearing Mexican ways she was all too familiar with, remarking 'There go the lions again.' For one of them had roared out in his cramped cage in the little zoo on the island.

Honorio the houseboy, a married man long in the service of Alfredo Calles, glided to and from the kitchen where Maria his wife was preparing something good. He wore natty Bermuda shorts and a serious expression.

Big Alf was applying himself seriously to the matter in hand: what his plate contained. He liked to pile on what he preferred and start eating. In Denmark it is customary and good manners to dig in as soon as food is placed before you, and the men are demanding seconds before their womenfolk (who double as cooks) have sat down. The same custom probably obtains in the cramped quarters of the zoo, always lions before lionesses. I wondered if the expression of lofty indifference covered the fatalism that must lie behind all cruelty. Mexicans had an affinity with cruelty, because they were adepts at inflicting pain.

'¡Ah Pájaro! Pájaro!' crooned Alfredo in his most cajoling voice. He was King of the Castle, the White Elephant bought as a sure-fire investment a week before the peso fell. Now on the market for nine years, it was still unsold. It would have been just the eyrie for a reclusive movie director; Kubrick was still alive, living somewhere in England.

After breakfast we would all go down the hundreds of steps for a dip off the private dock. The old Greek had a bad leg. Alannah swam like an otter and could not be got out of the warm water. A trimaran with two employees from the Acapulco municipality came and collected any scurf that might have accumulated on the surface overnight and was floating there, one man to keep the engine ticking over, the other to remove the debris with a net. Alfredo called out affable greetings; the sea was being prepared for him as though it were a large warm bath. He accepted all that, as if it was his due. The sea was warm. Jellyfish floated in it, trailing their stingers.

He was aloof in manner, not exactly standoffish but apart, like the dying James Joyce, lord of languages. He kept himself to himself, as we Irish say in our fork-tongued, sly way, denying all.

He kept himself to himself at a right royal remove from common clay; the distance between yourself and the King, the *Rey*, his Reyness, is immense, boundless and immeasurable as a state of mind. And I should know, having once shaken the hand of a king, and a Spanish king at that. It's not in the eye but in the firm but distant grip.

He was a striking-looking man who moved about the city on foot. He didn't drive a Sunbeam nor a Chrysler but a small yellow Toyota that no car thief worth his salt would look at twice, the King in mufti disguised as a civilian. He was as bald as a coot.

He had begun to lose his hair at an early age and seeing it was going anyway, he bethought himself '¡*Carajo!* I might just as well lose it all,' decided to go the whole hog and have it shaved off, offering to astonished bystanders a noble brown dome speckled as an auk's egg in place of the former thatch. And why ever not? Wasn't he himself the grandson of a real bad egg, addled by Mexican standards, a right *huevo malo*?

For a full decade, Mexico found itself in the firm grip of General Plutarco Elias Calles, says the quaint history book which never tells the truth. The man from Sonora came from a poor background and when his term of office ended, his name stank in the fastidious nostrils of all liberal-minded Mexicans.

Big Alf had the face of an Aztec Eagle Knight without the helmet, or maybe the ringmaster in a circus who controls the animals and stage-manages the whole show with that face and that deportment that you associate with such apparently effortless mastery, even before you witness it in action. It was a look, a port, midway between contempt and indifference; we do not *try* to amuse and we are *not* amused.

He was a king in exile. His astrological sign was the Lion, images of which filled his house, with paintings of generously rumped ladies of easy virtue. Deprived of all hair, maneless now, he had become not less but positively more king-like. He had been manager and owner of the night-spot Tiberio on the Boulevard Miguel Alemán in Acapulco; he puts us up in his odd appartment in Mexico City. It was the city of the future, highly dangerous, jungle-like in its extremes of wealth and poverty, its ferocity. You had to keep your wits about you, otherwise you'd be clawed to bits in short order.

The lordly and lion-like Alfredo Calles showed us tenderfoots (Alannah had married a Mexican, had lived there; it was Rory's first and last visit) the place to have breakfast (The Biscuits), the place in which to have lunch ('all you can eat for forty pesos') the place not to go to (Sanborn's), the best bookshop (Casa Lamm) all on Colonia Roma, lent us his chauffeur (Don Cutberto), tried without much success to 'Mexicanise' Rory. But even a lion-tamer couldn't manage that. He couldn't do it. We should never carry passports or much money about with us. He moved like a man who knew his way about: thirty of his friends had been mugged, but not him. His manner was menacing.

But to tell you what Alfredo Calles (Big Alf) is like, I must first tell you what he is not like. His son Alfredito (Little Alf) he does not resemble in the least. They are poles apart in deportment, character, temperament, upbringing, favours. One is quite bald and lordly, the other is not. Big Alf (to further confuse matters) has a double in the same building: a painter who unlocked the door and stepped out carrying canvases and, seeing Rory's look of recognition, said 'I am not he' and crossed the road, laughing.

If I tell you that there is something in his dark Mexican eyes that reminds me of a turkey-cock which seems to be permanently in a furious temper, bridling, it does not mean that Big Alf in any way resembles or reminds me of any turkey-cock I ever encountered; but in attempting to describe the cross look in the turkey-cock's eye I seem to be describing the history of Mexico, divided and subdivided by successive waves of conquerors, one more rapacious and bloodthirsty than the other in its greed, from the time of the Incas and the Aztecs to Pancho Villa and the

President (deeply corrupt, like the others) who succeeded Calles; to Lazaro Cárdenas.

As we crossed the great sunbaked plaza after viewing the Diego Rivera murals, I heard a most joyful and tuneful melody coming from under the shaded colonnade and who was it but a one-armed beggar playing a tune by blowing on a thorn leaf as one might twang a Jew's harp or vamping on a harmonica (Marzy dotes). Rivera had shown me a previous Mexico and the barbarous cruelty of the Spanish conquistadors, and then the Americans came with their cartels and their arrangements, their plans for Mexico, hated by Diego with all his simple and trusting big heart, the man who had swallowed some of the ashes of his maimed woman, Frida Kahlo.

Not anything as grandiose as the Plumed Serpent, then, but more domesticated and just as savage in its own way, the turkey-cock comes strutting, lord of the Mexican farmyard, boss of the patio, whom even the dogs fear, its fury, its ill-tempered ways, its contrary nature, warped and disturbed.

They are ill-natured creatures, the male of the guinea-fowl (*Numida meleagris*), hostile to all, forever bad-tempered, gobbling at intruders, with inflamed ugly wattles erect. As retrievers or pit bull terriers are bred for specific purposes, so turkey-cocks are bred to vent their spleen, their bile.

They are choleric, expect no quarter from enemies; always expecting the worst, and rarely disappointed in that. For a violent end awaits them; a cruel fate has so arranged it. In order to live with any dignity they must suppress any instinct of tenderness within themselves, knowing that their fate is to be decapitated by a cook with an axe in her hand. Or she is for hewing their head off with a hatchet on a block of wood, cursing them as ungrateful creatures. They have no love for their offspring whom they consume, purple with rage, in embryo in hens' eggs. They will gobble up whole generations, not bothering to distinguish one lot from the other, pitiless as Saturn.

Sometimes, livid with fury, wattles suddenly flooded with blood, they spread out their tawdry wings as though this were a general's bemedalled cloak, a cloak of glory, as if to cry out, but only to expose their dungy hindquarters, the awful anus, as if 'mooning' or cursing their Maker, wishing they could fly. They feel lost in the evolutionary chain of being.

But Big Alf is not like that at all.

A disdainful, baleful look characterises the hooded eyes of turkey-cocks, protected by a flap of skin that hangs down rather like the leather windbreak before the western door of Málaga Cathedral. Their eyelids are permanently inflamed as with acute conjunctivitis and the hardboiled gangster eyes have an oily sheen, adding to the menace of these farmyard creatures not quite as big and belligerent as buzzards. They seem to look down their beaks at you, their head level with your crotch where they could do much damage, had they a mind.

They have no respect for anybody. Fearlessness with them is a kind of vice. They could turn on you.

They have no graces. Their call is unpleasant, more caw or phlegmy clearing of mucus from a constricted throat. They are not particular about what they eat and disdain to clean their arses. They shit in unexpected places, knowing you will tread on it, carry it into the house with you.

With them the act of love is gross, a display of supreme power and contempt over those whom they despise (the clucking hens); with claws like spurs they spurn the cowering hens, putting their full weight down on them, drawing blood. They cackle like witches.

But Alfredo Calles is not like that at all.

History, wrote Octavio Paz, has the cruelty of a nightmare. Presumably he meant Mexican history. And who can gainsay that, seeing that there is nowhere a crueller history?

In a monochrome, slightly foxed, photograph taken during a banquet at the National Palace in Mexico City in December 1914, the waiters (male to a man) standing behind the distinguished company appear blurred and smudged as if caught in the act of fleeing from the dining room, leaving this dangerous assembly, for the President, Gutierrez (a monumental bulky presence), is flanked by the *pistoleros* Pancho Villa (to his right hand) and Emiliano Zapata to his left, dangerous company for any sitting President. The eyes of Zapata glitter like topaz or, better, gleam like a tiger's in a thicket; possibly 'touched up' by a nervous photographer. You can see by the fixed stare caught by the nervous photographer that he (Zapata) has felt the finger of destiny rest on his shoulder for a split second, as surely as the cook came for the turkey-cock, or the Plumed Serpent for the unfortunate Cuauhtemoc whose very name sounds like a death-rattle.

A white silk scarf is knotted about the neck of Emiliano Zapata, lending a dandyish look to the reformer who crouches in his seat, hands on the table. Pancho Villa appears to have something in his mouth and he too crouches a little as if preparatory to catapulting himself across the table to have it out with whoever has the stomach to face him. Both are obviously outdoor men, with their scorched complexions and heavy moustaches. Anybody with a moustache like that is asking for trouble.

Attendants bearing plates of food are stationary for a second, caught in mid-stride. Glasses of what looks suspiciously like water are set before the diners, with no wine bottles on view, and a centrepiece of roses before *El Presidente*, who appears quite calm in the midst of these troublemakers and killers with scant respect for authority. The revolutionary fervour that burned in their eyes and hearts could not be quenched, could not be suppressed, much less put out.

Who was it wrote that thinking about something you know nothing about is not very helpful? When I thought of Mexico before I set foot in it I thought of a country askew, a great bony protuberance coming out of the USA and extending down to Guatemala and Honduras. The names of states sound like cries of pain: Guadalajara, Guanajuato (birth pangs for a big baby who was to become the pistol-toting pug-ugly muralist Diego Rivera), Oaxaca; sores and suppurations, acts of unbelievable cruelty, the brave Emperor with the impossible name from whom a cry could not be wrung.

I thought of congruences in no particular order:

Stout Hernan Cortés grown lean, the hideous syphilitic being in the angry murals of Rivera; of Cantiflas and colonialism; of hangings and insurrections; of those two feathered serpents, Maximilian and Carlotta; of figures hung on gibbets like crows roosting on a tree; of disembowellings aplenty; of *indigenismo* and *Chamools* (whoever they were); of Uxmal and Quetzalcoatl (whatever they were); of *insurgentes* and *tormentas* (lots of these); of Cuernavaca and Morelos; of fantasy and fact; of Rivera's Zapata leading on his white horse in the mural; of the courage and cool cheek of Frida Kahlo maimed for life; of Totonac and Huastec; of an open coffin and tears, idle tears (buckets of those); of rusty weaponry in a courtyard where the wind blows dust about; of men in huge sombreros cantering into town, brandishing revolvers; of Montezuma's revenge; of Cuauhtemoc being tortured and not uttering a cry, biting through his lips, and his torturers laughing at him; of David Alfaro Siqueiros and José Clemente Orozco and their terror-inspiring murals like big blisters that would never go away or be lanced or cured; of horses rearing; of obsidian-tipped spears.

Of the astounding spectacle that was the sudden twilight on the road (all tolls) from Mexico City to Cuernavaca, when Roxy drove like the wind and the little Greek counselled slower driving, or let Alannah drive. Of the cartoons of the great José Guadalupe Posada, a man of the people; of communal *ejidos*. I thought of a scorpion in a shower stall and how small it was; when I thought of Mexico, I thought of all that. I thought of much more, that must also be Mexico; how big it was, immense really, stretching away for ever, and the two volcanoes bowing politely to each other: Popocatepetl and Iztaccihuatl like two kettles boiling over, lids hopping up and down, or two turkey-cocks fighting to the death.

When I thought of Mexico, where I will never go again (once was too much), I think of history immobilised, gone septic, much more immobilised than mere Irish history (history small and shrunken, scratching its sores); history as a hump on the back, a pain in the neck, an acute pain in the arse. I thought of Mexico, the whole of Mexico, the same grim, goaty land that Graham Greene had walked into, confronting his worst fears, his horrors.

63

The *Zaca* Sails Again!

W hat have Little Mo, Gorgeous Gussie Moran (famed for her frillies), Binny Barnes, Myrna Loy and Gloria Graham got in common?

They all reminded Rory of Roxy. She had that 'arrested' look that you get on the faces of pretty girls who know they *are* pretty and are excited by the prospect of playing tig and forfeits and hide-and-seek and blind man's buff in the shrubbery with the boys. She was 'it'. There would be hiding and running and much shrieking in an extensive garden with tall trees and food and soft drinks laid out on a long table and servants serving and the sun would shine, oh yes it would surely shine.

Her adult life would be a continuation of that game. She had looked into the mirror and liked what she saw. She had reached her goal in fast clever moves, like getting 'home' at tig. Modelling and what her daughter ungallantly called 'face-fucking' (using oneself as bait, like supermodel Naomi Campbell) led to the movies and they led to clothes designing, the rag trade, and then she was 'home'.

There was more to her than face and body flaunting. You might learn something of the mother by studying the daughter, but not much. Big Alf's pet name for her was apt, for she was bird-like, with thin bones and a beaky face, exotically tinted hair. You knew this little bird came from the tropics and had flown far. She was always alert, picking at her food, batting her eyes; given to sudden flights of fancy.

She was a somewhat confused Californian lady who read *Time* magazine and believed that the ETs or vegetable men from outer space had already landed on Earth and were living incognito in Baja, California; which may be God's truth for all I know. Stranger things have come to pass in our time.

I could see her as a daring *rejoneadora* mounted on a pure-bred palomino mare, galloping across the bullring just out of range of the bull's horns to rapturous applause from a great crowd that packed the Plaza de Toros.

Or as the scantily clad Lovely Juanita being hurled high from Ganjou brother to brother, from Bob to George and from George to Serge, twirling up like a spinning top in a bizarre musical act widely regarded as dangerous, performed to the strains of that perennial favourite, the Scheherazade Suite of Rimsky-Korsakov.

Nothing could be too extreme when it came to choices, provided these involved well-cut clothes or very few clothes and some pandering to vanity, theirs and hers, as was only a woman's right.

She thought that the pelicans that flew alongside the launch (ostentatiously hired by Alfredo, standing masterfully on his private dock; unobtrusively paid for by the Greek) were albatrosses. Like furry pets dreamed up by Disney's fun people, they flew alongside the launch, looking for scraps.

'¡Ah, Pájaro! Pájaro!'

She had never read a serious book in her life, or listened to classical music and certainly had never heard of Coleridge. Love between them may have gone cold but some affection remained, like eggshells in a nest abandoned. Pet names are a guard against loss, like primitive music – was that Dr Matthew Mighty-grain-of-salt speaking? One would have to take much of Roxy's fancies with a mighty grain of salt. One could almost see her being fired from the mouth of a cannon, wearing little gauzy wings like a butterfly, almost. She was, as they say, 'fun to be with', she *was* much fun singing mock-Wagner in a falsetto voice, in the dining-room doorway of the Old Post House in

Kinsale, her true home. From there she had shimmied down a rope, to be rowed out to the yacht moored off the Bulman in moonlight where a lover waited. She was full of life.

When we were taken out in the launch we may have passed the sea lanes traversed by Flynn's yacht *Zaca* so many years before, with Orson Welles and Rita Hayworth aboard; the helmsman, cocksman, rather in awe of Welles, rather fancying the lady. How could he not?

'Were this Dublin Bay, it would be chilly,' Rory remarked fatuously to the tall sunhat perched like a chimneypot upon the noble dome that was Alfredo Calles at sea. But he was deeply inhaling his own 'pot' and had little interest in such tittle-tattle.

The launch slapped against the oncoming swells, splashing Rory, a poor sailor, now feeling repulsed.

'Well, we're not in Dublin Bay now,' breathed out Big Alf snappishly, with implacable Mex disdain, 'pot' smoke pouring from both cavernous nostrils as if the famous twin volcanoes had begun erupting again; gazing knowingly the while at the coastline that was passing by, the whited sepulchre of the sinful city of Acapulco, where he had once run a famous night-club, sprawled out there in the sun. 'Thank God,' Big Alf, amended as closure.

Only in a school of draw-poker, playing for high stakes, where calling a bluff is a serious matter and the opponent (who may be holding a straight flush) either stares one out or scrupulously avoids one's eye, would you encounter such fixity of stare, probing and probing in a situation of knife-edge tension.

Rory stared at the city at which Welles must have stared, having scouted for locations. There was a hotel formerly run by Johnny Weissmuller and John Wayne, which they had grown tired of and given as a present to their doorman. Such high-handed acts were typical, it was something in the air, abruptly giving and as abruptly withholding, insulting.

Roxy was laid out in the bow, like Rita Hayworth on the aft deck of the *Zaca*, glamorously taking the sun. Now she was for everybody, the whole world wanted her; she was taking everything with great deep breaths as the launch cut through the waves, and the pet birds, Disney's furry creations, flew alongside, staring with their dopey eyes, close enough to stun or kill with an oar. The beer-cooler was being handed around. Rory, quick to take offence, felt a proper yokel.

'Pass the beer forr'ad,' said the little old Greek.

'I feel just like a beer,' Roxy drawled at the sun.

'You look just like Rita Hayworth,' said Rory, all gallantry now.

'Tut tut.'

She was in harmonious accord with her surroundings, like those exotic movie stars who can only play themselves. They are not required to play anybody else, the Garbos and the Garsons and the Hayworths, by directors shrewd enough to pander to such vanity; it was hardly vanity, it came natural as breathing. (Here Rory smiled to himself, seeing in his mind's eye, the eye in the back of the head, Garbo's Scandinavian hockey-player's shoulders in a heated winter pool.)

She (Roxy that is) was a woman of the future, whereas Garbo was a woman of the past, a nineteenth-century figure or effigy copied from some magazine. The woman of the future was a cool granny who had a grasp of essentials; what stories she would have to tell her grandchildren, of 'face-fucking' in the wicked twentieth century! The ladies of long ago played tennis in long skirts and headbands; it must have been more like softball than lawn tennis, Helen Wills Moody and Kay Stammers, dainty as porcelain shepherdesses or ladies at the spinet.

Those ladies had long gone. Women's tennis was now a savage game, with lesbians grunting and swearing under their breath, imparting topspin to crashing services.

She had worked and face-fucked in Mexico City, New York, Bali, London and Tokyo, the immense sprawling cities of the future, dangerous and creepy as the city shown in *Blade Runner*. Her grandchildren, if she had any, would be the highly neurotic progeny of the future. And what worse (louder?) sound could come after rock? Something calculated to burst the eardrums?

Aldous Huxley, long gone, had envisaged a future, our present, as 'the laughter of demons about whipping-posts and the howling of the possessed as they couple in the darkness'. Why, it sounded just like a rock 'in-spot', a Berlin cellar. Berlin would be everywhere, the cities would all be the same – horribly similar in their cacophony and crime; crime would be commonplace like sport. Sport would more resemble battle.

That would be our future, and I rejoice not to belong to it.

64

The Jogger on Coronado Shore

Whilst staying at the Rancho Pico, Big Alf's country seat, didn't poor Rory ingest a prawn that was 'off', bought at the French place Carrefour that sold everything imaginable; and by God he lived to regret it, spending three feverish days in bed, taking nothing stronger than milk and reading *The Radetzky March* from the peerless hand of Joseph Roth, a prey to nightmares.

'Montezuma's revenge,' mocked Big Alf in his pitiless Mexican way.

There was a scorpion in the shower stall. Tongolele (his brawny dog named after a night-club *chanteuse*) had eaten the cat's (Max's) food. A heavy palm frond had fallen in the night. Mexico had lost to Peru in the World Cup.

Big Alf, grandson of a president of Mexico, was a past-master of the bluff disclaimer and short, sharp deflatory rhetoric; but his greatest weapon by far was silence. His silences were uncanny. Rory was baffled. It was the enigmatic silence of the ringmaster who throws open a door and points silently up at the tightrope suspended above, across which the novice is expected to walk.

Once, going upstairs to a family get-together at the Old Post House, Big Alf had poked Rory in the back, intimidatingly: 'Don't dilly-dally, son. Keep moving', as if ordering a menial about in the presidential palace. And Rory saw his features darken and lengthen like a mask of Montezuma reflected in a mirror as they ascended together into the social mêlée that awaited them. It would include Father Paddy from Glenstal, the pink aunt and daughter already seated, drinks in hand, all flustered yet already in full conversational flow, an unabatable flood of trivia, a torrent of talk, a river forever flowing backwards. Talk about the froth of dreams!

Alfredo had a distinctly lordly manner, walked as if brandishing a cane, distant and aloof, carried himself like a king, but a king who read *Time* magazine and went jogging in lurid tracksuits with goofy insignia, jargon and numerals, a joker in the pack.

He had a kingly manner of high disdain, knew how to treat his subjects; his generosity had the quality of a king's bounty.

Big Alf out jogging resembled a *palo* aloft on the shoulders of sweating bearers, one of the three kings who brought gifts to Bethlehem, in costly raiment: the disdainful features might have been carved in wood. He never became flushed because he was naturally dark-complexioned. Jogging didn't become him, he was naturally a sedentary type, naturally lazy, the President accustomed to issuing orders for minions to carry out. Big Alf was high and lonesome as the snore of Christy Mahon's da; abstemious with alcohol, high on hash, which kept him on an even keel. Quoting some Mexican statistic of astounding import ('*five million pesos*, my friend!'), he was King Melchior mounted on a camel, a dispenser of symbolic charity in the form of handfuls of sweeties flung down to shrieking *niños*.

His consort Roxy had a good figure, liked to keep in condition, liked to be seen in shorts showing off her Californian knees; possessed by that desperate fear that all American women have, of losing one's looks, one's husband, the fear of growing old; she liked to get a good 'burn' as though she were a Pratt and Whitney Boeing engine burning off fuel at 33,000 feet; that was Roxy's way, ever the mettlesome lass.

When they went out jogging together on the roads around Charles Fort or over the bridge at James Fort on the way to Ballinspittle, they were a sight to see; a terrific display of well-muscled thigh and tanned knee, gabbing volubly away as they went pattering by, very exotic and foreign-looking to

encounter passing on a narrow Irish road, as if you had met
the Emperor Maximilian and Queen Charlotte out for a stroll,
taking a breather.

One day Roxy would be heard of in Bali, next day she was
doing a deal in Tokyo, flew on to New York, was seen shopping
in Chicago. She was next heard of in Cuernavaca, taking a short
break at Rancho Pico; then she was in the condo on Coronado
Shore, jogging on the private beach where dogs and vendors
were not permitted to set foot. Then San Diego was left behind
and she was in London or flying to Paris to take in the spring
collection. Faxes flew ahead of her like confetti at a wedding.
She couldn't manage joined-up writing. Roxy was a scream.

She wore shorts because she liked to show off her legs. They
gabbed while jogging; animated chatting and jogging didn't seem
to go together, as with chewing gum while singing arias from
light operas.

An old love had died, a clockmaker named Christopher Stokes
with a clock shop on MacCurtain Street in Cork, not to be
confused with Sigismund, King of the Clocks. He had been
buried in Douglas's Protestant cemetery. Roxy was devoted
to the dead man and arranged for Alannah to lay wreaths at
anniversaries. She was like that.

Loyalty was almost a vice with the Buxton Hopkins; birthdays
and anniversaries were remembered, faxes flew, long-distance
phone calls were made, the fat chewed. Good intentions were
rampant here; the family must stick together at all costs. That
was the big idea.

¡Oh Pájaro! Pájaro! The fat's in the fire.

In the cool of the evening, sundowner time in South Africa, and
the time for imbibing of Lion beer and Oude Meester brandy,
Acapulco was enjoying a stupendous sunset over the water,
promising another such day tomorrow, with a young fellow
monkey-like shinning up a tall Royal palm to trim off some
of the decayed fronds with a machete. The stand of palms
rose higher than the third floor of Alfredo's Palacio, with a
view over the bay and the lighthouse beginning to wink on
and off as a warning to mariners. We sat with drinks before

us on a glass table, summoned thence by Tiberio himself, the message conveyed by Honorio the houseboy, padding silently along the corridor, barefoot and in Bermuda shorts, silent as though he had been castrated by order of the Emperor. Drinks on the upper terrace tonight and pot-smoking! So we were all assembled, and the little old Greek was getting the sharp edge of Alfredo's tongue in what passed as friendly raillery but wasn't quite, and Roxy and Alannah were murmuring together as two sisters should, and Rory was drinking gin and tonic in a tall glass as Rory liked to do.

The evening calm was rudely disturbed by the heavy grunting and honking and farting (drunkard barging into quiet room, hippo foraging in a marsh) of the love-boat making its leisurely pleasure-cruising way between Boca Chica and La Roqueta.

The love-boat *Acatiki* was out and about, fairy lights dangled between two masts, picking out the shape of the celebrated organ, seat of one's innermost thoughts and secret feelings, suspended between mast and mast, below which the snoggers snogged, close in each other's arms, the girls in thin frocks proudly displaying love-bites like tribal markings, the not-so-young dancing with the not-so-young, those past it, just as the sun went down, and Rory's own heart sank into his *espadrillos* for he hated with all his heart piped Muzak in public places and no public place seemed free of it. The love-boat went gobbling across the bay, the dancers danced, the music played, call it music.

'Some people's idea of tropical dance music,' murmured Roxy.

'Some people's idea of fun,' murmured the small old Greek.

Tiberio offered no comment. The great hooded eyes were closed, the blinds down; he was not at home, or he was sleeping. He was not saying anything. If he was a true Emperor Tiberius whose every whim could be gratified, why then with one imperious wave of the hand he could have all three hundred dancers chucked overboard, the worst offenders castrated, as he had had Honorio castrated, or, better still, flung off on the island and the Jardín Zoológico cages thrown open and the pleasure-cruisers fed to the lions, to implement their boring diet of horse-flesh. Sink the damn *Acatiki*; then all would be quiet.

Alfredo's house in Calle Valladolid in Mexico City was full of ceramic lions both rampant and *couchant*, little lions and large lions in different material; he was obsessed with lions. His own languid indifference was based, unconsciously, on the MGM lion logo, the one that roars briefly and looks away indifferently, bored to death with MGM.

The lions (or was there only one?) roared in their cages at sun-up and sunset on La Roqueta at feeding time; it was the Island Where Lions Roar. The jungle and the authentic wilderness have been dispensed with and all the wild animals hunted to extinction, replaced by a fake substitute wilderness for the amusement of tourists, created by clever ad-men, con-men; a sort of chic wilderness made of cardboard where you wouldn't be devoured by wild animals, into whose natural habitat seemingly you had been permitted, for a reasonable charge, to stray.

The wildly gesticulating lewd statuary in bronze, of manly parts, gleaming torsos and Olympic legs, had been arrested in a somewhat similar way; not permitted to stray over into outright indecency, of provocative pose and outsize bronze member fully erect; there was merely a suggestion of it, a hint. The male torsos sighed mutely with a lover's insistence, *Oh touch me! O please do!* It was a Zoo of Dreams. The architect who had erected the extraordinary house of mirrors had been homosexual and also practised as a sculptor; the gesticulating bronze parts were all his work. Alfredo walked about in flip-flops and shorts, as though walking through the cloisters of a monastery, cool as a cucumber.

Banana boat rides were popular on Acapulco Bay between La Roqueta and the Boca Chica. The yellow thing vaguely banana-shaped, a long phallus that curled up at each end with enough seats to take eight or ten screeching pleasure-seekers in life-jackets was pulled behind a speedboat with throttle wide open, bouncing across the swells and wakes of other pleasure craft plying between the hotel and the island, the screaming girls also bouncing up and down and giving themselves risky orgasms and pissing themselves with sheer excitement: riding on the swells, they skimmed across the surface of the sea. In the distance, but approaching, could be heard the unmistakable farting and grunting of the good ship *Acatiki*, she was coming around again.

Clam-divers swam out beyond the point into the open sea beyond, holding on to an inner tube which carried a lethal array of knives and machetes for prising clams off the seabed; a flutter-kick carried them along, only head and arms visible, like otters or beavers moving slowly through the water. They ignored banana boats and the cruising love-boat with its fake heart lit up, a sore gone septic.

One morning, swimming off Alfredo's private dock, with the beer-cooler and the avocados stashed in the shade, Alannah encountered one of these dark-skinned, silent otter-like clam-divers and engaged him in conversation in the sea as she likes to do. He was pushing his inner tube before him, flutter-kicking very slowly. Why was he returning so soon? What was amiss? (Her Spanish is excellent.) It was a long swim back to where he had set out, the place where the glass-bottomed ferries set off for La Roqueta, the place where they return to at dusk.

'*¡Hay agua mala!*'

The sea was full of jellyfishes waving their stingers beyond the point, with more of them in the open sea; he wasn't going to swim through them, explanations were superfluous.

'They're not great conversationalists,' Alannah said, lolling about on her fun-tube in the sea.

65

The Martinez Couple

D on Alfredo Calles was the owner and manager of the very fashionable Tiberio nightery on the Boulevard Miguel Alemán in sunny Acapulco, *the* place for cool cats to divert themselves. It was a splendid night-spot done up in vertical black and white stripes like a zebra pelt or a painting by Franz Kline, and Alfredo himself was an exotic match for the fancy décor.

El Patrón favoured the casual look – all-white cotton jeans and shirt, no necktie but white silken cravat, embroidered white waistcoat, white loafers and white socks, very tanned, a way-out cool cat with one gold earring like a pirate, but more a ringmaster in a grand circus, dapper as Bryan Ferry of 'These Foolish Things' fame (haven't we all got em?); but a more kingly presence: Don Alfredo Calles was the Boss and no mistake.

It was a way-out place to be, the whitest, coolest place in all Acapulco night-life. It wasn't cheap. It was there that Yul Brynner (who *had* worked in a circus) complimented Alannah: 'Nice ass you got there, kid' were his very words. He had arrived with a Hollywood crowd of big spenders and show-offs. Elsewhere, at another time, Chuck Berry had a feel, as also Charlie Haughey.

Alfredo Calles was by nature an easygoing type who conveyed the misleading impression of inflexibility. I never heard him lose his temper or raise his voice; but this was part of the kingliness, he didn't have to raise his voice when he issued orders around the Palacio or in Tiberio.

His manner with the servants was that of a feudal lord. He liked to give long detailed instructions. The houseboy or *mayordomo* Honorio, the non-swimmer, the silent one who glided about the Palacio in Acapulco, looked after the place in the months when it stood empty, with the maimed German Alsatian dog that Alfredo had adopted; he, Honorio, took the orders nodding that he understood. He had security for life; the feudal lord would see to that.

The Martinez couple of the Rancho Pico below Cuernavaca were gatekeepers, lodge-dwellers, who swept the lawns clear of leaves, a veritable labour of Sisyphus, for the leaves always fell, and the breezes blew all around Cuernavaca. They used brushes made of twigs, rarely spoke to each other, and were a couple straight out of the Conquest as portrayed in the Diego Rivera murals in the Palace of Cortés.

You could see in the Martinezes how passively and with what fatalism the Indians had bowed to the will of the Spaniards; they were born slaves, but they believed that their time would come. It hadn't come yet but it would come, in time.

When Alfredo Calles was about to leave again for his office in Mexico City he issued detailed last-minute instructions to Eliseo, not standing as a servant might, submissively before the master, but seated alongside Alfredo by the swimming pool near the sauna under the tree that nobody knew the name of; they spoke then as equals might discuss the running of the place, the fowl-run, the vegetables, the upkeep of the long bungalow, the pair of them with their heads together.

Eliseo Martinez had his own car, his own house. One daughter was a nurse, his son Miguelangelo was studying to be an engineer, his wife Graciela could iron clothes like an angel: she was one of the pigtailed peons offering their produce to the raping and rapacious Spaniards. They might inherit the estate, in time.

When Alfredo came to Summercove for his vacation he brought something of Mexico City with him. He and Roxy mingled with the locals at drinks parties; they socialised, they

were not 'stuck up'. Big Alf liked a pint of draught Guinness at
the Bulman.

Señor Alfredo Elias Calles (baritone) of Mexico City and
Acapulco and the Señora Roxy (alto) of San Diego and Cuernavaca
– international guest stars of the Kinsale Opera Society – by popular
request sang their famous Papageno–Papagena duet from *The Magic
Flute* under the inspired baton of Frank Buckley, the local musical
maestro.

Francis X. Buckley, the Kinsale *Kapellmeister*, was a veritable
Fortunio Bonanova on the podium, which he occupied with
the maximum dash and verve, sprightly and emotional with the
baton, in smart dinner jacket and tails, swinging tails – Arturo
Toscanini in style and swagger. This was very well received by
the local cognoscenti, the music-lovers.

With his back to the audience, shoulders moving energetically,
coat-tails swinging, he was as wild as the sorcerer's apprentice, yet
meek as Little Sir Echo, odd as the performing seal in a circus.

With a rush of blood to the head, he had rocketed headlong
into *Ruddigore*. His mother sat in the front row, astounded. She
adored him, as did the choir, made up mostly of girls from Super
Valu, who stood enthralled. Oh the sweetest man you would
ever hope to meet in a hall full of half-wits was our Frank!

PART VIII:

How the Century Ends

The rath forninst the oak wood belonged to Bruidge, and Cathal belonged to Aedh, and Ailill belonged to Conaing, and Cuiline and to Mael Duin before them – all Kings in their turn. The rath survives; the Kings are all covered in clay.

Anon., Sixteenth–century notebook

66

The Three Brothers

T'ree brudders . . . wan wit a bad eye

B elow Ringenane bridge in a field tilted down towards
Oysterhaven Creek stand three mobile homes mounted
on breeze blocks facing into opposite corners like boxers
between rounds or as the stone heads with two faces buried up
to their necks on Boa Island, set and fixed solid in the earth for
all time, staring off in different directions.

They seem to avert their eyes from each other, as do the
three brothers who occupy them, long-term bachelors not on
speaking terms and having no direct dealings knowingly with one
another, as if in accordance with some Kikuyu tribal custom at a
fly-blown *manyatta* where they pretended not to see each other.
'Doll's Eye' neither saw nor wanted to see 'the Belgooly Flasher',
who never spoke to nor acknowledged 'The Fascist Beast', who
neither saw nor spoke to either of the other two. This dour trio
of lackadaisical dimwits had long been unemployed and lived
only for dole day, which fell every Thursday; it was their day
for stocking up on provisions and getting pissed. The Belgooly
Flasher, a lurker at convent gates, was a small-sized crafty-looking
fellow who gave the impression of ever being caught in the act
of departure, abruptly leaving, dressed for winter, pushing an old
bike weighed down with provisions in plastic Super Valu bags
hooked on to the handlebars. He sometimes passes by. We live
in Upper O'Connell Street between the convent (closed) and

the pie factory (closed) in the Guardwell. Below us formerly was Sheehy's auction yard and warehouses used as storage, since knocked down and replaced by a block of flats with its own car park.

You said: 'The town is simply seething with cousins.'

The Belgooly Flasher went by manhandling his pushbike, head down as if fighting against a north wind. You said: 'There goes the flasher . . . his flashing days are over, thanks be to God.'

The three brothers are still not talking in the field that slopes down to the river that for Rory would always be the curlew river.

I myself, having been born into a family of archly uncommunicative brothers who rarely spoke together, the two elder with the two younger, I mean, like lifelong enemies, in a previous existence down the country in the days of Aladdin paraffin lamps and horse-drawn hay-bogies, know these sullen silences only too well.

I rarely communicated with any of them after the family split up; the youngest has taken offence at how he and his wife are represented in the pseudo-autobiography preceding this one, the middle brother died in Ealing and is now beyond all communication. The eldest, I am told, divides his time between Largs in Scotland and Hobart in Tasmania, formerly the penal colony called Van Diemen's Land.

I never had much dealings with my eldest brother: more than ten years separated us and he was closer to brother Bun, younger by two years. They had been brought up together, as had the Dote and I. The Dodo had been inclined to despise me as a convent boy with provincial accent and awkward manners, who associated with the snotty-nosed Keegan brothers in the front lodge.

In boarding school special rules obtained for him. He couldn't be pandied or punished in any way for failing exams and spent much time confined to bed in the infirmary, laid low by psychosomatic ailments brought on so as to avoid classes, the subjects he detested, such as Irish. Special rules had to be made to accommodate his strangeness; he was given 'lines' as though he was in an English boarding school. He was a lifelong secret subscriber to the school magazine, the *Clongownian*.

The Dodo was opening bat on the college XI, a stonewaller who took no chances, refused to take easy singles. He was a great 'gardener', forever poking and prodding at the crease, awkward in protective gear, the box, the gloves with ridged rubber webbing, the outsize leg pads shackled his movements, always requiring nice readjustments, making running difficult.

He was a bundle of mannerisms, based on famous cricketers whom he admired; never having seen them in action (in the days before television), he had to imitate styles caught by the still camera or confine himself exclusively to defensive strokes or none at all, just occupying his crease, staying in and not scoring. It was the same strategy he used to get into the infirmary.

His defence was gritty, poking at the crease, calling 'No!' to a partner anxious to chance a quick one. He wasn't one for sneaking cheeky singles or attempting anything forceful on the leg side, sweeps to the boundary, rattling the picket fence. The school cap down to his nose, shirt collar up around his ears, the eyes watchful, the bat tapping, raised up as the bowler was about to deliver, he was a sight to behold.

Does he get a tickle? They've held him in the slips, the umpire's finger is raised and off goes the Dodo, bat tucked under arm, gloves peeled thoughtfully off, slowly wending his way back to the pavilion, to scant applause – 'Bad luck, Dodo!' In his diary will appear: 'Wrong decision.' *Nota bene*.

Bizarre.

67

In the Long Ago

I t happened in the time when sons feared fathers, as fathers before them had feared their own fathers, their hard fists and exasperated ear-twisting and royal rages reaching back to the black times of the forefathers, the crusty old patriarchs themselves in their nightshirts and long white beards, their hard ways and prohibitions ('Thou shalt not . . .'); sticklers for form, their right hand resting on the good Book of Manners in two hefty great volumes, the Old Testament and the New.

Then, as if to make up for the loss of the love of the father (for how could you love someone who beat you?), didn't they go and love their mothers all the more; they *adored* them with an anxious and longing love that reached out and could hardly be appeased.

Looking back through the fully extended telescope that measured off the three score years and ten allotted to human life, time appeared to contract; and there was Mumu dealing out a hand of Pelman Patience on the study table, placing the cards face down and palming the deck before shuffling, wondering if it would come out right this time.

And Dado, who rarely if ever engaged in work about the house, once he had come in, stood on the front steps in castoff cricket boots, a handkerchief saturated in linseed knotted about his neck, rotating a safety match in one ear, then the other, a vacant look on his face. His jaw had fallen and his mind, ah his mind, a total blank, unless he was admiring the scuffling job he had done on the front gravel.

At all events it had all begun a long time ago and as though it had happened to another person in another country in another time. Before rural electrification had brought electric light as the greatest comfort into the home in the late 1940s; and before the monster TV, the greatest curse, had choked off the old life. When the elderly men had gathered at gates and leant on walls to gossip at evening time, watching the light go. All that had gone too.

As for myself, now aged seventy-one and well advanced into the sere and yellow, why I can hardly recognise that other puny and positively emaciated male child with matchstick arms and legs and face squeezed up into what the family called the bear's face. A shy slip of a thing, nervous as a whippet, with that worried frown caught in the Kodak snaps gone sepia with age.

Mr Doorley of Monkstown by the sea, a Dublin dentist by profession, had invited Rory to his place for a holiday to 'fatten him up' and enjoy some healthy sea-bathing in company with his daughter Evelyn. Brother Bun was to keep me company, for I was too timid to go by myself.

So it was porridge and fry-up for breakfast, and Seapoint for a healthful dip, and a walk on Dun Laoghaire pier after lunch, and a glass of milk and Gold Grain biscuits before bed and 'Did you move your bowels today, sir?'

A human life, in the scale of boundless time that we are adrift in, is but the duration of one indrawn breath that is then expelled; the passage of Halley's Comet through 'everchanging tracks of neverchanging space' in its circuit about the sun, coming into sight and going away again every seventy-six years, a reasonable human lifespan; such is our time marked out in the sky.

The Dote and I had made a pet of an elderly hen whom we named Ma Duggy White. Her body feathers hung down like soiled linen, a dirty shift showing under a skirt, and her hinder parts were always clotted with dung. Scratching about in the back yard she made a sadly droaning regurgitative noise in her throat, the distinct sound that hens make when foddering, sad music on a descending scale. This we called 'Years–Gone–by'. It was the sad music of the passage of time, the very sound of its passing.

The great Parisian organist Messiaen had heard the call of an unknown bird in the evening, in Persia, and put the sound into his triumphant devotional work as the voice of God, a sound hardly audible, a very remote, distant clear and perfect call, as the sound of the sea in a shell held to the ear, thought to be the sea itself but is only pseudo-sound, a false sea sound, only the memory of real waves or surf breaking on a real shore somewhere, tidal shifts and changes, capricious winds, all that.

When the Birr bus passes the front gate, Dado knows that the evening papers have arrived in Celbridge a mile away, flung from the bus in bundles on to the pavement outside Breen's Hotel, and he can stop poking in his ears with a match. It's time to send one of the Keegan boys for the *Evening Herald* and *Evening Mail* and on Saturday, *The Field* and on Sunday half a dozen London papers, with a penny or tuppence to John Joe for sweets or Woodbines or himself.

The young masters, Dodo and the Bun, are off at Clongowes pursuing their serious studies, sending weekly letters home with reports of their progress or lack of it, tales of their prowess (or lack) on the playing fields.

I had been 'held back' two years so that the Dote and I could start as equals, so that he was big enough to walk to the convent a mile away in the village. In fact it was I who was never able to catch up with the steady and conscientious progress made by Colman, the exemplary student at all times, whether put through the slapdash educational methods of the Sisters of Mercy (who favoured the strap) for beating the Catechism into us, teaching us our tables and all the singsong lessons by rote. Or later at boarding school in Killashee with a French order of nuns who had their own punitive methods.

Madame Ita Magdalene stood you in front of the dais and cut at you with a ruler edged with lead that could draw blood, if you got French irregular verbs wrong. Her face within its shadowy coif lengthened like a horse's and all flushed darkly with blood, her dander rising and the great horse-teeth clamped together. 'You'll get this right if we have to stand here all day.'

A long rusty freighter in from Bilbao occupies the whole length of the loading bay, the claws of the grab dipping into the open hold and swaying back to release another load into the truck waiting on the quayside to carry it off to Good's Mill on the hillside above the town.

When the south-westerly wind activates all the burglar alarms in the vicinity of the yacht club and out to the new houses on Viking Wharf, it sets the halyards of yachts moored in the marina a-jingling and a-tinkling as merrily as wind-chimes. No, not wind-chimes or chattering teeth; more the sound of ice cubes striking against the sides of a long-stemmed good-quality glass three-quarters full of Gordon's gin and tonic.

A young and fully grown voracious jackdaw has its head halfway down the gullet of its mother, near where the RMS *Aycturus* is offloading its cargo of soya beans and pig nuts.

It all happened long ago, even though it seems but yesterday. A decisive battle was fought and decided in the mud and filth and gore in midwinter with much slaughter by the well-trained English cavalry. It was over in three hours, with consequences that would last for centuries. At sundown the battlefield must have presented a melancholy sight, worse than the Cork municipal dump, when flacks of crows and gulls came down to join the pillagers and feed off the corpses. We know less of this battle than we do of the first battle of Kursk or the slaughter of Stalingrad. Mountjoy's army of four thousands were outnumbered more than two to one by O'Neill and O'Donnell; we do not know how many Irish were slain or how few the English; of the Spanish none at all.

Don Juan del Aquila and his army of four thousand had been bottled up in the town for three months and food was scarce; they made sorties by night, spiked two cannon that had been annoying them. For days after the defeat they waited for news of the Irish, who had marched from the north in semi-darkness, marching sullenly, cursing their Maker. Mountjoy, standing on a slope of wetland with several Grand Marniers inside him, awaited the arrival of the drenched Irish army; he seemed to be able to read O'Neill's mind. He sent Sir Henry Folliott and his cavalry to engage him across the stream near the Ballinamona bog, caught him off balance, and the rout had begun.

O'Donnell was proceeding in a westerly direction to Mill-water; his pikemen following too close, some dozing as they stumbled on to regrouping infantry and caused the frightened horses to charge into the men, who were now certainly awake. Whereupon, in the great confusion and much cursing, his soldiers left the battle and were fleeing to the west, not to enter it again except as corpses floating down to White Castle in what was to be called the Ford of the Slaughtering. For there was no waving of white flags or status as prisoners of war or seeking sanctuary; Wingfield's horses came on like avenging angels with drawn swords, showing no mercy.

When the Spaniards offered to parley and Mountjoy acceded they were given shipping and safe conduct and sailed for La Coruña with band playing and flags flying. O'Neill submitted to Mountjoy at Mellifont the day after Queen Elizabeth had at last expired. The three brothers up on the tilted field were still not on talking terms. The clan system hadn't worked.

But I ask you, Golubchik, did brothers ever hit it off since Cain and Abel? Has a brother ever been a good *amigo*, a pal, a trusted confidant and friend, since Damian and Pythias were steadfast buddies? A person close to one to whom one can open one's heart, as the saying goes, even if the different lives that you lead have long separated you, given you different interests, driven you far apart? The brother you knew in childhood has long since departed, tiptoed silently away, become a stranger, passed away, or died.

In heavy musty old family albums with immensely thick pages you see the face of the late mother or late father in the faces of the young grandchildren playing on swings. But don't I see my dead father's hands (those of a shiftless fellow, a born idler) duplicated in my own hands, the hands of a writer, even to the dark liver spots on the backs of the hands stretched out before me for closer examination, like the darker circular markings on a blackbird's egg (or am I thinking of the thrush?).

My three brothers fly away in the clouds, like the umbrella lost in Dublin that was found again in the echoing cavern called Open Hole on the Old Head of Kinsale, through which the intrepid Alannah once sailed in a small yacht.

What have we got here, then, amid the gall and wormwood, the floss and flurry, fact and fiction? The Goncourt brothers involved themselves exclusively with French writing, but did they see eye to eye? They did not. And the *Brüder* Mann, Thomas and Heinrich of Lübeck, how did they hit it off? They didn't. And the fictitious Karamazov brothers, what of them? And what about the boozy half-brothers Geoffrey and Hugh Firmin of *Under the Volcano*, who can neither stop drinking nor blathering ('They are losing the battle of the Ebro'), the latter got up as Tom Mix, able to neigh like a horse.

Then you had the far-fetched pair of brothers in P.C. Wren's fable *Beau Geste*, doing the decent and honourable thing, the elder joining the French Foreign Legion, followed by the younger brother; heroic fighters against the tribesmen from the Riff. The brothers, dauntless characters, true scions of the house of Brandon Abbas and her ladyship, were *white clean through*.

What about the beastly Bulkiah brothers, Sultan Hassanal and playboy Prince Jefri, who never did a stroke of work in their lives? Borneo was always bad. As in the olden times, all were at each other's throats: Guelph versus Ghibelline, city state versus city state, Florence versus Venice, Verona versus Bologna.

We know that James Joyce had a younger brother, as indeed did Willie Yeats. Sam Beckett had an elder brother Frank: he mourned when Frank died of cancer.

Henry David Thoreau had a brother who died of lockjaw.

A London merchant, one Francis Rogers, newly arrived in Kinsale from the West Indies in October 1703 'amid foul weather' wrote: 'The town lyeth on the River Banny [*sic*] which runs far up . . . we did not a little indulge ourselves, with very good French claret drunk in the taverns at an English shilling, Brandy at three shillings & sixpence & four shillings per gallon.'

There were two ships called *Kinsale* on the high seas at one time. HMS *Kinsale* was built in the Royal Naval dockyard where the present-day Trident Hotel stands. Master Shipwright Stacey and one Chudleigh the foreman were the men who put the work through.

There is also a place of that name (Kinsale) in Montserrat in the Leeward Islands.

68

The Great Battle

O'Neill had set off from the north, bringing the foul weather with him, crossing 'o'er many a river bridged with ice', to arrive in a poor state for fighting under such harsh conditions. His Spanish allies (three thousand eight hundred of them cooped up in the town) were also in poor spirits, having been bottled up in the harbour for three months and provisions low, finding it difficult to feed themselves, they had begun to hate Ireland and the awkward Irish.

Between the bottled-up Spaniards and the frozen Irish at Coolcarron there were approximately four thousand English armed and ready, stoking their fires, priming their weapons, biding their time, raring to go.

The hot-blooded Spaniards finding themselves on short rations were fit to be tied. Mountjoy had set up a battery some six hundred yards to the east of Cork Gate on high ground and coolly proceeded to land penalties from all angles, making the Hispanics throw up the supper they had missed. When the two severed halves of the Irish Army had eventually come together, six thousand five hundred foot and horse, they made early use of the 'garryowen' tactics, devised by inferior Irish rugby teams down the years from the time of Eugene Davy and the Mauler Clinch. In my day a back line of Quinns playing for Old Belvedere were still wasting possession, following up futile high kicks and hoping that something good would come of it, Paddy, Kevin and Brendan running like hares.

Skipper Hugh O'Neill was the Irish hooker. A great lardy lump of a man of some sixteen stone plus, hard in the tackle and an adroit tactician. A great man for putting in the boot, getting the head down and pushing, farting and cursing, grunting as he shoved, not averse to some eye-gouging in the close work. Up-and-unders were his speciality, the fabled high garryowen. 'Lots of garryowen today, lads. The wind is swirling. Hit them with all you have, knock the shit out of them!'

'Red' Hugh O'Donnell was the Irish stand-off half, erratic, dodgy in defence, but brilliant on his day; a safe pair of hands, with a devastating drop kick, he could sidestep like a stag.

The English, the old foe, played their usual game, the scrum tight as a drum, heavy as a Churchill tank. At once they sent in their two heavies, Johnson and Rodbar, men not lacking in bottle, adepts at taking out their opposite numbers, maulings that might land them in hospital, playing to the weak side of unsighted referees, their crash-tackles calculated to capsize a bullock. Mountjoy, the English captain and fullback, of Harlequins and England, read O'Neill's mind as if his battle strategy (supposing he had any) was sketched out clearly on parchment. The back line, the so-called line of attack, O'Donnell and the two centres, Des Thorpe the nightmarishly sluggish scrum half who seemed to send the ball out with glue on it; the two wings, all could have stayed in the Bective Rangers changing room for all their effectiveness on the field. Many a green jersey was torn from a brawny Irish back, or a skinny back (Brendon Quinn), on that freezing December day.

The very topography of the place, undulating and marshy, with pools six foot deep in places, seemed to throw them into dire confusion and disorder, as if it weren't their own ground. Ireland playing 'away' internationals at Cardiff Arms Park and Murrayfield in the centuries to come had recourse to garryowens and then more garryowens, and then still more garryowens.

The English were encamped on high ground, hitting the walled town with two batteries placed strategically to do most damage; they continued to hit and hit until put out of action by the crafty and now very hungry Hispanics, creeping out under cover of darkness on a daring night raid to spike the cannons. The English and Irish could see and smell the smoke of each other's camp fires, hear their doleful songs. The poor condemned Irish sang of imminent death, knowing their bad time had come.

To join the Spaniards, their allies, the Irish had to cross low ground and break through the English lines at Campbell or Ardmartin where the ridge drops to the valley level at Millwater. The Irish had hoped to proceed along the ridge and creep unnoticed around the English and join the Spaniards in the town, with only a small English defence at Cappagh to overcome.

The Munstermen complained that there were too many Leinstermen on the Irish team, the Connaughtmen said there were too many Munstermen, and the Ulstermen thought there weren't enough Ulstermen; but in one way or another the Irish tasted defeat again, that bitter taste like gall to which they had grown so accustomed. The so-called clan system was finished, all washed up.

With one practised savage backhander, a swipe with a sabre as calculated as the stroke that sent the polo ball goalwards at a chukker in the Phoenix Park, the screaming head of the unarmed pikeman went tumbling into tussocky marsh, the truncated body with outstretched arms begging clemency to the last and still in the act of falling as the horseman thunders by, hallooing, flourishing his bloody sabre.

'Seventeen, sirrahs!'

The exultant cry came from the plucky leading trooper Walter Hurlingham of Hendon riding Vulcan from the stables of Sir Henry Wotting, a magnificent bay charger of some seventeen hands.

The trooper of Wingfield's Horse came on at a rapid canter, flourishing their sabres and hallooing. Hal ('Nut-Case') Hosty of Leeds, then Alex ('Crank-Case') Pringle of South Shields, then the trio of foul-mouthed swashers Burns, Bedford and Nye; then hell for leather, making up ground, massive Dugdale and Cornfield, with Egglington and Barnacle far out on the right wing, followed by Campbell-Goulding of Island Magee; coming on fast as if beating for hidden frightened hares, the troopers hallooing and laughing.

The Irish Army was running away. They were beaten all right. You could smell the defeated army across the fields sloping down to the river where many of them fled, discarding pikes on the way, but finding no mercy, no pity there, where death awaited them.

Hosty had cornered a pikeless yokel gibbering with fear, down on his knees begging for clemency, beshitting his pants and holding up the palms of his dirty hands. But the Nut-Case was having none of that, his face turkey-cock red with hard riding; he was about to let him have it. War was a messy business, but sharp lessons had to be taught and learnt well. Hurlingham, sweeping past on Vulcan, was ever loyal to his Queen; he served her with a loyal heart. Vulcan was farting like a two-stroke.

'Paste him one for me, the rogue!' he called out jubilantly. 'One for good measure, give it to him good and hard!'

'I'll paste him one all right, I'll do for this fucker.'

The high-pitched scream of the victim, the trooper's grunt and sabre thrust were instantaneous. Nut-Case cleaned his weapon on the flanks of the piebald, laughing and waving.

The pursuit went rapidly on as far as Dunderrow, chase and kill without much grace, and with no mercy shown. The Irish had buckled as soon as they engaged; O'Donnell had gotten his knickers into a hopeless twist; he was finished as soon as he came in. Mountjoy had ended O'Neill in double-quick order in the bog. The Irish – and so many of them! – were finished; the sorry butchering went on until dark. The troopers grew sick of killing; the tally was great, it was a square dance without partners. The Irish had simply withered away. Weak cries of a man dying were heard down in the river, and a trooper cursing him as he floated beyond reach.

The Irish were decimated as the sabres rose and fell; hack followed thrust. They would have to be finished off so that the Queen could sleep untroubled in her bed. They had no stomach for such hard fighting. They had come frozen into battle. The day had dawned overcast and chilly, with a cold north wind driving a murky drizzle before it; it was not good for riding. Any foul weather would do for fighting: it was better not to see some of the barbarities done on that day, better to keep your mouth shut about what you had seen.

Still the killing went on. The sadists were having a field day. Hurlingham himself was sick of it, but satisfied at what had gone on, how it had ended. English casualties had been minimal; the surgeons had a quiet day. The English had fought well, cannily, using their nuts.

You'd have to feel sorry for the defeated, to go into battle so ill-prepared, so badly organised, and there were so many of them, more than double the English Army, not counting the Spaniards skulking in the town. O'Neill had worked wonders with untried, untrained volunteers, who had little stomach for battle; perhaps it would frighten off further volunteers?

Now the way was clear, the Queen had Ireland on her plate to do with it as she pleased; offer parts of it to the victors. Peace was assured, the Irish will had been broken: that was all that mattered, in the long run.

These heroes, relatives of Nym, Bardolph and Ancient Pistol, would re-emerge in North Africa in World War Two, to begin to swing another way a war they were losing, the Head-Banger, Nut-Case, Fast-Forward and the others were now being broiled alive inside tanks. The place names they chalked up on the sides of their tanks were like citations of valour, good as medals – Benghazi, Wadi Halfa, Sidi Bel Abbès, Tobruk – telling of hard-won victories in battles fought in cruel heat in the Libyan desert, of pipers inflating bagpipes and going in before Scots troops. They had punched holes in Jerry's defences, knocking Rommel out of Africa for a six, so that they could go home again to Leeds and Birmingham and Bolton and Hull. They were Monty's men as surely as Nym and Pistol had been Prince Harry's men, as sure as Hurlingham and Cornfield and the others had been Wingfield's Horse, in the long ago.

In the plantation before the house where I had been innocently amusing myself, I slipped on a branch and split my nose on a forked holly bough and ran across the front meadow, blood pumping from both nostrils on to my jersey, bawling for my ma. The grass was high, it was a summer of the early 1930s before the war. I wade through it, weeping, bleeding profusely, calling for my ma.

Later on the threshold of puberty, one day in a game didn't I beshit myself with excitement and must have confessed as much to Mumu, who ran a shallow bath and told me to take off those trousers (shorts) and get into the bath. And when I stood up in it she washed me down and when I sat down in it she threw the big sponge to cover my privates. So how old was I then, if I was embarrassed to expose my privates? And was she too embarrassed?

One day when I had been guilty of some misdemeanour in the garden or in the front yard, or in the rockery, Dado ordered me into the house as punishment on that lovely sunny day: 'Get into the house, you little pup!'

He followed me in, his dander rising, as mine was too, and pushed me in the back with his fingers, jabbing.

I turned on him, as if to go for him, glared at him; and he was shocked, took a step back, lost his authority, blustered.

'What what what . . . did you say?'

I turned my back on him, gave him best, received a hard prod in the small of the back.

'Get up those stairs, you bold little brat!'

'I'll tell Ma.'

'What did you say, you pup?'

'Maaa!'

'No supper for you, my lad. Up with you!'

I mounted the stairs with offensive slowness, prodded and poked in the back. My father was fuming. I was bawling. All was in order. Mumu was nowhere to be seen.

69

Sir Walter Raleigh and
the Cockadoodledoo

Sir Walt in Cork, the butter hairy, his troops strutting
on the Mall, the native kerns deceitful, liars by necessity;
not a virgin in the land.

Balcony of Europe

O ne grey Sunday morning in the bad summer of 1603,
two years after the fiasco at Kinsale, Sir Walter Raleigh
was taking his usual constitutional along Merchants'
Quay in the sorry port of Cork; he liked to perambulate
thereabouts because all that pertained to the sea interested him,
he being a seafaring man for most of his life. He walked on the
balls of his feet like a black bear on a chain, his nose discoloured
from much wine-imbibing; he wore dark grey hose and a
half-cape of a lighter grey trimmed with ermine and, as behoves
a gentleman, he wore a sword (to defend a lady's honour, should
she be insulted). On his head a Highland bonnet of faded blue
from which a single peacock feather depended, held in place at
an acute angle by a garnet brooch. He was cock of the walk.

He had been presented with seventeen thousand hectares of
confiscated Desmond estates following the Kinsale débâcle that
gave generous spoils of war to Englishmen of good standing,
which he had sold on immediately and profitably to the Earl of
Cork who was ambitious and no fool. Raleigh himself therefore

did not lack means.

He was disinclined to take up residency in Myrtle Grove, a much-banged-about Elizabethan mansion which was his freehold in the fishing village of Yawl (in Gaelic *Eochail*, meaning yew tree). Congreve the dramatist, who gave *The Way of the World* to the London public, had spent his early infancy there; but Sir Walter did not care for Yawl.

He was a true sailor in that he frequented Bankside bawdy houses *before* breakfasting on beer and chops, for he was a manly man high in blood, attempting to modify his bear's pace to accommodate a gross high-rise early morning horn that threatened to burst itself free of the containing and restraining codpiece in its hempen stitching and stirring like a weasel in a sack.

Towards him came two fresh-faced wenches with a little dog, out for an early morning stroll like himself. They were clutching each other and giving out peals of laughter while engaged in close and intimate feminine gossiping; their bright eyes sparkled and their nostrils flared when they spied who was advancing towards them with measured tread, a roguish rogering smile already beginning to play upon his lips; about to sweep off his bonnet and do the honours as befitted a gent and a highborn one who, moreover, had the ear of the Queen of England. With ballooning skirts furled about their hips and cheeks ablaze with rude health, they were blown towards him, surprising him in the middle of a most pleasurable reverie.

He was puffing away on his curlicue pipe bought in Barbados, with enough smoking tobacco to last him a year, and smiling fondly to himself at the recollection of a certain blushing but compliant lady-in-waiting to the Queen (Elizabeth I, the regal woman in the ruff with the glazed eyes of the bream, or a cod – when she was being skittish – or the wobbly eye of a doll when she had a drop taken), who was a real handful with her heaving milk-white bosom bared to the nipples, whose favours he had once enjoyed, standing her upright against the bole of a great beech tree that stood alone in the corner of the palace gardens. On a sudden impulse, then and there, he had positioned her as impatiently as a window-dresser might roughly manhandle a helpless female dummy.

The tall beech groaned deeply down all its mighty length as a freshening southeaster poured steadily into its top-heavy summer boscage, blowing steadily from beyond the London Mall, and brought into play a great rustling and tittering and general unrest in the mighty tree that towered above them.

As he pleasured her with a deep-pronged pleasuring, the flustered lady had groaned in unison with her impatient debaucher and the great deep-breathing tree that swayed to its roots; this during the intermission of a motet by Palestrina or one of the lesser Venetians, anyway a small string ensemble that was busily sawing away inside, to amuse their tone-deaf Queen.

Finding themselves conveniently alone in the great garden now being thoroughly drenched in a sudden heavy summer squall that had sent the rest of the gossips scurrying for cover, they had seized their chance there and then, or rather the bold circumnavigator had seized *her* and pushed her up against the beech and made it very evident that his intentions were dishonourable. Oh sweet Sir Walter! You undo me!

The rain fell pattering amid the huge straining canopy and press of leaves but left the ground they stood on dry as tinder. Sir Walter, at the peak of his ardour, had lifted the lady up in his arms, pronged her with his overmastering passion that could neither be (by him) controlled nor (by her) resisted; for that was the way things were.

Was this what is called happenchance? The summer breeze coming up the Lee brought that other summer breeze in its wake, brought back the avid lady-in-waiting (what was her name?) into his arms. The red-cheeked hussies were giving him a bold eye as they passed by. 'It's him, it's him I tell ye! It's Raleigh! Ship ahoy, up the Jolly Roger! Lovely day for it, Sir Roger! Will it hold up?'

Will you look at the perfidious state he's in! No woman could feel safe on a sofa with the likes of that one! Morning, Sir Roger. Grand morning for it!

The choleric Queen was crying out testily, 'Where *is* Sir Walter? Where *has* he gone to? Bring him here *immediately*!' The Queen's every word was law.

70

Fisher Street and Environs

We are to be found in the second house on the one-way traffic system ordained by the Local County Council; in the second-last house if you come the wrong way by car along Upper O'Connell Street, the system terminating at Casey's Corner where the road dips down by what used to be the Fishermans' Recreation Hall but is now a private dwelling-house with family already in residence, as you can tell from the toys scattered about the yard.

Directly opposite this stands Bruno's Tower, a brave renovation job by the tireless Breton from Pont-Aven, working from sun-up to sundown creosoting railway sleepers that were to be his rafters. The former architect and garden designer built his tower on the site of a previous lighthouse and it (the tower) sprouts out of the living room like aberrant growth on top of a clump of toadstools. The heavy Breton cross set up on the wall was brought all the way from Pont-Aven and has already acquired its own growth of lush Irish ivy.

Bruno Guillou has installed an arched window to match the liturgical effect of the corresponding one opposite, the architrave much favoured by the roosting pigeons who leave their droppings below, as though the place had been there a long time.

Upper O'Connell Street, presumably named for the Liberator,

is one of the cleaner and less dog-fouled of the streets hereabouts, the new pavements laid down by the municipality going as far as the bottle bank near the marina where the yacht *Cassiopeia* out of Corpus Christi, Texas, had been moored all winter.

The dialects of the fishermen here are distinctive, as if they spoke different languages in Scilly, World's End and the Flat of Town. The one-way systems and short interleading streets make the place confusing; you could walk out and come back to what seems a different town, depending on which way you re-enter; walks taken clockwise and then anticlockwise along the embankment to the new bridge below Folly House yield up quite different views, as in Lacan's famous mirror-distorting effect; studying one's face in a mirror and seeing a stranger staring back.

Mazzer, a retired nurse from a psychiatric ward (of whom more anon), drives her small white Fiat down the wrong way past us, sounding her horn, not quite in control of the car, down on its springs. She drives atrociously.

'Why shouldn't I?' she asks defiantly. 'Wasn't I born here, and my mother before me? There's nothing in the deeds of my house to tell me which way I can drive my own car up or down the street.'

Mazzer is a portly lady bordering on the outsize, a stalwart big-bottomed battering-ram of a woman built along the lines of the well-corseted Margaret Dumont, Groucho's imperturbable stooge, massive and commanding who can neither be browbeaten nor downfaced. Mazzer controls the street rather as did Chaplin's fierce, baton-wielding cop with autocratic circumflex eyebrows in *Easy Street*, bending street lamps to pavement level with his bare hands.

The other ladies who live in the street are rarely seen and then only as clusters of gossiping noddies with tinted hair. One noddy is always in full spate; the rest you never see, they seem to live indoors, like the Swedes, their doors rarely open. One of the elderly Arnopp sisters, of ancient lineage, is said to be poorly, having taken to her bed, and a coal delivery comes regularly. After their brother, Piercy, died there was no man to dig the garden. A retired butcher, he passed away last year; butchers from all over the country attended his funeral, butchers being close as Freemasons. They are not very neighbourly neighbours, the Arnopp sisters; dressed like a Russian peasant one of them tears at the weeds, visible over our drenched stockade. Is it Dora or Kitty? I never know which is which; but one had not been seen out for months, maybe a year; smoke curls from their chimney early in the day. Kitty or Dora is dying.

The walled garden of flowers and vegetables and rustic arbours abutting on St Multose cemetery over the wall must come as a surprise. We have those quiet well-behaved Protestant neighbours, *los muertos*.

It poured rain all this winter and cattle died in the open fields. The farmers didn't get the prices they wanted, fodder became short, livestock bawling with hunger in the waterlogged fields, up to their hocks in muck.

Rain fell incessantly, coming down like a hard penance, and in court the accused perjured themselves, threatened witnesses, swore at the Guards. Strange and unheard-of crimes occurred in remote places, the consequence of drunkenness and disputes about land and property, and the foul weather.

A man trimming a hedge slipped and fell from a collapsing stepladder, slit himself from ear to ear on the opened clippers, crawled in his blood across a lawn, his face chalk white, expiring in his wife's arms.

The Pope was tireless at performing good works, flying far, kissing the ground, saying Mass for two million of the faithful in Mexico.

A new and horrible new Ireland had begun to emerge. Skulduggery was exposed in high places, but those concerned seemed immune, hard to nail down; protesting their innocence, they lied under oath, denied all their misdeeds, slippery as eels. Priests, formerly trusted friends of the family, part of the family, for God's sake, were found to be guilty of committing unnatural acts with children under their care; the finger was even pointed at bishops. Nuns went to bed with other nuns.

We have four butchers' shops, one turf accountant, two banks, two postal deliveries in morning and afternoon, letter post on foot, and parcel post by green van in the afternoon, the parcel (books) given into your hand by a surly fellow out of uniform who will not catch your eye, sour as though permanently out of sorts. Alannah said wittily that he might feel happier if he was working in an abattoir; hadn't his da, sour as the son, been a butcher?

The sounds that wake us in the winter darkness are not the downpours of rain sloshing into the yard nor the dripping aftermath but around 4.30 the sound of Concorde 'going supersonic' as it invades Irish airspace, heading out across the Atlantic for New York.

Shortly after that we hear the same early car (coming the wrong way down the one-way system) stopping outside the narrow block of flats to pick up a colleague heading off for the day shift at the Eli Lilly chemical plant at Dunderrow.

They work a twenty-four-hour day there, spilling drug effluents through the muggy winter air, and when the wind blows in the wrong direction the Beugs get it, and close their windows, having already lost four peacocks to a neighbouring farmer laying down poison alongside their land.

These are the sounds that wake us in the darkness, and in winter that means fifteen hours of night with no exultant cockcrow to announce daybreak as the darkness leaks away and a wan purposeless sort of daylight takes its place. Small wonder that the 'mere Irish' are a lethargic breed. As said before, 'the smaller the island, the bigger the neurosis'.

The low sun shines at an acute angle into Upper O'Connell Street, coming between Mary Lane's wine bar and Satin & Lace boutique, lighting up the lemon-yellow door of Spring Cottage, so named on a scrollwork of entwined flowers, where Mazzer sleeps and snores and holds sway.

Two baskets of flowers are suspended on either side of the door and two printed cards with the prohibition NO PARKING, to be repeated in other windows. Such prohibitions are catching. Don't do this, don't do that. This house is mine. This way is mine. Keep out.

A recurring annoyance in summer months is the passing drunkard who knocks on the door at 5 a.m. on his way home, sometimes pulling out flowers from hanging basket and trellis. Mazzer believes that this may be a retired bachelor postman who is unable to break the habit of early rising and therefore has time on his hands. She threatens to empty a full chamberpot on to his head from an upstairs window one of these days.

Fidgety crows balance themselves on the telegraph wires near Good's Mill and drop down to snatch spillage from the lorries that ply between there and the dockside loading bay.

Great herring gulls escort the trawlers into the harbour and take the scraps discarded over the side. An otter fishing from the dock clings to one of the car tyres lashed to the sea wall. Jackdaw and crows take the easy pickings from Mamma Mia's skips and sly cats are fed by an old nun at the gate of the convent now empty of students, foul-mouthed girls puffing fags, boasting of conquests and rebuffs. The clear voices call up – 'suck-off, blow-job, mickey'. Their whores' language is purple.

The Urban District Council has supplied hygienic wheely-bins and imposed a charge for the Thursday collections. Before that the resourceful rooks were slashing open the plastic bags with their sharp beaks and the dogs dragged out the refuse for the birds to devour.

Blackbirds, thrushes and magpies assemble about the French prison where in January 1749 fifty-four French prisoners suffocated to death in a fatal fire. The nocturnal whistler passes in the night, always alone, whistling melodiously with trills and grace notes and arpeggios, going on his way so tunefully and cheerful. Curlews overfly the house in the darkness, sending down their lovely liquid calls. A single heron flies over the garden in the daytime, cranking herself forward, legs stretched out behind, heading for some fishpond. In the lane below the Friary Church the bats flit to and fro in summer, hunting insects. There are few dogs on the loose and cats seem to stay indoors or use the hidden gardens.

Wrens too I have seen in the garden, though seldom, woodpeckers never; for a while a piebald blackbird came and went and then did not return any more, perhaps killed by the cats. It was more white than black, more odd-looking than a magpie, odder than an ape painted white.

Crows sound guttural as old fellows gasping for breath, throats rusty with catarrh. The jackdaws give urgent mating calls on the roof opposite us, the cock with trembling wings outspread, puffed up with lust; the hen hopping out of reach, affecting indifference; then he is upon her.

Mute swans paddle in the marina, passing the green hull of the yacht *Cassiopeia*; the trim yacht has been on its moorings all winter, the long foul wet winter that continued late into April, the swallows arriving late. The Earl of Orrery thought Kinsale in 1660 'one of the noblest harbours in Europe'. The old port of bond houses and sedan chairs, burgheresses and Kinsale hookers, Charles Fort and James Fort, the ramparts, Desmond Castle; reaching back to the days of Thurston Haddock and Norman de Courcey, Philip Roche and Andrew Blundus; 'where the Brinney meets the Bandon', is our home today.

All through this summer, the saddest summer of the century and the wettest on record, the swallows could be heard but not seen twittering overhead as in previous summers, the summers of long ago; now reduced to dots and spots caused by indigestion, blurs in the retina of the jaundiced eye of the beholder; just sounds in the air announcing the summer that had never arrived.

The nests of the swifts in the eaves of the other No. 2 at the top of the Stony Steps are no longer there, torn down by cruel tenants concerned about the limy droppings squirted on the footpath and doorsteps.

There is an old superstition in Kildare, that if the nests of these exquisite summer birds are destroyed, the milked cows yield blood. No longer was heard their high-pitched screeching as they tore through the air around the Stony Steps. Renowned for their spectacular aeronautics while feeding, every autumn they emigrated to Africa, slept on the wing: nobs of the air in their spotless white dickeys and midnight blue jackets, nattily attired they had their own schedules, their small dark eyes missing nothing.

The birds of Kinsale were as the birds of the Ark, sole survivors of the Great Flood; they sang as though their last hour had come. On an overcast Sunday in early August the seagulls were crying like cats over the garden of No. 2.

★   ★   ★

Judd Scanlan was sent down for twenty-two years for importing drugs from Arnhem and Amsterdam via Rosslare and Ringaskiddy into Cork, hidden in Donaghmore and Nad woodlands. Profitable connections had been made in Brixton and Maidstone Prisons with the Columbian drug cartels. Barbara Berg was bereft; they had a daughter whom he adored. He would be seventy-one when he left prison, an old man. The Gardai thought that he wouldn't be able to handle it. If you played with fire, you got burnt. The man behind the murder of Veronica Guerin on the Lucan Road was imprisoned in England, reputed to be a very bad egg indeed.

Hit-men were for hire in Dublin: if the price was right anybody could be rubbed out. Killing was like any other business; drug trafficking was carried out like any honest business, but what business was honest? Every nest had its bad egg. Cocaine and Ecstasy were worth millions, the tobacco of the twenty-first century. The villains had appropriate nicknames for those who had done time in the nick: the Bodyguard, Seedy Fagan, the Penguin Mitchell. In the dock they all protested their innocence; they were innocent men, they said. They had been got at.

Transport managers were recruited to facilitate drug trafficking from the continent; the rich villains took their vacations on the Costa del Sol, showed films of their marked victims, jeered at Veronica Guerin, who was marked down for murder. Ecstasy and cannabis importers were into the big time. It was a lark.

71

St Multose Cemetery and
the Commogue Marsh

I n St Multose cemetery abutting on our walled garden lie
the Protestant dead. Dead husbands lie by dead wives, dead
sons and daughters by dead parents, kinsmen and their
dutiful womenfolk, all dead Anglicans assembled here. Those
who had lived a long time and those whose lives had been cut
short, with modest gravestones commemorating them in a grassy
walled place within the arched gateway that leads into the church
grounds proper, the Protestant enclave.

Here lie the Arnopps and the Copithornes and the Drapers and
the Staffords and the Waltons and George Edward Stanley and
Margaret Flaherty (a Miss Barrington had married a Catholic),
Buttimer Byron, Newman, Kingston and Wing Commander
Ronald Sivewright (*Per ardua ad astra*) and Robert Johnston and
his beloved wife Peg (née Gregg) who died four years after,
aged forty-seven years ('Abide with Me') and Gertrude Mather
who lived ninety-four years, and Hodgkin the kleptomaniac who
hadn't lived so long, and Heathcote and Crawford and Donald
Dean Marleau (born in Canada) buried near the wall under the
great yew tree, since removed to accommodate another block
of flats, a youth hostel.

This is a Protestant redoubt in a republican Catholic heartland
where Anglican Protestants intermarry and breed with their
own, keep faith with those of their own persuasion and keep

themselves to themselves: the Goods and the Grahams, the Lucases and Daphne Daunt keeping the bloodline pure, to worship in St Multose and sing their doleful Anglican hymns amid the monuments and memorial stones commemorating those brave soldiers and officers who had offered their services and given their lives to the English Crown.

It was the site of the great battle, a cannon shot away, in the dead of winter in 1601 when Protestant English put O'Neill and O'Donnell to flight, watched by Catholic Spanish from the inner harbour. It was an afternoon's slaughter.

The Catholic cemetery of St Eltin is out beyond Good's Mills on the road to Summercove, and there roil the mortal remains of Joe ('the Trapper') Revatta and little Billy O'Brien (not to be confused with little Willie O'Brien, publican of the Bulman) and those other brave hearts who have passed away in our time, going out from the Bulman bar one damp day and stepping into the afterlife, wherever it may be, free of all encumbrances pertaining to the living, with benefits and rewards that scorn profit and loss.

The layabouts and loungers lounge about the Temperance Hall, sitting on their idle arses on the public bench supplied or resting themselves against the walls, Dicky Rock (RIP), and gouty Garr, still with us and mad as a brush; from World's End, the Fish, beery O'Leary of Barrack Street, the loonies and wiseacres, gossips and tosspots of the town. I recall the time when elderly men gossiped all day by gateposts in Ireland; but the instant TV arrived they went indoors and haven't been seen since. These old knowalls who hung about gateposts at dusk, travellers in time who maybe never put a foot outside their own parish are no more.

'St Multose, and St Eltin, who are they when they are at home?'

'Our patron saint. They are one and the same.'

'But one is Protestant and the other Catholic, how can they be the same?'

'They are the same chap.'

'How come?'

'I don't know.'

'Well, I'll be damned!'

In Loving Memory Of
ISABEL DOROTHEA JAMES
Dearly Beloved Wife Of
JOHN NEVILLE ABRAHAM JAMES
Born Oleby
22nd November 1896
Died Kinsale 16th July 1977

On unadorned white marble headstones the names were cut. Cheek by jowl the James man and wife lay underground.

In Loving Memory Of
JOHN NEVILLE ABRAHAM JAMES
Dearly Beloved Husband Of
ISABEL DOROTHEA JAMES
Born Dublin 17th November 1891
Died Cork 25th September 1979

In Loving Memory Of
MICHAEL NEWMAN
who died 16th June 1928
and his sister KATHLEEN
Died 14th July 1965.
And of their mother
KATE NEWMAN
who died 18th April 1978

'BLESSED BE THE PURE IN HEART
FOR THEY SHALL SEE GOD.'

Late April pansies of russet and orange with black hearts nodded their heads to the breeze that blew through the little walled graveyard where the Newmans slept their last sleep, as Rory strolled by, took note of their names and the year of their decease.

The recently mown lawn of the little Anglican cemetery was carpeted with a profusion of daisies and dandelions, numerous as

the fields of poppies that sprang up from the blood of slaughtered
Serbs, become the red poppies that grow only at Kossova.

JPR (Russell) NORMAN
25–12–1923 to 1–1–1999

PERKINS
HOWARD AND ANN née BUCKLEY
1911–1997.
Christ Our Light.

In Loving Memory of My Darling Wife
ELIZABETH ANN RAYMOND
Who died 10th October 1974
and her loving husband
TERENCE GEORGE RAYMOND
Died 23rd January 1994
Resting Where No Shadows Fall

Happy and loving memories
GERTRUDE MATHER
Lived 94 years
30–8–1899 – 5–6–1994

A clump of dandelions below the headstone, that read:

In Loving memory of
BARONESS MC M.C.A. DIBBETS
Grandmother of ASTRID WILLIAMS
29th April 1963–13th May 1997
Beloved wife of TOM WILLIAMS & loving
mother of Thomas Neal? [undecipherable].

In loving Memory of my husband
DONALD DEAN MARLEAU
Born October 1939 in Canada.
At rest September 1988.
'Until We Meet Again.'

In Loving Memory Of
PAT HEATHCOTE
Born 6th September 1909
Died 13th March 1997.
Beloved wife of
FRED HEATHCOTE
Born 12th December 1908
Died 5th March 1991.
At Rest

In loving memory of
ADRIAN JAMES WENSLEY WALKER
Born 6th March 1932
Died 4th October 1996.

In the cement below the headstone was cut the name WALKER, above an unweeded headstone of black marble.

In Loving memory of
GEORGE N. BEASLEY
Born; Kent 5th December 1915
Died; Kinsale 1st November 1996.
At Rest

In Loving memory of
GORDON ALEXIS GOOD
Born 20th June 1926
Died 6th July 1987.
In Heavenly Love Abiding.

Below the proud running header COPITHORNE lay the dead Copithornes in their serried ranks:

In loving memory of
JAMES RICHARD COPITHORNE
Mullendonny, Kinsale. Died 12–12–85
aged 67 years.
The Lord is My Shepherd.

DORMAN
In loving memory of
HENRY HOBART GEORGE
'Raffeen,' Scilly,
Born 19th January 1906
Died 4th May 1991
And his wife
GWENDOLEN ALLEN
Born 13th January 1908
Died 16th March 1997.
'Love One Another.'

In loving memory of
our dear brother
GEORGE ARNOPP
Died 5th October 1989.
Also our dear sister
MARGARET
Died 18th September 1990.
Well done, thy good and faithful
servant enter the joy of the Lord.

In loving memory of
MARIGOLD SLOCOCK
Who died 24th May 1986
Aged 92 years.
At Rest.

In loving Memory of
THOMAS CHAMBER
Coolbawn, Ballinspittle
who died 7th September 1982.
His wife Mary, née Blennerhassett
Died 6th July 1991.
Forever with the Lord.

The curious names of villages and townlands are presumably
Anglicised versions of the Gaelic originals:

Ardbrack
Ballinadee
Ballinamona
Ballinspittle
Ballynacubby
Ballynagrumnoolie
Bawhavota
Cappagh
Commogue (Creek)
Crossbarry
Currahoo
Dromderrig
Dunderrow
Knocknabohinny
Knocknacurra
Ringfinnan
Timoleague
Tisaxon Beg

Our ship's chandler John Thullier has itemised the fowl of the marsh at Commogue and the life thereon.

Little grebe and dabduck keep diving, turning over weeds and stones to feed, as do the turnstones. A flash of russet orange betrays the presence of the kingfisher. Golden plover fly in formation towards Timoleague, their favoured habitation. You know the shelduck by its pied plumage, the widgeon by its chestnut-coloured head, the mallard by its gorgeous vivid green. Oystercatchers, cormorants and tufted mergansers feed here, herons perch on the branches of alders; little egrets have come from the Mediterranean to take up residency on the south coast. Mute swans stay all year round, paddling by the dyke and the Dog Pond near the road to Dunderrow and the Doon. Greenshanks and redshanks occupy the right bank under Knocknacurra (these slender birds easily take fright), lapwings assemble in large flocks facing into the wind. The little dunlin feeds near the curlews, the godwits have upturned bills, ducks and waders feed from mid-October to mid-February, a grim time of year that gets longer and longer, wetter and wetter.

The causeway across the marsh at Commogue was built 150 years ago. For thousands of years the river has been flushing tides into the open inlet. Sluice gates under the road allow salt water to mix with fresh water coming down from the streams that enter the marsh from the surrounding hills. This brackish water, together with an alder grove in the northwestern corner, provides a diverse habitat for various flora and wild life birds. (Thullier)

The Fella says that John Thullier, bearded like a sea-captain, is 'perfidious'. Treacherous and deceitful, they have fallen out over some small seafaring matter that would not trouble landlubbers such as you or me, hiding in the shadows of the rushes.

The upturned mallards show their arses when feeding upside down, unconcerned with such disputes, that make life in the country what it is: medieval. Is it not so? We never had a Renaissance nor a Reformation; we never needed them.

The Gangrenous Hand

Scott of the Antarctic

He died amid the snow blizzards on his return journey from the South Pole and has been carried 35 miles from the spot where he recorded his last words.

He is buried on an ice shelf that is moving, so we can work out where the bodies must be today. Scott and his two companions, Dr Edward Wilson, the expedition's chief scientist, and Lieut. Henry Bowers, have been covered over with just a foot of ice each year, and are now 90 feet below the surface. Scott's final journey will take another 250 years.

Daily Telegraph, 9 November 1998

The will to live must have eventually left them, been drained out of them; for nothing could change the prolonged inertia until death had dealt his last hand, freed them; best to slip away in sleep and be carried off into unconsciousness.

The minute hand and the hour hand were both nailed to the clockface and time stood still, waiting for them to do the decent thing and die. They stood outside Time, it was finished with them, held captive in a dark place like miners asphyxiated in a deep coalmine out of which the oxygen is being drained, or blindfolded hostages held captive in dark quarters by terrorists or madmen.

If one roused himself to speak, the other two listened apatheti-cally without any signs of emotion, heard him out in stupefied silence, huddled together for warmth, breathing their hound's breath into each each other's faces, emitting sour wind and sighing. The blizzards closed around them; the brown air in the tent was bad, the stink of putrefaction lingered, all that remained of Evans who had died six weeks previously of a gangrenous hand cut on sledge runners. Exactly a month before, Larry Oates had stumbled out of the tent on his frostbitten feet, after pronouncing the famous epitaph, never to be seen again, as if he had gone off the edge of the earth. Someone had blundered!

The moan of the Arctic wind rose to a psychotic whine, dragging at the guy ropes. Was it day or night? There seemed little enough reason to hope for any improvement in their miserable lot, no human voices carried on the wind and each night they prayed never to awake. They were already in the Nether World. They stank like corpses.

The blizzards blew themselves out but the rescue party never arrived. Snow fell silently on the tent, a great mantle of snow laid down gently layer upon layer, year after year, obliterating them.

The tent with its three bodies intact became a sarcophagus, a snow-covered, iced-up hearse with no mourners to accompany it to its final destination. Scott and his two companions had now drifted beyond the camp which he had failed to reach eighty-eight years before at the end of March 1912. They were on a moving ice-shelf carried along at a slow and stately rate of just under half a mile a year; the slowest funeral cortège in the world would take another two hundred and fifty years to reach the Ross Sea. They still had some way to go, buried ninety feet deep in the ice like flies in amber.

'Outside the door of the tent it remains a scene of swirling drift,' the cramped fingers had written. Wasn't it Yeats who wrote, 'Too long a sacrifice can make a stone of the heart'? Captain Robert Scott's achievement is considered a success, like the siege of Stalingrad, the retreat from Dunkirk, the London Blitz, the Windmill never closing, a tied Test match at the Oval: such rearguard actions and tactical retreats are proof of man's mettle, reveal the human spirit.

By December 1999 the tent had passed One Ton depot where the rescue party had waited six days to no avail. In about 2250 the frozen grave will break up into giant icebergs and the three bodies sink to their last resting place on the bed of the Ross Sea.

The Siege of Stalingrad

When the Russian winter descended upon besieged Stalingrad with its heavy tread the temperature sank by eighteen degrees and ice-floes began to build up and grind together on the Volga, buckling up and groaning deep groans. Crossing the frozen river, Beevor wrote, had become perilous as a Polar expedition. The Sixth Army awaited its fate in dugouts 'grouped together like a troglodyte village'. In their deep misery the steely-hearted citizens of the encircled city had begun to hallucinate. And to such effect that Stalin, their great leader, was seen stalking amid the ruins in his heavy military greatcoat, moving silently and stiffly as if already cast in bronze. He had come to comfort them in their hour of need in the suffering city named after him.

Starving mice broke into stationary Tiger tanks of the Panzer Corps and ate the cables off the power installations, effectively putting them out of action. When the city was retaken by Zhukov and his generals a great silence fell and the wind off the steppes whistled through the rusty skeletons of Sixth Army tanks put out of action by Russian mice.

The courageous Captain Scott had chosen to die in his own way, a fate no worse nor any better than suffocation with the crew of the submarine *Thetis* sunk in the mud of Liverpool Bay; or drowned amid the loose pianos and stiff-lipped gentry who had gone down with the *Titanic*, holed by a drifting iceberg off Newfoundland.

Towards the end, the last three breathing their last breaths, Scott, Wilson and Bowers, all equal now in misery, stinking to high heaven, with spirits flagging, they may have come around to the view that the whole sorry enterprise had been ill-judged, if not rank foolishness. What was the South Pole to them but a cairn of stones built in the Antarctic wastes by Amundsen and, as a final insult, the Norwegian flag limp on its pole?

They had come to detest the sight of each other, the awful proximity, the gloomy bulks looming in the cramped tent, their hoarse voices and insufferable patience; the courage to survive so obstinately in such squalid surroundings was demeaning, detestable.

Oh all the fishes in the sea that swam upriver under the arches of the Archdeacon Duggan bridge opposite Folly House (whilom home of the Simpsons) agreed:

> Bass
> Codfish
> Codling
> Conger eel
> Dab
> Dogfish
> Flounder
> Mullet
> Plaice
> Pollack
> Whiting
> Wrasse

all were in full agreement. As were the birds that wintered in the Commogue Marsh:

> Bar-tailed godwit and black-tailed godwit
> Black-backed gull
> Common gull and black-headed gull
> Common tern
> Curlew
> Dunlin
> Greenshank
> Grey heron
> Lapwing
> Little egret

Mallard
Merganser
Oystercatcher
Peregrine falcon
Redshank
Reed bunting
Ringed plover and golden plover
Sedge warbler
Shag
Shelduck
Snipe
Teal
Whimbrel
Wigeon
Woodcock
Yellowhammer
Yellow wagtail

as itemised by ornithologist Damien Enright and limned by Steve Pawsey.

Consolation for the defeated is that all lost battles are considered (by the losers) to be triumphs, moral victories on the field of sport and battle, defeat seen as a glorious victory (the tryless draw at Lansdowne Road), in the cant of history.

Verti la giubla!

73

Warning Shadows

W henever I'm working well on a book, scorning the
mundane, the humdrum and the norm; or say rather
when it is working well on *me*; as one might speak
of gangrene working in a wound or of a powerful prophylactic
calculated to fire up the sluggish system – I might receive the
summons from what Saul Bellow calls the Hidden Prompter
(who never sleeps, always alert for messages) who now wishes to
convey an urgent message coming direct from the unconscious,
central recording communications system or CRCS: for me to
rise up pronto, take up my bed and walk from even the deepest
sleep (it could be 5 a.m.) and, on going upstairs into the living
room (up from my sea cabin, my sea gown scarf'd about me in
the dark, groped I to find), to find the room where I work, lit
from three windows from two sides like some irrefutable point in
Euclidean geometry, now bathed in the most extraordinary light
imaginable.

You might say it was the ambient light found in the Dutch
Old Masters with the Dutch darkness driven out of the sky to
reveal an ancient amber light known to those circumnavigators
who had come into a bay in the Dutch East Indies just at sun-up
and found it flooded in this light.

Let me put it another way. A man is walking briskly through
a city become strange to him at an early hour when normally

he would not be up and about. Walking at a brisk pace through a Berlin emptied of traffic and pedestrians and become strangely silent, Vladimir Nabokov ('Sirius' the Russian novelist) makes his way towards the nursing home where his new-born son (nameless and still in the shock or stupor of birth) awaits the father troubled by the unearthly light that floods the sleeping city, familiar buildings casting strange shadows at awkward angles.

The shadows fall at such strange angles, that Nabokov feels he has slipped or fallen between the gap of one day and the next, dropped into a no-place, into the *Neveneinder ineluctably*. That part of the city he now traversed walking briskly, perspiring and nervous, was doubly unfamiliar to the new father now approaching a still unknown, unseen, sleeping son; and to be sure already held under threat, by the sinister Prussian shadows cast across the unfamiliar narrow streets and by shadows that were positively UFA-like in their menace, as though awaiting the arrival of Werner Krauss or Conrad Veidt and give them (the shadows) veracity, to deliver their lines; as the babe (now awake and bawling to be fed) awaited the father, now breaking into a trot, the nursing home (a strange home never seen before, lit by an unearthly light) at long last hove finally in sight.

But, then, neither was it quite like that.

I'd come up into the living room that I had left in total darkness six or seven hours previously to discover it now flooded with an extraordinarily calm orange effulgence, certainly an unearthly light; as a yachtsman leaving the darkness of the cabin for the open deck after daybreak finds all about him a double light, so that the yacht seems to sail in the air, sea-reflecting sky and sky-reflecting sea become one light bearing up the yacht, gushing from beyond the horizon, announcing the arrival of a new day.

Something as marvellous as that awaited me in the living room in spring or summer at that early hour. In winter, of course, the room would be in darkness, a cat sleeping, the ashes cold in the wood-burner, the automatic heating not yet on. It had something of the strong purposeful Prussian daylight, sunrise light, known to me in Berlin when I had left Hannelore and had to kill time walking round and round Schlachtensee

(Slaughter Lake) or Krumme Lanke (an old German song?), laden with guilt.

The colour that bathed the living room (the cat now awake and silently begging to be fed) was such an orange that orange will hardly do to describe it with any accuracy. I would have to say it reminded me of the truly phenomenal colour of the dead orchard that Calnek and I chanced upon in our marathon walk from Cómpeta in the hills to Canillas de Albaida; we never found the fish trail to Granada but at least we found this. The fruit unplucked on the small orange trees had rotted or been stricken with some blight or killing canker that left them black and hard and wizened on the trees; the useless last crop hung there in tatters like hand grenades that had not 'gone off', or rather had half gone off, enough to partly destroy the casing; the sections of the fruit that were not black with blight were this vivid orange, an infected colour, the freshness of the fruit thwarted of their natural growth. It was a peculiar place to be in; like something in Grimm again.

The light was already beginning to flood the village too. The sea to the south-east (normally out of sight for anyone standing at the window) seemed to have drawn closer, flooding part of the village, so strong was the reflected emergent daylight now pouring or streaming over the roofs of the houses where the sleepers still snored, for now smoke rose up from the chimneypots, announcing breakfast.

This house, formerly in Fisher Street but now Upper O'Connell Street, was once the home of Creswell, who lost his wife and moved elsewhere with his children. I kept encountering him or his double at drinks parties at Folly House (home to Mary Alice and Howard R. Simpson, late of the American Consular Service at Marseilles) or at Ardnacorrig, on cosmopolitan and posh Compass Hill (where lived historian Robert Dye and Tessa, a Hawaiian princess by blood), and knew him at once, for he always stood in the same posture (sundial) in the same outfit – red and white striped shirt, tan slacks, shod in Hush Puppies, holding a drink, a third depleted (red wine) with a social smirk on his face, standing a little apart from the other drinkers, silently brooding, deliberating upon something. Then I'd sidle up to him and say, 'Creswell, I believe.' To which he would respond with the utmost gravity and politeness: 'You've got the wrong man again. I'm not Creswell.'

'No? Well, you're the spitting image of him.'

'Nevertheless,' said the man who was not Creswell, looking over my shoulder with a crafty smile, as though he knew I was having him on, 'I am not Creswell.'

We painted the front of the house white, installed double glazing in three windows overlooking the narrow street, put a brass porthole into the front door to lighten the dark hall, painted the door Commodore blue, put in window-boxes.

We are No. 2. There is another No. 2 halfway down by the Stony Steps. Below us is the Guardwell. What can it be guarding so well? Search me. More puzzles in the labyrinth of our life. Lift me up, let me see!

If you examine the house from the outside (in the narrow street dividing the Guardwell from Casey's Corner or what used to be but is now Bruno's Tower) you might be looking at any semi-detached two-storey *casa* in a narrow *calle* in Palma de Majorca, say Calle dos de Mayo, and the surprise continues in that the hallway leads directly to a sunken patio with whitewashed walls and hanging baskets of flowers, a throughway admitting daylight while it lasts and affords admittance to the walled garden beyond, a half-acre of lawn and arbours and flowerbeds and a crazy-paved path of flat stones from a beach near the Old Head, and three apple trees and a tall twelve-foot brick wall at the end, with Protestant *cementerio* and twelfth-century tower and weather vane (missing salmon) with Canon Williams's Anglican bell tolling beyond the nearer wall where honeysuckle has been trained against a trellis.

The interior developed in as arbitrary and haphazard a fashion, the hit or miss Spanish manner of adding rooms to accommodate new-born babes, with the bedroom downstairs off the hallway and the living room and kitchen upstairs, the kitchen more galley than anything else, behind a clapboard division that screens it off. The floor to ceiling window with sliding door has been enlarged to admit more daylight, with access to the deck and teak rail overlooking the herb garden and arbours. You climb upstairs via a narrow gangway without banisters into the living room where sunlight penetrates to the street wall and two windows overlooking the street. A Welsh window-cleaner puts up his collapsible steel ladder once a month and ascends, full of wind and fresh gossip (he had stayed in a Chicago hotel ninety-two storeys up), one of a company of Jehovah's Witnesses from Bandon. His previous and late confrère Higginbotham had departed into Ecuador where he died of cancer while presumably engaged in proselytising, not window-cleaning.

74

Countess Markiewicz and the Siege of Derry

... a great perturbation of sweaty heroes ...
watching the hurlers above in Kilmainham.
Samuel Beckett, *Whoroscope* (1930)

i

The gun, which had never really left Irish politics but had always been secretly there, under the counter as it were, used as a bargaining ploy in dirty deals, was back again. Ever since Sir Roger Casement had imported arms from Germany on a ship that had carried sewage pipes as legitimate cargo, the gun had been there. It was still being used for plea–bargaining in political deals that referred to the disbanding of a secret army that had no intention of ever surrendering its arms while any remnants of the British Army remained in Ulster, the Orange province that would always fight and would always be right. Their Green counterparts still prated of a free united Ireland, turning their backs on the grim reality that the Protestants, the Orangemen, were implacably opposed to such a scheme; for those who have had power once do not readily surrender it.

Provos imprisoned in Portlaoise had smeared the walls of their cells with their own excrement, as heated up as their politics, the dirty protest of babes and revolutionaries in arms. Others had taken hunger strikes to the limit, died for their convictions, now

375

cadaverous and stinking in soiled sheets. Neither camp would budge an inch from the position they had adopted; neither had one iota of mercy for the opposition, no matter how gallant or foolish in their mutual efforts to infiltrate enemy lines, to annihilate each other and all that was theirs.

Captain Robert Nairac, purporting to be Danny from the Ardoyne, had given them 'The Broad Black Brimmer' and three other rebel songs at the Three Steps Inn at Drumintee. He had then been taken out, beaten insensible with fenceposts and whatever other implement came to hand. Nairac, with not much life left in him, was then shot out of hand like a mad dog and the sorry remains chucked into a meat-grinder.

The Provos refused to give up their arms, their dangerous toys; they scattered about the bodies of their victims as heartlessly as cannibals would discard human bones after a cannibal feast on some desert isle where they had repaired for a celebratory repast. They weren't admitting what may have happened to Captain Nairac. These facts could never be publicly known; the hatred on both sides was implacable; the dead were dishonoured, thrown into unmarked graves, not even graves, not even recorded; they would like to forget them, forget all that had ever happened, what they had done to Nairac, what they would do to others. The victims were dumped as casually as the Mob disposed of its kills in the marshes and wasteland beneath the Pulaski skyway, discarded like carrion.

The weapons sold to them by Gaddafi were brought in secretly and wrapped in oil-soaked coverings as if they were holy relics or the shrunken bodies of mummies in sweet-smelling preservatives; buried in secret places at night in woodland and bog, and records kept of their precious whereabouts. Those entrusted with such secret nocturnal burials were told to keep their mouths shut, if they knew what was good for them.

When the great day came they would be dug up, resurrected for the uprising that was to free Ireland, so long in bondage to the hated enemy, perfidious Albion, the bad neighbour, the masterly manipulator of political skulduggery down the long centuries when Ireland was in bondage.

The country was riddled with arms caches and now with dead

bodies buried in shallow graves, grudged even the respect owed to the dead, but every indignity heaped upon them, cursed as they were put down, hidden away. The weapons got more respect than the dead enemies; no single reverence could be accorded them; they were as hated in death as they had been in life. The sacrifices had been too great; the fight had to go on.

Killing had its own price that had to be paid – the weapons were not cheap, transporting them was expensive, bribes had to be dropped. One paid for the other in the bigger calculations of a secret war, a war of attrition against civilians and informers, and wrongdoers who deserved punishment and would get it, knee-capping, all part of the unacknowledged legislation of dreams, deals and bonds sealed with handshakes, nods and winks.

And how could anything good come out of such dishonour-able and mean-spirited and twisted activity, carried out at night, when the hit-men struck again, out of sight and hearing of honest people asleep in their beds, dreaming of a free Ireland? How could it?

Ireland didn't deserve to be free. Ireland was in bondage, had always been in bonds. Dreams of sudden wealth had come to certain citizens of another island – was it Mozambique? – of treasure buried by pirates and the exact place where it had been buried seen in dreams with enough exactness for the sleeper when awake to draw a rough map, sell up everything and buy digging equipment and start digging. Those benighted dreamers gave up their jobs and went on digging a huge hole and then other huge holes near the first one. They found nothing and were ruined, for all their savings and hopes of wealth had gone into the digging equipment, and now they had nothing, the fools, the fools, the fools!

I have seen a dog digging for bones in much the same frantic manner on a beach near Bundoran, firing the sand back through his hind legs like a power-hose. At least the dog gives up, quits the demented digging and leaves the beach. Not so the Provos; they have their own itinerary, their dreams that they will never relinquish. Every race to its own wrestling. Every race has its own particular craziness. And Ireland? Ireland is no particular exception; every dog has its own fleas.

ii

As a precocious youth of sixteen summers, Orson Welles had travelled through Connemara in a donkey-trap, painting scenery until his money ran out, then he acted for the Edwards –MacLiammóir company at the Gate in Dublin, as is well known. There he began to find himself, began to develop his prodigious talents.

In October 1931 he played the Duke Karl Alexander opposite Betty Chancellor in *Jew Süss* and received good notices. He offered Alexander Korda the outline of a satirical film; it was to be set in Italy, on the Mediterranean coast, in one of those mythical kingdoms the size of Luxembourg, a farce about capitalist imperialism. Two towns had hated each other for seven hundred years.

It brought to mind the true story that Flora Jessup had told me of the last siege of Derry and her small part in it. For she herself had been on the Derry walls during the famous siege, and was 'had' there thrice by three of the boys in the course of one night. Liverish and with the direct stare of puck goats with stinking breath, they had enjoyed her favours, one by one, each unbeknown to the others, in different rooms, between patrolling the walls and coming upon Flora, dauntless daughter of desire, a Botticelli page from the fork down.

She may not have been the Countess Constance Markiewicz in her uniform of Citizen Army green, brandishing a heavy service revolver but at least she was serviceable and one of their own, for was she not herself a countess of the Holy Roman Empire? She had some such distinction, bestowed upon her by the Pope in the Vatican.

The three heroes who had enjoyed her favours in the course of one night may have feared it was their last on earth. The third was Cathal Goulding himself, quartermaster of the 'official' IRA, who encountered her preparing breakfast and had her there and then, under the table. She was his porridge and his Holy Communion.

During the siege the lads grew beards; Flora had had a rash for days after their attentions but had offered herself up freely for Ireland. She was, after all, to be the consolation prize for a brave soldier ready to offer up his life for Mother Ireland.

The notion of an uprising had excited them and no two ways about it; the hard men, the renegades, had been looking forward to Easter, for wasn't it to be their time? It was woven into the very tapestry of our history; implicit in the national anthem ('The Soldier's Song'), repeated in the story of Casement's weapons concealed under German sewage pipes, the thirty pieces of silver, the crowing of the cock, Christ's reassuring words to the Good Thief. It was all there, and in their credulous hearts they believed it, every word of it.

The traitors and informers, the turncoats whom James Joyce said we would always have with us as part of our heritage and history (as Christ told us we would always have the poor), the ratters, big and little grasses, those who had been 'turned', or were about to be turned, were now all united, like a Churchman pack with twenty cigarettes (extra strong) intact in it, presenting one stern face set and resolute to the common foe, perfidious Albion.

English Anglicans, hard-boiled Protestants, in their credulity believe that Queen Victoria slept everywhere they were pleased to put her up in: hotels and the rich private houses of England suitable for their Queen. As we in our credulous Catholic way believe that Saint Patrick slept all over Ireland, generally in the open on the sides of hills that became places of pilgrimage named after him. We also believe that the Devil, Old Nick, dined out all over Ireland and was royally entertained.

At least that's what they used to believe in County Kildare and may still do, for all I know. Satan rode with the Killing Kildares and dined with Speaker Conolly at Castletown, now taken over by Desmond Guinness and the Irish Georgian Society.

75

The Americanisation of Old Ireland

'Have a nice day!'

i

The Americanisation of Ireland began with the baseball caps. After that came the shopping malls; then it was every man for himself, the pell-mell downhill race of the Gadarene swine. Let me tell you about it.

Of all the countries in the world to emulate, we had to pick the worst. Baseball caps with goofy logos and slogans were worn by young and old, often back to front. Old codgers wore them, as well as farm-workers driving slurry wagons. A general uniformity such as you get among soccer supporters ('Who do ya support?') was established. Then came the rash of shopping malls from Tallaght in Dublin to Crazy Prices in Portlaoise.

Then came the bypasses around Cork city, as the large provincial town was called; as though some city engineer had taken leave of his sense and built roundabouts everywhere he could, and also where he shouldn't, slavishly following some road system he had seen in Sweden and Portugal.

Cork and Cobh were trying to join up, arterial hands reaching across the Lee; new caravan routes were opened up and the gravy-trains converged on Cork from all directions; the besieged city under attack from its own clogged-up road system, as a virus can eat its way into sound tissue or what had been healthy tissue previous to the onslaught of this particular pernicious disease.

It was all part of our new opulence and greed. Cork believed in the Celtic Tiger with all the credulity of its easygoing provincial heart; the hearts of simple Munstermen and womenfolk shallow and commonplace as bedpans.

They believed in the Celtic Tiger in the same way as they believed in 'Jackie' Charlton, that honorary Irishman, moving statues (wasn't Ballinspittle just down the road?), proportional representation, the Immaculate Conception, the Mystery of the Blessed Trinity, Healy's honey, the Mass, Yeo Valley organic yoghurt and the Sam Maguire Cup.

When Cork was victorious on the field it (the cup) was carried in procession about the streets by coach Larry Tompkins who raised it aloft as though he were Buckley, Bishop of Cork and Cloyne raising up the monstrance to display the Blessed Host for the people to adore and venerate. They were only adoring themselves, the preordained correctness of being what they were, in Cork.

The slogan was a misnomer in any case, if not an outright crib, suspiciously close to the adman's 'Put a Tiger in Your Tank', just another catch-phrase or 'sound-bite' like 'Guinness is Good for You' or 'You're Never Alone with a Strand'.

Tigers were threatened with extinction in India, except as sport for maharajas hunting them from howdahs mounted on elephants; rarely seen in the Dublin Zoo and not any more in Duffy's or Fossett's Circus. The old authentic Celts themselves would soon be as extinct as the tigers of the wilds, replaced by *amadáns* in pink and purple baseball caps worn back to front.

A tunnel had been cut to facilitate the flow of 'urban' traffic about Cork city and ease the great Dublin–Cork nexus, divert it elsewhere and give the city an 'infrastructural edge' in bringing in foreign investment. 'Road rage' was not unknown; next there would be talk of 'downtown' and the 'inner city'; whereas it was only a provincial dump, full of insistent beggars and citizens of all ages and stripes sucking ice-cream cones even in the depths of winter. Winter and summer were indistinguishable, were it not for the foliage. The riverside walks and the bridges were dreary; in Dublin at least you knew the Liffey was flowing out into Dublin Bay, and the Corrib ran friskily enough through Galway, braced up by its keen Atlantic air.

An import–export drug business had been set up illegally between Cork and Amsterdam, and where you get big money easily come by, you also get crime and protection rackets. Cork was only imitating Dublin.

Tribunals had been set up in the capital to try to weed out malfeasance and skulduggery in high places; in the last quarter of the century High Court judges were found wanting and a former Taoiseach found himself in deep water. There was much talk of settlement and appeasement, the old wounds long open and going septic might still be healed. Miracles never cease.

Then the miracle happened. In Belfast, the very seat of the grievous infection, and on the twelfth or last month of the passing century, the Lion sat down with the Lamb. The jackal had consented to share spoils with the hyena.

A new access road was cut into Kinsale from Belgooly, haunt of contentious blacksmiths, a feuding family and Provo-sympathisers or outright Provos; elegant (the road, that is) as it followed the curves and twists of the Curlew River wending its way to the sea.

The local chief of the fire brigade was taken up by American entrepreneurs and flown out to California to be trained up as a caddy master, flown home and installed in the Old Head of Kinsale Golf Club and made for life. Green fees were steep, the course windswept and exposed on a plateau near Hole Open.

Only foreign golfers were acceptable. In a small shack similar to a Balkan border control point with armed soldiers checking passports, the former fire chief kept an eye on the elongated ruin of the Geraldine castle, in case of falling masonry, collecting dues from those prepared to stump up thirty bob for the privilege of walking on ground that had formerly been free. On paying their fee, they were issued with a ticket and let in.

The old de Courcey castle ruin stood crookedly on its base, sad as an old man's mouth with gums and broken roots of teeth; below it stood the Balkan customs shed or toll gate or ticket office manned by the gingery-haired caddy master for the rich

Kerry brothers who were developing the links, so that Tiger Woods himself could play a round with Payne Stewart one misty day in July.

Tiger Woods meets the Celtic Tiger! The land was swarming with tigers. Girls in public utility services and shops, pharmacies and doctors' receptions were taught not to keep the customers waiting but to advance with a welcoming smile as fixed as falsies, as winsome as Kewpie dolls. They dressed stylishly and showered regularly, exposing more flesh in summer, even navels; the models here were the swinging Corr sisters from Thurles, a trio of songbirds very popular with the Irish young, our Fizz Girls. All were pert and pretty like rubber dolls, quick with the magic formulae taught them in business schools: 'No bother!', 'There you go!', 'Have a nice day!' even if it's pouring rain. 'No problem!' 'No *bother!*'

No longer were the tall green double-decker buses of the Dublin transport system malodorous moving places of Virginia tobacco fumes and rotting shift-straps. In the rapid Americanisation of Ireland, this was a point in its favour; Americans were as hygienic as Scandinavians. They strolled up and down Grafton Street and called out to their spouses: 'Gee whiz, honey. Hey, getta load of this, honey!'

ii

The things we do badly are public monuments, always too bulky or set in an inappropriate place on a pedestal too high and mighty for their own good: witness Nelson lording it over the Coombe; or the upended blue ploughshare on Wilton roundabout in the outskirts of Cork, or our very own Monument in Kinsale, beyond the Sovereigns Inn, formerly the Sea View Bar, purporting to be a 'wave', in processed (corton) steel, with a small 'fountain' attached. It cries out for graffiti as a poor text cries out for the blue pencil. Or dynamite.

The only useful thing the Provos ever did with dynamite was to blow Lord Nelson off his pillar in the centre of the capital's main thoroughfare, O'Connell Street, formerly Sackville Street.

The Irish Army engineers shattered every window in O'Connell Street when they in their turn attempted to dynamite the stump.

It may be said that the main thoroughfare is as uninspiring as Stalinallee in what used to be East Berlin, or the main road that runs through Prosperous, Swords or Newbliss near the Border, as if anxious to be elsewhere. An architect has given his view that the only hope for O'Connell Street would be to paint it a uniform purple from end to end, from the Rotunda to the bridge, royal purple, the colour of fly agaric or a cardinal's cap that signifies sanctity, here intended only to signify a throwing in of the sponge.

Degeneration upon degeneration upon yet more degeneration was Cork's (Cark's) dreadful fate. O Lord deliver us!

Gaelic games as organised by the GAA are nothing but a form of apartheid in sport, no 'foreign' games allowed (meaning no English games). Bullfighting should be introduced to broaden the public taste; a corrida in Croke Park for Easter, *every* Easter, might get them baying for blood.

76

When Rory First Tasted
Wiener Schnitzel

T he involuntary striptease that had begun on a boulder below the Temperance Hall, aptly named Eden, when a brazen schoolgirl had exposed herself for Rory's benefit, continued; the flush-faced schoolgirl had been a regular Gerty MacDowell for teasing display; there would be others after her. Yet more came later; the involuntary striptease was to be resumed years later in another country, when the Jacaranda Street stripper performed for Rory and for him alone in Johannesburg, after the puppet tour was over.

It was continued, very briefly, years later in a street in Munich where a handsome couple were walking, the tight jeans of the brunette wide open to a glimpse of gossamer scanties through which dark pubics erupted; a riot below the waist that belied the calm, beautiful, made-up face with the disdainful aloof expression.

Goldbronze panting, sighing, Lydia Douce and the famous smackbang *Sonnez la Cloche*. Everything reminded Rory of something else; now it was the cane-brake near the swimming pool at Rancho Pico; a gauzy furred miracle of a Mexican butterfly, vivid blue and earth-brown, trembling on a leaf, unaware of its beauty, its uniqueness, its aloneness; a rare species that one does not see much of, because there are not so many of them to be seen. They don't care to be seen; that's the way it is with them. They are so shy.

Today you can have me, I am yours today.

Was it in Berlin or in Cologne that I first tasted Wiener schnitzel? It was winter, and we were touring with Wright's puppets in Germany, heading for Holland, having left summer behind in Yugoslavia. We were going on to tour South Africa and both Rhodesias with the puppets; it was to be a two-year tour.

Ever since I have been disappointed in Wiener schnitzels, for I never got as good a one as the first I had tasted with Coppera in some humble German or Austrian eatery.

In Johannesburg I became friendly with Bernhardt Adamczewski. He was the German-Polish second husband of Fiona, Coppera's best friend from King, her home town in the Eastern Cape. Adam gave me the idea for extending and widening out the novel I was working on sporadically. I called him Otto Beck and included him as the catalyst and mediator between the Langrishe (Hill: Higgins) 'sisters', who in reality were my three brothers and myself in drag; wedged between an Irish past and the European present. Jeremy Irons played Adamczewski ('Beck') in the television production directed by David Jones, where Springfield garden and the father and daughters resembled emanations straight out of tsarist Russia, life in a *dacha* there, in that time and place.

Otto Beck was Adamczewski, his pedantry and his pipes, his past as a shepherd in the Dolomites. He died a few years ago in London, having married his wife's best friend, who had been kind enough to tell him that his daughter was not his own.

The Berlin I knew there in Die Brücke with Wright's puppets was not the Berlin I got to know later when I lived there with Hannelore. As the Málaga that I knew first when passing through with Callus at the wheel of his DKW late at night, was not the same Málaga that Coppera and I had known later with the kids when they were growing up and their Christmas toys were stolen in the Alameda Gardens by old men lurking in the shrubbery.

One's first impressions of a place are always wrong. Foreigners speaking a strange language were always misleading; one got the wrong idea of them, although Dubrovnik continued to remain strange for me, the people having coffee at seven in the morning in the great heat of August.

The pretty brunette with long legs jay-walking across a street in Berlin, skittish in her high heels in summer dress, crossing the wide street to where I was walking on the pavement, threw me a quick look of unambiguous intent. She crossed the wide street that was free of traffic while the lights turned from red to green and threw me this look that reduced me to a jelly.

When Hannelore spoke to her *Mutti* on the white phone she had installed in the little chocolate box flat in Prinzregenten-strasse, she spoke as a loving daughter should regularly once a week, and used the softest sweetest tones: '*Mammylein*' so softly, permitting me to listen to her mother's voice, such a frail neurasthenic voice speaking beautiful German, like a wind in the fir trees. Hannelore spoke the most intimate German to her mother, in a voice she would never use with me.

Rory found that he could bring dead people back to life. Even when treated in a fictional manner, they came back to life. He could bring them closer. Rory could bring my mother back, as long as I called her 'Mumu' and not Lil; and my father, as long as I called him 'Dado' and not Da. I had to turn my back on the real parents in order to evoke this other pseudo-anonymous couple who were more real than my real parents, Bart and Lil. I thought, not quite believing it, that one day I would write a book about them. Well, this trilogy is it.

There was a time in the early 1950s when the CIE roll-ing stock, on first-class non-smoking carriages, the suburban service from Dublin to Greystones, was almost as grand as the Trans-Siberian Express and grand ladies travelled in the first-class carriages, on their own or with a child, on the way to the Grand Hotel. One such covertly eyed Rory, immersed in a book, in the reflection of the window. Passing through the tunnels at Bray Head, the carriage became as intimate as a *fiacre* in the Bois de Boulogne. Rory was reading, or pretending to read *Mademoiselle du Maupin*. The pretty fellow-traveller spoke and said: 'He isn't going to talk to me.'

And of course Rory never would. To have a real woman wouldn't be the same as an imaginary one; he wouldn't know how to take her; it was all dreamy stuff, all dreams.

The old puppeteer Wright had died in his bed in Islington, amid family and puppets and well-wishers; he died in harness.

With his young wife Lyndie he had travelled to Hvar in Croatia, which smelt of lavender. The widow and his young children, the brother and sister, had scattered his ashes on Devil's Gulch on the slopes of Table Mountain.

Harry Calnek, my old *amigo*, did away with himself at Malaspina Road on the Powell River in British Columbia, after alerting the local police as to his intentions and the whereabouts of his remains. He had bad cancer, which had also killed Howard Simpson.

The century was ending badly, as badly as it had begun, with wars and rumours of more wars.

77

The Regional Hospital, Cork

'Just sit up now, like a good man, and let me take a quick peep at your heart and lungs,' said the nurse briskly.

On the night following my admittance to the Regional Hospital in Cork, the Cardiology Department, for an angiograph in BI ward (Surgeon Peter Kearney) I supped lightly on fresh orange juice, half a block of HB ice-cream with wafers stuck in like sails and two peaches cut into segments, and retired to bed early, to dream again of Mumu.

Mumu transformed miraculously into what was no longer the deep fish Sedna, mother of all mothers, but reduced now to the dimensions of a slosh ball for Russian pool, the cerulean blue of a blackbird's egg found in the hidden nests I used to search for in Springfield shrubbery with the young bride Mrs Dilly Ruttle, my very first love or first inkling of what love might be. The blue ball struck delicately, a softly angled cue shot by a player who knew what he was doing, rolling slowly across the green baize to hover on the edge of the left centre pocket, before toppling in. The dream went on in absolute silence; what struck me most was the tender blue of the ball that had vanished, and I wondered was it something to do with Mumu's buckets of flowers, long-stemmed delphiniums, calla lilies (her Christian name was Lily), red hot pokers, daffodils in spring, taken in the Overland by Dado (for Mumu didn't drive) to Celbridge and Straffan Catholic church to decorate the May altars and the high altars for Mass and Benediction, which she would not attend herself, owing to claustrophobia. I was dreaming back thirty-five years prior to the heart-probe in a hospital on the outskirts of Cork city, watching the clock above the reception desk in Ward B1, and Nurse Elaine Walsh was smiling in through the glass at me, third in a ward of four male patients with heart conditions awaiting the gurney to roll us into the operating theatre where Dr Kearney awaited his quota for the morning.

78

Adieu in the Form of a Letter to Mrs Mary Alice Simpson (widow) of Chevy Chase, Maryland

Howard R. Simpson, RIP
US Consul General in Marseilles, 1974,
d. Chevy Chase, 1999

My dear Mary Alice,

Greetings from a far wet place. Stocks of Howard's much-appreciated Vietnamese pickled whole-grain high-class chillies are much depleted and will soon be gone, like Howard himself, gone with the wind.

But the blackthorn is out and its white blossoms very luminous, as also the gorgeous gorse very orange, all along the banks of the tidal Curlew River which you may never see again.

By mid-May the hedgerows give off the tangy scent of wild garlic; the perfume of hawthorn (which hits you on horseback) delicately fragrant is everywhere, and the elder-flower in full bloom with an over-sweet aroma suggestive of the sickroom but suggesting too the fullness of summer.

I'll end as helplessly as I began seventy-two years back, with nothing to love with except the heart, the only reliable organ left; and that's not so reliable either, per the angiograph in the hospital that you know only too well.

Do I hear a dog barking in the corridor?

It's been a bleak midwinter in the months since your hurried departure for the new life in Chevy Chase, Maryland. The opening of the cricket season was delayed in England by snow at Fenners, but the *Novillaros* (not yet in their *trajes de luz* but got up sharply enough in tightly fitting well-cut grey uniforms like bellhops in five-star hotels) strode proudly into the Madrid bullring for the first corrida of 1999 as they have been striding since the days of Lope de Vega and Calderón de la Barca. Or Philip the Fair, whose corpse was transported about the dusty highways and byways of Spain by the semi-crazed widow, until the head of the departed one had turned as green as weathered bronze and shrunk to the size of a small pumpkin.

She buried him with some pomp, as befits a king, within sight of the convent she had retired into to pray for his soul. They were a strange pair. He died of drinking a glass of water following a hard of game of tennis.

Death, then, is shrinkage, declining and wilting away out of life; no more ice-cold Margaritas at Folly House. Well, the years roll by, as roll they must. So, how are things in Gloccamorra?

Ever,

Rory

PS Gloccamorra or no Gloccamorra, how are you sleeping in nookshotten Chevy Chase? Something wakes me at 3.30 and I get up to work on this book I'm finishing, but I suspect my mother is writing it. She always felt that she had a book in her. Now it's coming out.

I took a break at 11 a.m. and searched high and low for my teeth (mi teef), the frontal bridge that produces such a winning smile (if I care to use it), compliments of P. J. Power, dental genius of Kinsale, without which (and whom) I am a sorry sight. The search proved fruitless, as lesser writers would put it. Guess where I found the teeth?

In my mouth.

79

The Old Moon with the New Moon in Her Arms

U nder the table are boxes of tissues, aerosol cans and Hargate roach spray, an oxygen tank and additional breathing apparatus, the Divibus pump for use thrice a day to control asthma. As the blood's impurities build up the other organs, particularly the brain, are poisoned.

Her attempts to write poetry get mixed up in grocery lists for Jefferson Market on the south side of 10th Street. Her bowels are not functioning properly, nor do her dentures fit; it becomes an ordeal for her to collect the mail two floors below. She has become generous with abuse, finding fault with everybody. Her friends, for the most part, are long dead or live far from New York, though she has a brother who is still alive. She no longer receives any magazines or newspapers other than the *TLS*. It was, as she put it, her Trappist period. A Trappist period for Djuna Barnes.

What went wrong with *The Antiphon*?

'Tis a very odd verse play involving incest in the Jacobean manner that she had worked at for nigh on fourteen years, wasted years, if wasted they were. It was a nagging obsession to do with the father, himself an American version of old Karamazov. It was a move in the wrong direction, moving into a bogus seventeenth century. She had to write indirectly of the horrors that befell her long ago. Wald Barnes, the father, was involved.

By right she belonged to Europe, was its frustrated chronicler along with Edith Wharton, Henry James and T.S. Eliot. To stay out of Europe was a mistake, hence her silence, the Trappist period; whereas Freya Stark worked on well into her old age, learnt Persian in her eighties. Baroness Blixen (1885–1962), though afflicted with amoebic dysentery and tertiary syphilis and an invalid for the last third of her life, yet 'found' herself in Kenya and wrote *Out of Africa* in English. She found a way out of her misery (the loss of the coffee farm, the death of Denys Finch-Hatton); whereas Djuna Barnes (1892–1982) had sunk down under hers. There were leopards about the farm in the Ngong uplands where the air was like wine; the Baroness shot lions and leopards, made shift to learn native languages, loved the second son of the thirteenth Earl of Winchilsea who by night shot two marauding lions while Karen held the torch. She wrote of another daytime kill:

I went right up to it and watched the light ebbing from its eyes; it was my first meeting with a lion and I shall never forget it. In their build, carriage and movements lions possess a greatness, a majesty, which positively instils terror in the human being and makes one feel later that everything else is trivial – thousands of generations of unrestricted supreme authority, and one is oneself set back 6,000 generations – suddenly comes to feel the mighty power of nature, when one looks it right in the eyes.

Karen Blixen, *Letters from Africa,* 1914–31

February 1958, touring with John Wright's Marionettes

One night near Kariba Dam, still under construction, a lioness loped for a quarter of a mile down the road, trapped in the headlights of the Bedford truck. I sat beside Wright, who was driving, and watched it moving; it didn't seem alarmed. I thought perhaps it was a donkey, from the movement of the haunches; until it leapt off the road into the darkness and I saw it was a full-grown lioness, very pale, almost luminous in the headlights.

Wright stopped the Bedford, killed the lights, and we stepped out. I stood on the ground above the great river they were damming and I felt that power that the Baroness was referring to: lions and lionesses were moving freely about in their own native habitat into which we had trespassed; it was their ground. The deep imprints of their great pads had marked the wet cement of the tarmac on the new Kariba airstrip.

'She was a very private person and on more than one occasion called the police to remove weeping women from her doorstep,' so wrote Frank O'Neal, the last helping hand to reach out, since Berenice Abbott would not bring herself to help.

Could Djuna Barnes have progressed beyond *Nightwood*, had she remained in Paris, or lived in Berlin or Vienna? It didn't happen.

Wednesday, 12 October 1994, twelve years after her death, Derek Mahon, Alannah Hopkin and I visited Patchin Place in Greenwich Village; then Patricia King drove us over the George Washington Bridge and out along the west bank of the Hudson through a very lush land with the verges mown all the way to West Point and the railway line and the road narrowing, on a superlatively blue day in the fall, to Cornwall-on-Hudson for lunch at Painter's. After lunch we visited the post office and Derek Mahon bought stamps in order to inquire whether there were any Barneses living there. No, no such family; so we went to the library. An aged female historian of the town was in the basement, we were informed. She grudgingly conceded that the Barnes family had lived briefly there, but the family was 'not respectable' and never considered part of the community. But Djuna Barnes had asked that her ashes be scattered in a dogwood grove on Storm King Mountain; she wanted to come back, I said. Well, yes, maybe, the aged historian conceded; so we left it at that.

It was a lovely blue day in Cornwall-on-Hudson. We looked for the Barnes house on the way to Storm King Mountain but couldn't find it. We never found it. Many fine houses stood thereabouts with balconies and porches and an almost Austrian look to them; wooden homes.

Djuna Barnes was born on 12 June 1892, ten years after James Joyce, at Cornwall-on-Hudson in upstate New York. She was to live for the last forty years of her life in Patchin Place, Greenwich Village, where she died on 17 June 1982.

How the Century Ended

I know that time is passing because I cannot walk any distance without discomfort and hills are fast becoming impossible. I know of the passage of time because the beech sapling from Springfield (planted for my grandson Paris) was about nine inches when planted seven years ago in the garden here: it is now twenty-two feet high, whereas Paris, at twelve, is five feet three. His ambition, he tells me, is to be an international rollerball champion. He was born to blade.

One sunny day in Bavaria so many years ago, I went walking in the Alps with Karen Reece. The Agatha Christie long-runner, *The Mousetrap*, is into its forty-eighth year and may be good for another half-century, a London cultural pilgrimage for Japanese tourists.

Alistair Cooke's *Letter from America*, begun when Rory was nineteen years of age, has been transmitted from the same BBC studio for fifty-four years.

Passed away in that time that is passing, some by their own hands, I remember

Bernhardt ('Adam') Adamczewski, who died in London.
Zbigniew Herbert, who died in Cracow.
Henning Mortenson, who died in Copenhagen.

Michael Morrow, who died in London.

Mike Poole, who died in Cómpeta, laughing like a jackass to the bitter end.

Geoffrey Rowe, who died in Greystones, having risen from his bed one Christmas morning, to fall dead at his wife's feet.

Brendan ('Brother Bun') Higgins, who died in Ealing.

Howard Simpson, who died in Chevy Chase, Maryland.

Anthony Kerrigan, who died in Illinois.

Not forgetting Gerard, Paddy and Philomena, all gone to their rest.

Rita Hayworth who died in Hollywood, at sixty-eight. She was prematurely senile; her looks and memory gone.

Madeleine Carroll who died in Marbella, where she had been a recluse since the death of her daughter. She was eighty-one.

Two of my lifelong friends did away with themselves when threatened by cancer: Donal Farrell, by an overdose in St Amour, and Harry Calnek, by hunting rifle in Canada. May they find peace, wherever they went thereafter.

Petrushka Karr would have turned thirty. On the last day of the century, the tides splash in and out twice a day in Copenhagen, Cork, Dublin, Cape Town and Amsterdam, going with the rollings of the earth ball and her moon through everchanging tracks of neverchanging space.

Ponting or Hobsbawm, or some such pundit, informs us that genocide has marked out our century. But before the so-called Holocaust, the Germans slaughtered the Hemeros in Africa. The Turks slaughtered Armenians; the Hutus slaughtered the Tutsis in Rwanda; the Croats slaughtered Serbians, then the Serbs went in for some ethnic cleansing of their own in Bosnia and Kosova. Predators pattered after victims like stoats in search of blood.

Epilogue

Past It

Age does us no favours. Advancing years do not bring serenity; our end is likely to be as untidy and messy as our beginning, when we came bawling messily into this world.

The carnal clinch can be left behind as an embarrassment. Eyesight failing. Teeth gone to pot, bridges installed; hearing only so-so, memory likewise, nostrils and ears sprouting hair, pubics offer scant cover; the metabolism getting into the swing of it before the final dissolution, the final descent into the grave, to be scattered as ashes about some favoured spot, tipped into some river, lake or sea.

The rotting metabolism, past it now, bursts in terrific slow motion from the coffin six feet down and goes rampaging away to join the other maggot-moved corpses, joining up with the teeming subatomic life underground.

The long red tresses of Rossetti's beautiful model Elizabeth Siddall filled the coffin to overflowing when it was opened, years after her demise, for the poet to recover a Morocco-bound volume that he had laid upon the dead breast of the beloved.

Human hair grows out of hand in the sleepy stagnancy of the grave, before falling off in fistfuls as the monitoring death-moths engender and come forth in force, probing and rummaging, having a field day. The skeleton scatters out of the coffin's last embrace in bits and pieces and goes wandering off. Coffin boards are removed elsewhere by busy termites, wriggling worms going at it, at it; human bones scattered all over the place, appendages – eyeless sockets and hairless skulls – dropping off and devoured in our final dissolution into the teeming earth. We all roll with the earth's turning, asleep for ever on its broad, deeply breathing bosom. Thinking of dead friends is the price we pay for our rest. Very dear friends all gone home. *Vale*, Harry, Donal, Adam, Geoffrey, Gerard, Paddy, Vera, Philomena. *Adieu, adieu*, Anthony and Howard gone from Majorca and Chevy Chase, Maryland, fled out of life.

In May of this year, a survey published indicated that 20,000 citizens a year were emigrating from the Republic, Celtic Tiger or no Celtic Tiger. The island called Ireland was still draining away like sanies into a bucket.

Happy New Year, all you suckers out there, preparing to set foot gingerly into the twenty-first century. Have a nice day! *¡Feliz Año Nuevo! Bonne Année! Glückliches Neujahr!* Give my love to the sunrise.

On a marvellously sunny late May day in the new century with swifts screeching overhead and jackdaws guarding their nests in the chimney pots there came a letter in a hand that seemed familiar and what is more from Copenhagen. It was from Anna Reiner, the old flame twenty-five years on. She wrote:

'Why do you call yourself Rory? And how can you be seventy-one in the year 2000 when you are born in 1927? Or more interesting where did you spend the lost two years?'

Za vaschyezdarovyie!